PROGRESSIVE TAX REFORM AND EQUALITY IN LATIN AMERICA

EDITED BY

James E. Mahon Jr.

Marcelo Bergman

Cynthia Arnson

WWW.WILSONCENTER.ORG/LAP

Available from:

Latin American Program
Woodrow Wilson International Center for Scholars
One Woodrow Wilson Plaza
1300 Pennsylvania Avenue NW
Washington, DC 20004-3027

www.wilsoncenter.org/lap

Design and Layout: Station 10 Creative, Columbia, MD, USA

ISBN: 978-1-938027-43-7

THE WILSON CENTER, chartered by Congress as the official memorial to President Woodrow Wilson, is the nation's key nonpartisan policy forum for tackling global issues through independent research and open dialogue to inform actionable ideas for Congress, the Administration, and the broader policy community.

Conclusions or opinions expressed in Center publications and programs are those of the authors and speakers and do not necessarily reflect the views of the Center staff, fellows, trustees, advisory groups, or any individuals or organizations that provide financial support to the Center.

Please visit us online at **www.wilsoncenter.org**.

Acknowledgments

This book represents the culmination of the Latin American Program's three-year project on the politics of progressive taxation in Latin America. We are grateful to the Tinker Foundation for its generous support of this initiative.

We are also grateful to numerous colleagues from throughout the region who have contributed their expertise at various stages of the project, either as conference participants at events sponsored by the Woodrow Wilson International Center for Scholars in 2011 and 2012 or as authors of previously published case studies: José Roberto Afonso, Martín Ardanaz, Alberto Barreix, Carlos Elizondo, Laura Frigenti, Juan Carlos Gómez Sabaini, Juan Pablo Jiménez, Stephen Kaplan, Santiago Levy, Eduardo Lora, Nora Lustig, Marcus Melo, Gabriel Ondetti, Natalia Salazar, Saulo Santos de Souza, John Scott, and Vito Tanzi. Their comments, perspectives, and advice have greatly enriched our inquiry.

In 2013 and 2014, we collaborated with institutions in Mexico, Costa Rica, and Colombia in sponsoring regional forums on tax reform. For their leadership and cooperation in these joint efforts, we express our thanks to Hugo Beteta, of the Comisión Económica para América Latina y el Caribe, in Mexico; to Jorge Vargas Cullell, of Programa Estado de la Nación, and to Armando González, of *La Nación*, in Costa Rica; and to Leonardo Villar, of Fedesarrollo, in Colombia. Colleagues too numerous to mention in all four institutions provided indispensable help in organizing the conferences and issuing the resulting publications; to them we owe a collective word of thanks.

Finally, we owe our deepest thanks to Verónica Colón-Rosario, program associate of the Latin American Program, for her research assistance and oversight of all phases of the project's implementation.

Cynthia J. Arnson
Marcelo Bergman
James E. Mahon Jr.
December 2014

Contents

INTRODUCTION

The Political Economy of Progressive Tax Reform in Latin America—Comparative Context and Policy Debates

James E. Mahon Jr. and Marcelo Bergman,
with Cynthia J. Arnson

Over the course of more than a generation of vibrant and mostly uninterrupted electoral democracy, Latin American governments have done almost nothing about the fact that the region suffers from the highest levels of inequality, on average, in the world.[1] On the spending side, what little has been done has been quite innovative, and this has brought new attention to redistribution through programs such as conditional cash transfers and universal noncontributory pensions, which have been credited by some with a small but measurable improvement in equality in several countries since about 2000.[2] But taxation across the region is still generally regressive, relying greatly on revenue from consumption taxes and (with a handful of minor exceptions) hardly at all on revenue from personal income taxes. The long coexistence in the region of elected governments, enormous inequality, and inattention to progressive taxation ought to puzzle us—and not just because it directly violates the expectations of the most widely cited model of the political economy of taxation.[3]

The background papers and case studies of the Latin American Program's Project on Taxation and Equality can be found at http://wilsoncenter.org/publication-series/taxation. Thanks to Richard Bird for generous and perceptive comments on a draft of this introduction.

However, more recently, and especially since the Uruguayan tax reform of 2006, some policymakers have in fact begun to consider what might be done on the revenue side of the ledger to address inequality. The Chilean tax reform of 2014 is the best example. Still, progressive tax measures have faced a variety of obstacles, as we discuss in more detail below, including the doubts of some experts and practitioners about their effectiveness or political feasibility. Hence the questions: What kinds of reforms would be economically efficient, effective at redistribution, and politically possible? And what conditions and strategies might be most conducive to such reforms?

This book seeks to answer these questions, in pursuit of two objectives. The first is to update the literature on tax reform in Latin America by focusing on *how progressive tax reforms take place*, with special reference to important recent examples of success and failure in this regard. The second is to glean *advice for reformers*, drawn from the same literature and examples, emphasizing factors that are within the control of policymakers. The literature on tax reform in the region has produced a large volume of work on the optimal design of reform from an economic and administrative standpoint. But much less has been done on the determinants of reform, especially on the success or failure of progressive tax initiatives.

In this introduction, we offer a historical and comparative context for the political economy of progressive tax reforms, while also reviewing the most important recent policy debates in the field. The subsequent case study chapters then describe the most important tax reforms recently proposed and implemented—or not—in Chile, Uruguay, Colombia, Guatemala, and Mexico, explaining the outcomes and drawing lessons for future reformers. The book also features two commentaries from local experts, one on the recent reform in Chile and the other on the more disappointing recent record in Guatemala. The conclusion pulls together these threads, while reflecting on the political economy of fiscal reform in Latin America and offering tactical lessons for tax reformers.

PROGRESSIVE TAX REFORM

We begin by defining progressive tax reform. We consider a reform "progressive" insofar as it shifts the tax burden, on average, toward wealthier households and away from poorer ones. Now, admittedly it has been hard to calculate tax incidence with a great deal of confidence, especially in a region as data-poor as Latin America, leading scholars to rely often on estimates of the net incidence of a package of policy measures. And even the best post hoc calculations of a reform's effect will be confounded by many simultaneous changes. Still, based on several decades of estimates, we feel justified in considering net relative increases in the revenue burden carried by personal income and property taxation (especially on real estate) to be progressive, and net relative increases in revenue from consumption taxation, especially on basic necessities, to be regressive.[4] We will also refer to income taxes on firms and payroll taxes from time to time. However, the incidence of the former is still disputed, despite a large scholarly literature, even with regard to countries with better data than those discussed here.[5] The latter is an important issue, which has recently entered the conversation because of its likely impact on the demand for labor.

Of course, Latin America has seen many tax reforms; but a quick survey shows that different kinds of initiatives have predominated in the region at different times. Since the 1960s, three periods can be identified. The reforms of the first generation (c. 1967–94) generally focused on raising revenue, in part to compensate for the customs income lost to trade liberalization, and mainly to address large fiscal deficits derived from growing government spending.[6] They featured the introduction or expansion of the value-added tax (VAT) and emphasized simplification and base broadening. The second generation of reforms, between the early 1990s and mid-2000s, most commonly involved amendments to minor taxes and to VAT rates or bases, while continuing, in most countries, the overall expansion of tax revenues relative to gross domestic product (GDP). Revenue agencies improved collection by expanding administrative tax capacities and adding new technology. Finally, the most recent period, which we provisionally call the "third generation," began with the reform in Uruguay in 2006 and continued with the smaller (and less progressive) Mexican tax initiative of

October 2013 as well as the major 2014 reform under the second government of President Michelle Bachelet in Chile. Although it is too soon to say whether progressive tax reforms will predominate in the years to come, they surely constitute the most notable novelty on the reform landscape.

Granted, most tax reforms are mixtures, involving packages of measures with different goals and effects. Many reforms might not be easily classifiable according to the three periods suggested above, simply as revenue raising, amending, or progressive. Often the least salient or controversial measures (say, improvements in administration) later make the most difference in terms of the size or composition of revenues.

LATIN AMERICAN TAX SYSTEMS IN COMPARATIVE PERSPECTIVE

In comparison with the rest of the world, several features of Latin American tax systems stand out. First, contrary to common perceptions about neoliberalism and the "Washington Consensus," Latin American countries have, on average, increased their ratio of tax revenue to GDP more than any other region in the world between 1990–96 and 2004–10.[7] Nor is this entirely a product of the region's new left-wing governments after 1997.[8] Colombia, which was never ruled by the left, has almost doubled its tax income over the past two decades, as Gustavo Flores-Macías shows in chapter 3.[9] Guatemala, whose president is a former general and a man of the right, finally saw a modest revenue-increasing tax reform in 2012, as we also see in chapter 4, by Maynor Cabrera and Aaron Schneider. In fact, the most distinctively left-populist governments of the region—those of Venezuela, Ecuador, and Bolivia—have relied more on wealth from natural resource rents than on taxing their citizens' consumption or incomes.

At the same time, despite the recent increase of tax revenues, most Latin American governments still tend to lag behind comparable countries in terms of the share of taxes they collect. Figure 1 shows a scatterplot of 107 countries reporting data to the World Bank's *World Development Indicators* for 2012, with log10 GDP per capita (purchasing power parity, constant 2011 dollars) on the horizontal axis and central government tax revenue as

Figure 1. GDP per Capita and Tax Revenue as a Percentage of GDP, 2012—Latin American Countries Highlighted and Labeled against Trend for All Countries

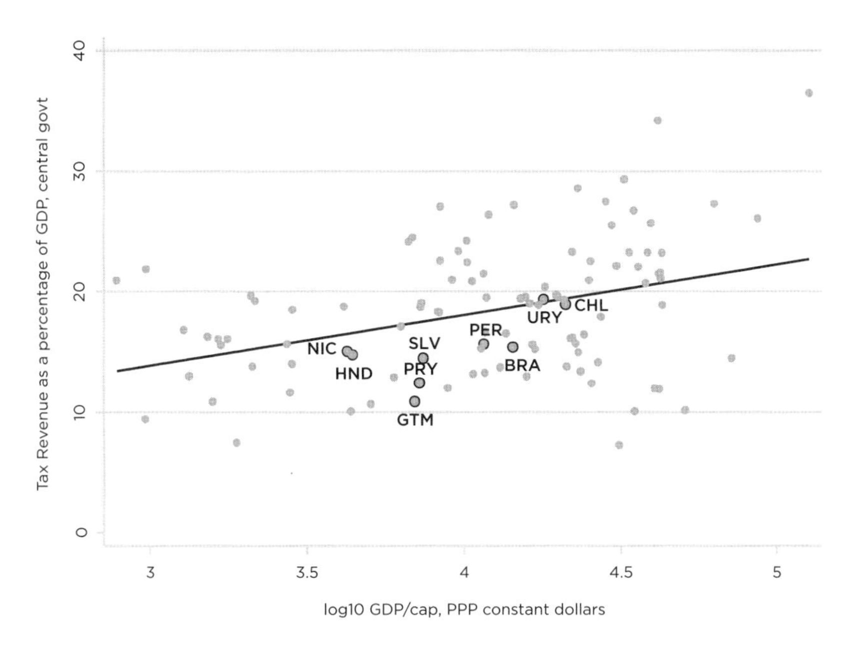

Source: World Bank, World Development Indicators (Washington, D.C.: World Bank, various years), online database.

a percentage of GDP on the vertical axis, with a fitted regression line. The Latin American countries in the data set fall almost entirely below the line. Brazil, for which the revenue figure excludes important subnational income that would place it above the norm, is the only clear exception.

Finally and most important, as mentioned above, the Latin American countries also have a highly distinctive and regionally consistent mix of tax revenues. Compared with other parts of the world, personal income and property taxes raise very little revenue, while governments rely to an unusually high degree on consumption levies.[10] Table 1 shows the percentages of total revenue supplied by personal income taxes and taxes on consumption for seven groups of countries in two recent periods. Although World

Table 1. Recent Regional Averages of Relative Weights of Personal Income Taxation and Consumption Taxation in Total Revenues, Two Selected Periods (percent)

Region or Group	1993-99			2000-2006		
	Personal Income Tax	Consumption Taxes	*N*	Personal Income Tax	Consumption Taxes	*N*
OECD Europe	19.4	27.9	15	19.5	30.4	14
United States and other rich ex-British colonies	39.7	17.6	2	38.3	19.8	5
Latin America	2.5	37.3	7*	2.9	38.1	8*
Latin America IDB-CIAT				4.63	37.04	10**
Sub-Saharan Africa	11.2	22.5	16	13.1	26.8	20
Eastern Europe and Eurasian ex-communist	6.9	40.0	13	7.6	41.2	21
South and East Asia	10.8	25.5	13	9.5	29.6	15
Middle East and North Africa	3.3	11.1	10	8.2	20.7	8

Note: *N* = Number of countries contributing to the average by having at least one year in the period with reported data for both personal income taxes and consumption taxes; OECD = Organization for Economic Cooperation and Development; IDB-CIAT = Inter-American Development Bank–Centro Interamericano de Administradores Tributarios database.

* For 1993–99, Latin America = Brazil, Guatemala, Panama, Paraguay, Peru, Uruguay, Venezuela; for 2000–2006, Latin America = Argentina, Bolivia, Guatemala, Panama, Paraguay, Peru, Uruguay, Venezuela.

** Complete data for all ten countries in all years: Argentina, Bolivia, Brazil, Chile, Colombia, Dominican Republic, Guatemala, Mexico, Peru, Uruguay. Includes subnational consumption tax revenue for Argentina and Brazil.

Sources: International Monetary Fund, *Government Finance Statistics* (Washington, D.C.: International Monetary Fund, various years); World Bank, *World Development Indicators* (Washington, D.C.: World Bank, various years); Inter-American Development Bank–Centro Interamericano de Administradores Tributarios database, 2012.

Bank and International Monetary Fund data are missing for many countries and years, we see a strong contrast between Latin America (the shaded rows) and every other group shown in the table. Using the more complete data from the Inter-American Development Bank and the Inter-American Center for Tax Administration (Centro Interamericano de Administradores Tributarios), although its denominator excludes large nontax revenues for several countries, the contrast persists. In terms of property tax revenue, Latin American governments collect, on average, much less than any other region. Considering only the portion derived from real estate taxes, according to the Inter-American Development Bank, receipts from urban and rural property averaged only 0.37 percent of GDP in the 2000s—about half the amount collected by other developing countries and only one-sixth of the average reported by the Organization for Economic Cooperation and Development (OECD).[11] In sum, two taxes that are considered the most likely to be strongly progressive in their impact—personal income taxes and real estate taxes—are remarkably weak in Latin America, while consumption taxes, usually regressive on balance, play a notably important role.

This does not deny the important differences across the region, especially on the overall levels of taxation and the importance of resource rents to the treasury. For example, Brazil and Argentina collect a much higher share of GDP in taxes than do Mexico and Guatemala. Venezuela and Bolivia rely greatly on hydrocarbon-based income. Table 2 depicts total revenues, tax revenues, and revenues from the more progressive (personal income tax, property tax) and regressive (consumption) kinds of taxes, as a percentage of GDP, for the period 2006–10. The most striking conclusion is that despite the different rates of tax collections, one pattern remains stable: Progressive taxes remain for most countries a minor component of total taxation.

Very little has been done to change this tax structure. Despite the expansion of tax revenues, the region's high levels of inequality, and its embrace of democracy, Latin American tax systems have not become more progressive in the past several decades.[12] In the major reforms of the first generation, governments cut top rates for both corporate and individual income taxes, while often reducing the number of special tax exemptions. Reformers paid more attention to efficiency and "horizontal equity" (equal treatment for different sources of taxable income) than to "vertical

Table 2. Total Revenues and Tax Revenues in Latin America as a Percentage of GDP, General Government, 2006–10 Averages; Property Tax Revenues, 2012; and Estimated Levels of Tax Evasion (revenues in percentage of GDP)

Country	Total Revenue	Total Tax Revenue (without SS Taxes)	Consumption Tax Revenue (Domestic)	PIT Revenue	Ratio of Consumption to PIT Revenue	Property Tax Revenue	Estimate of Tax Evasion Level
Argentina	32.09	26.06	10.86	2.64	4.1	1.8	Medium
Bolivia	28.60	16.05	9.97	0.20	49.9	1.1	High
Brazil	33.98	27.27	14.19	3.56	4.0	2.1	Low
Chile	28.24	20.02	9.45	1.25	7.6	0.8	Low
Colombia	23.49	15.92	7.45	1.10	6.8	2.1	Medium
Costa Rica	21.78	14.39	8.46	2.06	4.1	1.1	Low
Dominican Republic	16.33	14.43	8.31	1.56	5.3	0.8	Medium-High
El Salvador	17.52	13.56	7.64	2.22	3.4	0.0	High
Guatemala	13.03	11.11	6.40	0.48	13.3	0.1	High
Mexico	20.34	9.36	4.11	2.61	1.6	NA	Medium
Peru	18.39	15.21	7.52	2.13	3.5	NA	Medium
Uruguay	29.14	21.08	11.27	3.38	3.3	1.3	Low

Note: PIT = personal (individual) income tax; SS = Social Security.

Sources: First five columns, Inter-American Development Bank–Centro Interamericano de Administradores Tributarios database; property tax, UN-ECLAC, CEPALSTAT database, http://interwp.cepal.org/sisgen/ConsultaIntegrada.asp?idIndicador=821&idioma=e; property tax figures are for 2012, except for Brazil, Chile, and Colombia, which are for 2011; tax evasion, estimates by Bergman.

equity" (progressivity, or taxing proportionally more heavily those with higher incomes). International experts often argued that redistribution was to be achieved by spending the new revenue more intelligently to alleviate poverty.[13] This set of priorities remained dominant into the 2000s, as reformers tried to close loopholes while seeking other revenues in heterodox and opportunistic ways.[14] As a result, by 2012 it could be said that the region with the world's most unequal distribution of income also remained the world's laggard in redistribution through the tax code.

EXPLANATIONS OF THE LATIN AMERICAN PUZZLE

How did all this come about? In offering explanations, many scholars (economists above all) encounter an unfortunate obstacle when, in their search for defensible "microfoundations," they adopt the "median voter model," which has served as a workhorse in political economy more broadly.[15] As hinted above, the model unhelpfully confounds our efforts, because its prediction—that under a democracy with a broad franchise, greater levels of inequality will bring greater redistribution via fiscal policy—is strikingly at odds with the observed outcomes, either across Latin America or in comparing the region to the rest of the world.[16] Better explanations take account of the limitations on democratic choice, the importance of business lobbies, and the structural power of capital—summarized well, perhaps, in the old Latin American saying that political power is like a violin, to be grabbed with the left hand and played with the right.

The most important strand of the literature ties inequality itself, via porous and corruptible political institutions, to the perpetuation of inequality via regressive fiscal policy. An early example is a work by the development theorist Michael Best (1976), which observed that tax outcomes in Central America fit "the hypothetical preferences of the large landlords and in reverse order to the preferences of the majority of the population."[17] In pointing to the economic elite's control over the propagation of ideology, its investment power, and its influence over state administration, Best's study provides tools that could be applied to stable democratic systems today.[18] Other authors suggest that inequality predicts less fiscal redistribution because it entails a relative weakness of people in the middle-income sectors, who are often the most influential demanders of public services.[19] In particular, traditional elites have effectively resisted property taxation in Latin America since before achieving independence, and as the economic historian Kenneth Sokoloff and the tax law specialist Eric Zolt have observed, they did so even as such revenues were becoming the mainstay of local public goods provision in the United States and Canada.[20] The economist and Colombian finance minister Mauricio Cárdenas echoed this theme when modeling how elites would underinvest in state fiscal capacity in the expectation that this would be used to tax them in the future—an idea that helps explain not only the historically low taxation of landed property but also today's weak efforts to tax capital income.[21] In sum, inequality has itself produced unusually dominant elites who have successfully resisted direct taxation and have thus prevented the development of state capacities that could backfire upon their own interests.

Nevertheless (and consistent with the median voter model), redistribution in Latin America *has* increased under elected governments of the past generation, in the form of widely adopted conditional cash transfer programs, noncontributory pensions, other forms of social assistance, and increases in public health and primary education spending. But even as social spending has risen, its cash portion has still consisted mainly of social insurance payments enjoyed by the top one or two quintiles, and even in-kind transfers include well-funded services, such as tertiary education, used mainly by the wealthy.[22] Moreover, even though it makes intuitive sense to connect the spread of pro-poor spending to politicians' pursuit of votes, recent studies of the politics of conditional cash transfers suggest that the payoff to incumbents is modest, short-term, and significantly counterbalanced by defections among richer voters.[23] All in all, modest redistribution via spending has proven less threatening to political elites than progressive taxation. And of course, the latter also proved unnecessary whenever cheap credit and commodity booms facilitated politically popular spending.

Many researchers also point to capital mobility as an important constraint on Latin American tax systems, especially with regard to the balance between income and consumption taxes. This became especially important with the flight of capital in about 1982, in connection with the regional debt crisis.[24] The Argentine economist Gómez Sabaini observes that fears of lost investment and capital flight have made Latin American governments reluctant to modernize their income-tax systems up to developed-country standards.[25] In an earlier essay, Tasha Fairfield, the author chapter 1 in the present volume, vividly describes the political difficulties that the Argentine authorities faced in imposing a tax on interest income.[26] It might also be true that the threat of capital flight helps preserve democracy by taking populist redistribution off the agenda.[27] This has also been seen as consistent with the median voter model—a broad franchise, which makes the median voter a poor person who hopes to soak the rich, can persist only when asset mobility renders such a tax impossible.[28] Electoral democracy survives, though depleted in content and disappointing to the more progressive half of the voting public.

As we will see in the chapters that follow, Latin America's economic elites have many other ways to resist progressive taxation. Powerful business organizations, such as Chile's Confederation of Production and Commerce (Confederación de Producción y Comercio), and business-agriculture confederations, such as Guatemala's Coordinating Committee of Agricultural, Commercial, Industrial, and Financial Associations (Comité Coordinador de Asociaciones Agrícolas, Comerciales, Industriales, y Financieras, CACIF), often prevent or reshape legislation that could otherwise hurt their members' interests before it reaches the public eye. Meanwhile, the dominant conservative private media companies push progressive ideas to the margins of public discussion.

THE POLICY DEBATE

As noted above, when compared with the rest of the world, Latin American tax systems can be described as relatively underfunded and unprogressive. And as just described, there are plausible political-economy factors that could explain the lack of progressivity in taxation. But when it comes to policy responses to this underfunding and lack of progressivity, scholars and practitioners disagree about which of the two problems deserves higher priority and more immediate attention. At some risk of exaggerating the division between scholars, let us consider the main points in favor of giving priority to revenue generation and follow with a few arguments for an emphasis on tax progressivity.

The case for the priority of revenue rests on four pillars. First, there are several Western European examples of countries with effective welfare states yet regressive or nearly regressive taxation, Second, it is asserted that this approach (raising revenues rather than focusing on equality in the tax burden) would be more feasible politically. Third, it is probable that alternatives to tax revenue (borrowing and inflation) would be worse in distributional terms. Fourth and finally, nearly all Latin American tax codes contain a variety of tax loopholes and incentives that make easy targets for raising revenue.

Judging from a wide sample of countries, the incidence of spending is far more important to redistribution and social welfare than is the incidence of taxation.[29] This is emphatically true of the most important welfare states in Europe. Data for the OECD's member countries from the early 2000s showed that Sweden, Denmark, and Finland had regressive tax systems—but that once spending was considered, all three were highly redistributive, just like the rest of Europe (table 3).[30] Advocates of an emphasis on revenue over tax progressivity can cite examples such as these to argue that even redistributive goals are best pursued by fortifying and perfecting current, mildly regressive VAT-based tax systems—while making public spending more equitable.[31] This, the argument goes, is what some of the most successful welfare states have done for a long time.

The second, related, argument for emphasizing efficient revenue-enhancing taxation is that this pattern is more sustainable politically. The political scientist Junko Kato, for example, ties the historical growth of welfare states to regressive taxation.[32] The idea here is that in countries such as Sweden and Denmark, conservative elites had enough power to deflect large increases in direct taxation, leaving social democrats to fund expansions of welfare by the regressive (but efficient) means of broad consumption taxes. In its political logic, this is what political scientist Jeffrey Timmons calls a "fiscal contract" pattern, according to which governments exchange services, policies, and institutions for taxes, so that their spending mainly benefits those who supply the revenue.[33] To paraphrase his argument, whereas median

Table 3. Household Gini Coefficients by Country: Before Fiscal Policy, Post-Taxes, and Post-Taxes and Spending

A	B	C	D	E	F
Country (2001 Surveys)	Gini before Fiscal Policy	Gini Post-Taxes	Percentage-Point Variation, Taxes Only [(B - C) x 100]	Gini Post-Taxes and Spending	Percentage-Point Variation, Total [(B - E) x 100]
Germany	.3868	.3467	4.01	.3055	8.1
United Kingdom	.4705	.4610	0.95	.3434	12.7
Portugal	.4442	.4056	3.86	.3835	6.1
France	.3776	.3568	2.08	.3016	7.6
Denmark	.4373	.4580	-2.07	.3063	13.1
Finland	.4437	.4446	-0.09	.3233	12.0
Sweden	.4066	.4276	-2.1	.2940	11.3

Source: A. Barreix, J. Roca, and L. Villela, *Fiscal Policy and Equity: Estimation of the Progressivity and Redistributive Capacity of Taxes and Social Public Expenditures in the Andean Countries*, INTAL-INT Working Paper 33, (Washington, D.C.: Inter-American Development Bank, 2007), 55–60, and tables 32 and 34, calculated from data from the Organization for Economic Cooperation and Development.

voter models describe a world in which the state taxes A to benefit B, a "fiscal contract" view describes what the state has to give A in order to get resources from A. To fund welfare programs, it says, tax regressively.

This view also entails political limits to the taxation of the wealthy in Latin America. It has been argued that

> on the one hand, tax revenues in Latin America are substantially lower than in OECD countries or in the EU; on the other hand, the richest income quintile already contributes a much larger share of taxation than in the OECD and EU. . . . Because Latin American countries have much higher income inequality than OECD and EU countries, to support similar levels of spending, the richest income quintile must

> be taxed more heavily, at least in absolute terms. . . . Because the rich in Latin America contribute a substantial share of government revenue, raising their contribution even further may impose a strain on the social contract. The rich may resent contributing excessively to a welfare state that gives little back to them.[34]

Because the rich already pay the most under the current system, they will resist VAT rate increases—and especially, progressive reforms that target property and capital income.

Third, the common alternatives to additional revenue in Latin America—inflation and borrowing—are likely to be at least as bad as indirect taxes in distributional terms. Regarding inflation, a variety of studies have concluded that especially in the developing countries, it hurts the poor more than the rich.[35] The economists William Easterly and Stanley Fischer find that the subjective concerns of poor respondents with inflation correspond well with econometric results showing a significant negative relationship between inflation and various measures of poor people's income.[36] As for borrowing, if we consider the net distributional implication of future interest payments out of future taxation, the result is also likely to be negative.[37] For internationally held debt, the distributional issue has historically been less salient than debtor-creditor relations buffeted by cycles of boom and default. But as more Latin American countries' debt is held domestically and issued in domestic currency—both of which appear to have increased since 2000—the impact of regressive tax-to-interest transfers could measurably affect national income distribution.[38]

Finally, the work of efficiency- and revenue-minded tax reformers remains unfinished. For one thing, not every country has shared in the revenue increases of the past fifteen years. In the Dominican Republic, for example, revenues as a proportion of GDP saw an especially steep decline in 2007–9 and did not recover thereafter. Fiscal problems worsened in 2012, with weak tax revenues and a 40 percent rise in spending, leading to an estimated deficit of 8.5 percent of GDP for the consolidated public sector—all of which provided the background for the tax reform of October 2012.[39] For another, reforms that focus on efficiency and "horizontal equity" do not lack good targets. It is a general law of tax politics that loopholes multiply over time. On average, tax loopholes and incentives cost just over 4 percent of countries' GDPs in 2010, and the average includes some really egregious cases, such as the Dominican Republic, for which this figure was estimated at 5.8 percent of GDP.[40]

Let us now consider the points in favor of making tax progressivity a higher priority. The first and most important one is that pro-poor spending also faces formidable political obstacles. A detailed study of income distribution in five countries concludes that "what prevents Argentina, Bolivia, and Brazil from achieving similar reductions in inequality is not the lack of revenues but the fact that they spend less on cash transfers—especially transfers that are progressive in absolute terms—as a share of GDP."[41] In Latin America, spending well on the poor is almost as difficult, in practice, as levying taxes well on the rich.

Second, even if countries were able to supply high-quality public goods aimed squarely at the poor, a prior question still must be answered: How do we know that these goods are worth to them what fiscal experts suppose, compared with the consumption they sacrificed via taxation?[42] Tax policy specialists ought to put just as much effort into answering this question as they do into surveying households' incomes.

As all this implies, the worst outcome—an increase in revenue via regressive taxation that funds a rise in regressive or ineffective spending—constitutes an important risk for reformers under the political conditions that prevail in many countries. Here, perhaps, the case of Brazil stands as a cautionary tale for those who would forswear tax progressivity in pursuit of additional revenue. Although a relative success, its Bolsa Família program represents a small part of a social expenditure budget whose overall tendency is regressive. The country's high level of taxation as a proportion of GDP has not brought substantial redistribution.[43]

At this writing, such political economy concerns have helped attenuate the tension between revenue-raising and progressive goals, leading to a broad consensus to pursue both. An emblem of this consensus is a recent major publication by the Inter-American Development Bank, *More Than Revenue: Taxation as a Development Tool*. Its key reform ingredients include a dual income-tax system with low and proportional rates on capital, and with the highest rate on wage income equal to the (single) corporate rate;

the elimination of exemptions on capital income (of people) and special corporate rates; and the phasing out of exemptions and zero rates in the VAT, with a personal VAT or other form of reimbursement for poor households' consumption, along with a shift of social insurance funding from payroll taxes. Hence a major target is the proliferation of special tax regimes, while the report also shows a concern with informality and its effects on the fiscal sustainability of social insurance. But this agenda has an interest in equity, too—visible in its focus on effectively taxing capital income of persons (the proportional rate allows withholding at the source, while the low rate seeks to avoid motivating evasion) and its provision for finding compensation, within the tax system itself, for the ending of VAT exemptions on items of popular consumption.[44]

FACTORS THAT INFLUENCE REFORM OUTCOMES

This section classifies factors that might influence tax policy changes. These factors are also identified in the narrative country case chapters that make up the bulk of this volume.

We begin with *formal political power* deriving from a party or coalition's control of the presidency, the legislature, and the other institutions relevant to taxation. Other things being equal, more control brings a greater possibility of reform. Absolute majorities in presidential elections, especially in the first round of a two-round process, are an advantage. Parliaments matter, too; for example, the fate of progressive reform under the second government of Michelle Bachelet (see chapter 1) depended in large measure on the number of seats held by her coalition.

Political institutional factors would comprise not only constitutional arrangements (presidential vs. parliamentary systems, veto points, power to originate budget bills) but also the strength and cohesion of political parties and the apportionment of electoral districts. Such factors could also include the state itself—its relative autonomy, coherence, and performance. (We assume that although institutions are often seen as expressions of underlying structural power, they can also operate autonomously.) They are also hard to change. For example, historically poor performance on the spending side in Mexico (the low quality of public services and the lack of transparency) has led to a resilient distrust of taxation and a problem of tax insufficiency that has resisted a political solution for a long time.[45] For another, legislative malapportionment could block democratic impulses, thus entrenching elite power.[46] Finally, there could be a reciprocal relationship between administrative deficiencies and elite efforts to block progressive reforms: Where it is hard to evade or avoid income and property taxes, elites have a greater motivation to block reforms that increase these levies; where evasion is easy, they would care less.

Next, what chapter 2 author Tasha Fairfield has called the *instrumental* power of societal actors also deserves its own category.[47] This is the influence that derives from organization, access, and personal relationships—including those founded on wealth—as exercised in and around institutional arenas. For example, powerful sectoral or firm-level lobbies are more likely to yield tax systems with a variety of rates and sectoral exemptions. Highly organized and encompassing business or private-sector organizations, reflecting a high degree of unity among the economic elite generally, could stifle progressive reform in the legislature—or keep it off the agenda entirely. Here, Guatemala's CACIF is the most prominent example, while Chile and Mexico also stand out for the relative unity of their business sectors. The political scientist Gabriel Ondetti considers differences in business-sector organized power to be an important explanation for the stark contrast between Mexico's historically light tax burden and Brazil's historically heavy one.[48] However, in some cases, perhaps, highly encompassing business organizations could prove to be better allies in efforts to reduce sectoral tax exemptions and other types of opportunistic behavior.[49]

Structural factors include those related to the disposition and character of economic power in civil society and the shape of the economy generally. They are the hardest to change via ordinary policy, at least in the short run. For example, mobile capital and weak investment have been blamed for low taxes on capital and the proliferation of exemptions for investment in particular sectors.[50] For another, sectors dominated by large firms might be more likely to enjoy tax exemptions.[51] Finally, resource rents relieve states of the need to tax civil society in order to spend, so the timing of price changes might also determine the timing and urgency of tax changes.[52]

Another dimension involves *cultural* and *behavioral* considerations. These take on great importance in the practical politics of taxation because policymakers often try to influence public expectations about tax burdens (how will the reform affect your tax bill?) and tax compliance (will the tax authority start catching and prosecuting big evaders?). Tax evasion and compliance can be linked to a country's tax culture, which in turn relates to perceptions of fairness and accountability and also to expectations about how others behave, or are punished.[53]

Finally, a wide variety of *conjunctural* factors—circumstantial factors such as the electoral calendar, economic cycles (including price shifts that affect resource rents), security conditions, and protest politics—influence the agenda and the alternatives. (In this context, "alternatives" should be understood as what policymakers would consider the likely consequences of *not* reforming taxation.) As noted above, foreign exchange crises, accompanied by inflation and a trip to the IMF, predicted revenue-raising reforms that emphasized the VAT; these were also more likely to be enacted successfully by newly seated administrations.[54] Or, to take an example mentioned in a later chapter, the outbreak of street protests that include taxation demands could suddenly change the agenda for tax reform, as has happened in Chile.[55]

THE POLITICAL ECONOMY OF PROGRESSIVE TAX REFORM: MAIN CONCLUSIONS

To begin to offer conclusions, it is important to note that in each of the three "generations" of the recent history of tax reforms in Latin America, each dominant kind of tax reform seems to have had different determinants. The revenue-raising and simplifying VAT-centered reforms of the first generation accompanied the region's shift toward neoliberalism. These reforms were commonly ushered in by inflationary crises, often under new administrations responding to the imposition of explicit IMF conditions.[56] Reforms of the second period, dominated by amendments and adjustments to inherited tax structures, took place without the IMF's involvement, whereas reforms appear to have been more likely where political systems had an unusually high number of parties.[57] The progressive reforms of the third generation, which are the reforms examined most closely in this book, seem to have arisen in conditions notably different from those associated with either of the previous modes.

In the cases considered in this volume, formal political power and conjunctural factors appear to have been most important—above all, in explaining positive outcomes. The two major progressive reforms, in Uruguay in 2006 and in Chile in 2014, both took place under left-wing presidents with strong mandates, whose parties or coalitions had legislative majorities. In both these instances, the cause of reform was also probably helped by a tax administration with a reputation for competence and autonomy—and in both, reformers used this resource effectively in their communications strategies. In all four cases where reforms included net increases in revenue—Chile, Mexico, Colombia (2014) and Guatemala (though the revenue gain was much less in the last)—they took place in the first year of a presidential term, thus conforming to the pattern of revenue-raising reforms of the first generation. In Colombia (2012) and Uruguay, the proclaimed intent of revenue neutrality aided the passage of reform by diminishing expectations of an increased tax burden among the broad middle sectors. Especially where business or private-sector organizations were strong enough to block or limit reform in the recent past, a threat from the left (students in Chile, the specter of a Sandra Colom candidacy in Guatemala) helped overcome this obstacle, if only partially. Finally, the volatility of fiscal resource rents appears to have complicated the case for reform in Mexico and Colombia; and none of the countries, reformers or not, suffered a broadly felt economic crisis.

OVERVIEW AND STRUCTURE OF THE BOOK

This book analyzes the political economy of tax reform, above all progressive tax reform, in five countries: Chile, Uruguay, Colombia, Guatemala, and Mexico. The five chapters, one on each country, are written by scholars who have published extensively on taxation issues. The chapters evaluate the strengths and weaknesses of the reform initiatives, and suggest some reasons for their success or failure in each case. In addition, to broaden our understanding and indicate the range of views that exist regarding taxation issues, we have invited specialists linked to the private sector to present their views on recent reforms in their own countries—one concerning the successful passage of a major reform (Chile in 2014), and the other a reform that was passed but whose subsequent evolution has been nearly as problematic as prior reform attempts (Guatemala in 2012). Because the chapters also present clear variation in political conditions and policy outcomes, in a concluding chapter, we juxtapose them and attempt to identify the most important variables for explaining the fate of tax reform among the cases and, by bringing in other recent experiences from the region, across Latin America more generally.

Chile. In her wide-ranging analysis of Chile in chapter 1, Tasha Fairfield shows that President Bachelet's major progressive tax reform in 2014 followed more than two decades of pragmatic incrementalism on the part of the Chilean center-left. After the country's return to democracy in 1990, governments of the Concertación center-left coalition faced strong opposition from right-wing parties and business organizations, along with constraint from the institutional legacies of the dictatorship. In response, these governments employed a variety of strategies, from the rhetorical (e.g., tying reforms to the benefits they would fund) to the substantive (in which governments offered different forms of compensation to elites in return for tax increases). Fairfield compiles these strategies into a kind of catalogue for tax reformers. She then describes how the student protests of 2011–12 transformed the political arena, alarming business leaders and the political right, thereby making a significant progressive reform possible. However, even the 2014 reform showed the consensualist DNA of the center-left, as it was substantially modified in concert with representatives of business and the political right, even though the votes of the latter were not needed for its passage.

Chile—commentary. In his commentary on the 2014 Chilean tax reform, Francisco Rosende argues that the changes are likely to damage economic growth, savings, innovation, and equity. He observes that the controversial and now-defunct provision for Taxable Profit Funds (Fondos de Utilidades Tributables, FUTs) in the old tax law was instituted at a time of crippling indebtedness and financial weakness in the Chilean private sector. It worked, he says; FUTs served as useful sources of working capital and financial deepening. As for Bachelet's reforms, he characterizes them as a "tax shock," legislating rapid changes in tax rates and structures, over the objections of leading economists. He expects that the reform will favor large firms over small ones, not only because of the elimination of the FUT provision (for which the best alternative will be bonds or bank credit) but also due to new legal complexity (under which, among other changes, firms elect from two alternative tax systems).

Uruguay. In chapter 2, Andrés Rius describes Uruguay's first substantial progressive tax reform in recent Latin American experience, the 2006 package passed by the Frente Amplio (Broad Front) government of Tabaré Vázquez (2005–10; reelected in 2014). Rius asks a classic question for political economists: How can governments gain taxpayers' consent for tax reform? He argues that this tax initiative succeeded because it was revenue neutral, was backed by an effective communication strategy, and faced little resistance from the wealthiest Uruguayans. An innovative contribution of Rius's paper is the use of a behavioral economics approach, focusing particularly on strategies to overcome a loss-aversion bias. He spotlights the authorities' efforts to avoid activating the opposition of the extraordinarily broad swath of the Uruguayan public that considers itself "middle class." He also draws a sharp contrast between the income tax / VAT reform of 2006 and a subsequent initiative to increase land taxes: the former did not activate the weakly organized upper class, whereas the latter did—and was later defeated in the courts.

Colombia. In chapter 3, Gustavo Flores-Macías analyzes two recent and more modest tax reforms in Colombia. Spotlighting the 2012 reform under the first administration of President Juan Manuel Santos, the author finds that its main determinants were the government's legislative majority, the reform's revenue neutrality, and a persuasive argument that it would lead to an increase in formal employment. Although revenue neutrality reduced anxiety about an increase in the fiscal burden, the employment argument brought labor-intensive industries to the government's side, while appealing to the broader business community, for which informality had long been an important issue. Unlike the Chilean reform, this one was not launched at the onset of the administration, yet it still passed with overwhelming support. Flores-Macías also identifies several factors that reduced the resistance of the business sector, particularly the reduction of corporate tax rates. As for the reform efforts that culminated in December 2014, the author points to the revenue imperative (the result of declining oil prices, spending commitments, and fiscal rules limiting the size of the country's deficit) and sees the government's choice of continuity in the tax system as a pragmatic response. Comparing the two reforms, it appears that progressivity is best pursued when not under fiscal pressure.

Guatemala. During the past few decades, the governments of Guatemala and Mexico have not only failed to make their tax systems more progressive; but with tax revenue levels among the lowest in the hemisphere, they have also failed to fund their states adequately. In chapter 4, Maynor Cabrera and Aaron Schneider analyze the repeated disappointments of tax reform in Guatemala since the end of the civil war (1996), with a special focus on the 2012 initiative of President Otto Pérez Molina. The authors describe a pattern of legislative and party fragmentation that cannot sustain programmatic commitments, even for an entire presidential term. Despite repeated attempts to engage social actors in a "fiscal pact," reforms have fallen short due to party volatility, court interventions, and active elite resistance, led by the main private-sector confederation, CACIF. Although Pérez Molina's government has passed the country's most important tax reform to date, its revenue effect has been modest, and the state still collects barely the commitment of 12 percent of GDP spelled out in the peace accords almost twenty years earlier. In sum, the authors argue, Guatemalan elites have coordinated sufficiently to block efforts at state building, but—so far, at least—not sufficiently to advance a positive fiscal and development project of their own.

Guatemala—commentary. The commentary on Guatemalan taxation, authored by FUNDESA (Fundación para el Desarrollo de Guatemala, a think tank founded by progressive businesspeople) and CACIF, offers a glimpse of what this fiscal project might look like. Considering Guatemala's relatively low tax burden and the need for public investment to meet the country's development challenges, the authors argue that the main culprit is not the formal private sector, which has a strong taxpaying culture, but rather the high level of informality in the economy—74.5 percent of the economically active population. This also hurts VAT collection at the country's borders, because of uncontrolled smuggling. Along with a "national crusade" against informality, the authors also advocate that redistribution should not be a goal of the tax system. They prefer, for example, an expansion of the personal income tax base over the raising of rates on the highest incomes and argue that expanding the tax base is key to generating sufficient resources for the state to provide essential public goods such as quality education and security. Looking ahead, FUNDESA and CACIF consider that reforms of the Guatemalan tax system should be part of a comprehensive fiscal pact, along the lines of the agreement reached in 2000, and should include strong controls and greater efficiency and transparency on government spending.

Mexico. In chapter 5, Vidal Romero analyzes Mexican fiscal politics since the political opening of 2000, with a narrative centered on four main tax initiatives. He observes that most fiscal reforms in Mexico have taken place during times of poor growth and significant revenue needs, often when oil revenues were falling. As a result, there have been no comprehensive reforms but rather a series of uncoordinated measures, maximizing revenue from those sources that have been easiest to tap, then redistributing to organized interests through spending. The Partido Acción Nacional administrations of presidents Vicente Fox and Felipe Calderón did not prioritize progressivity, either. As a result, their reform initiatives failed to garner wide support in the Congress, while important provisions have been struck down by the courts. The author identifies several reasons for these repeated failures, including excessive dependency on oil revenue; antiquated jurisprudence on tax issues; a federalism that encourages irresponsibility among states and municipalities; and capital mobility across the U.S. border. Although the tax reform of 2013 could be described as the most successful in terms of both revenue and equity objectives, its achievements were very modest. It was initially described as a progressive reform, and like prior reforms, it was passed under conditions of revenue shortfall, so that the goals of progressivity and revenue gains each complicated the achievement of the other. Romero's chapter finishes with four practical policy lessons, drawn from the Mexican experience but applicable beyond it, beginning with the need to improve the effectiveness and transparency of public spending.[58]

Conclusion. In the concluding chapter, we pull together the analysis of these five country case studies as well as those of other countries—including Brazil, Costa Rica, and the Dominican Republic—identifying several variables that appear to correspond with different kinds of tax reforms. Finally, drawing from the case studies, we list lessons for would-be reformers, emphasizing things more likely to be in their control.

NOTES

1. See, e.g., M. Blofield, ed., *The Great Gap: Inequality and the Politics of Redistribution in Latin America* (University Park: Pennsylvania State University Press, 2011).
2. Felipe López-Calva and Nora Lustig, *Declining Inequality in Latin America* (Washington, D.C.: Brookings Institution Press, 2010). But for the findings of researchers who use tax returns to estimate a corrected Gini and find little change during the period, see P. H. G. F. Souza, M. Medeiros, and F. A. de Castro, "Top Incomes in Brazil: Preliminary Results," Social Science Research Network, October 23, 2014, http://ssrn.com/abstract=2511314 or http://dx.doi.org/10.2139/ssrn.2511314.
3. A. Meltzer and S. Richard, "A Rational Theory of the Size of Government," *Journal of Political Economy* 89 (1981): 914–27.
4. See the summary of estimates up to 2012 given by James E. Mahon, *Tax Incidence and Tax Reforms in Latin America," Project on Taxation and Equality* (Washington, D.C.: Latin American Program of the Woodrow Wilson International Center for Scholars, 2012), table 2, 7, http://www.wilsoncenter.org/publication/tax-incidence-and-tax-reforms-latin-america-0. Since 2012, a new wave of research using tax return data promises to substantially improve our estimates of tax incidence and income distribution, especially among the richest households. See, e.g., Souza, Medeiros, and de Castro, "Top Incomes," n. 3; and Tasha Fairfield and Michel Jorratt, "*Top Income Shares, Business Profits, and Effective Tax Rates in Contemporary Chile*," ICTD Working Paper 17 (Brighton: International Centre for Tax and Development at the Institute of Development Studies, 2014).
5. An important early work is by A. Harberger, "The Incidence of the Corporation Tax," *Journal of Political Economy* 76 (1962): 215–40. For a recent summary of the literature, see J. Gravelle, "Corporate Income Tax: Incidence, Economic Effects, and Structural Issues," in *Tax Reform in the 21st Century: A Volume in Memory of Richard Musgrave*, ed. R. Musgrave, J. Head, and R. Krever (London: Kluwer Law International, 2009).
6. Trade liberalization involved reducing tariffs and other taxes on trade, important generators of revenue for Latin American states in the mid–twentieth century.
7. A. Corbacho, V. Freites, and E. Lora, eds., *More Than Revenue: Taxation as Development Tool* (Washington, D.C.: Inter-American Development Bank, 2013), 7.

8. L. Caro, and E. Stein, *Ideology and Taxation in Latin America* (Washington, D.C.: Inter-American Development Bank, 2013).
9. See also N. Salazar, *Political Economy of Tax Reforms: The Case of Colombia* (Washington, D.C.: Latin American Program of the Woodrow Wilson International Center for Scholars, 2013), http://www.wilsoncenter.org/publication/TaxationColombia.
10. Even in Uruguay, the six-year-old PIT brought in less than 14 percent of tax revenues in 2013. Uruguay, Ministerio de Economía y Finanzas, Indicadores Económicos (Recaudación DGI), available at http://www.mef.gub.uy/indicadores.php.
11. Corbacho, Fretes, and Lora, *More Than Revenue*, 89, citing C. Sepulveda and J. Martínez-Vázquez, "Property Taxation in Latin-America: An Assessment and Options for Reform," in "Relaciones Intergubernamentales y Descentralización en América Latina," paper presented at CEPAL-GTZ conference, Santiago, November 2009.
12. In fact, based on sketchy data from the early 1970s, the personal income tax (PIT) seems to have declined slightly in relative importance by 1995–2000. The comparison countries include Colombia, Costa Rica, the Dominican Republic, Peru, Uruguay, and Venezuela. Of particular importance, they exclude Argentina and Brazil, for which the proportion from personal income taxes rose during these decades, but could not be included because of missing data on indirect taxes for one of the periods. J. E. Mahon, "Tax Reforms and Income Distribution in Latin America," in *The Great Gap: Inequality and the Politics of Redistribution in Latin America*, ed. M. Blofield (University Park: Pennsylvania State University Press, 2011).
13. See, e.g., Inter-American Development Bank, *Facing Up to Inequality in Latin America: Economic and Social Progress in Latin America, 1998–99* (Baltimore: Johns Hopkins University Press, 1999), 7.
14. A good summary of one type of opportunism, the financial transaction tax, is by T. M. Pecho, *Hechos Estilizados de los Impuestos sobre las Transacciones Financieras en América Latina: 1990–2012* (Panama City: Centro Interamericano de Administradores Tributarios, 2013).
15. Meltzer and Richard, "Rational Theory," n. 4.
16. P. Profeta, and S. Scabrosetti, "Political Economy Issues of Taxation," in *Tax Systems and Tax Reforms in Latin America*, ed. L. Bernardi, A. Barreix, A. Marenzi, and P. Profeta, (Abingdon, UK: Routledge, 2008); A. Alesina and D. Rodrik, "Distributive Politics and Economic Growth," *Quarterly Journal of Economics* 109, no. 2 (1994): 465–90.
17. M. Best, "Political Power and Tax Revenues in Central America," *Journal of Development Economics* 3 (1976): 50.
18. Ibid., 65–67.
19. M. R. Agosin, A. Barreix, J. C. Gómez Sabaini, and R. Machado, "Tax Reform for Human Development in Central America," *CEPAL Review* 87 (2005): 79–96, at 81, 93–94. The authors find this in regressions on a ninety-five-country data set. However, given that they use cross-national figures from the *World Development Indicators*, the results might be affected by the high number of Latin American countries, with low tax/GDP ratios and high Ginis, in the middle-income range.

20. R. Bird, *Taxation in Latin America: Reflections on Sustainability and the Balance Between Equity and Efficiency*, ITP Paper 0306 (Toronto: Joseph L. Rotman School of Management at the University of Toronto, 2003); K. Sokoloff, and E. Zolt, "Inequality and Taxation: Evidence from the Americas on How Inequality May Influence Tax Institutions," *NYU Tax Law Review* 59 (2006): 192–206.
21. "State Capacity in Latin America," *Economía* 10, no. 2 (Spring 2010): 1–45.
22. E. Goñi, J. H. López, and L. Servén, "Fiscal Redistribution and Income Inequality in Latin America," *World Development* 39, no. 9 (2011): 1564–66.
23. On the former, see C. Zucco, "When Payouts Pay Off: Conditional Cash Transfers in Brazil, 2002–10," *American Journal of Political Science* 57, no. 4 (October 2013): 810–22; on the latter, see D. Correa, "The Effect of Conditional Cash Transfers on Latin American Presidential Elections" (Ph.D. diss., University of Illinois, Urbana-Champaign, 2012).
24. V. Tanzi, "Taxation in Latin America in the Last Decade," in *Latin American Macroeconomic Reform: The Second Stage*, ed. J. A. González, A. O. Krueger, and A. Tornell (Chicago: University of Chicago Press, 2003), 327–56.
25. J. Gómez Sabaini, "Evolución y situación tributaria actual en América Latina: Una serie de temas para la discusión," in *Tributación en América Latina: En busca de una nueva agenda de reformas*, ed. O. Centrángolo and J. Gómez Sabaini (Santiago: Comisión Económica para América Latina y el Caribe, 2006), 111–12.
26. T. Fairfield, "The Politics of Taxing Latin American Elites: The Corporate Income Tax in Chile and Interest Income in Argentina," paper presented at Annual Meeting of the American Political Science Association, Chicago, August 30–September 2, 2007.
27. J. Mahon, *Mobile Capital and Latin American Development* (University Park: Pennsylvania State Press, 1996), 181.
28. C. Boix, *Democracy and Redistribution* (Cambridge: Cambridge University Press, 2003), 38–43.
29. Goñi, López, and Servén, "Fiscal Redistribution," 1559. Also see the compendium given by Mahon, *Tax Incidence*, table 2.
30. A. Barreix, J. Roca, and L. Villela, *Fiscal Policy and Equity: Estimation of the Progressivity and Redistributive Capacity of Taxes and Social Public Expenditures in the Andean Countries*, INTAL-INT Working Paper 33 (Washington, D.C.: Inter-American Development Bank, 2007), 55–60 and tables 32 and 34. See also H. López and G. Perry, *Inequality in Latin America: Determinants and Consequences*, Policy Research Working Paper 4504 (Washington, D.C.: World Bank, 2008), 18. The figures for these three countries in the Luxembourg Income Study are less dramatic—finding their taxation to be slightly progressive—but similar. See C. Wang and K. Caminada, *Disentangling Income Inequality and the Redistributive Effect of Social Transfers and Taxes in 36 LIS Countries*, Luxembourg Income Survey Working Paper 567 (Luxembourg: Cross-National Data Center, 2011), http://www.lisdatacenter.org/wps/liswps/567.pdf.
31. This is the conclusion of Goñi, López, and Servén, "Fiscal Redistribution," 1559: "Distributional concerns should not dictate the choice between income tax and VAT-based strategies to raise revenue collection, even for policy makers mindful of equity concerns."

32. J. Kato, *Regressive Taxation and the Welfare State: Path Dependence and Policy Diffusion* (Cambridge: Cambridge University Press, 2003). See also S. Steinmo, *Taxation and Democracy: Swedish, British, and American Approaches to Financing the Modern State* (New Haven, Conn.: Yale University Press, 1993).
33. J. Timmons, "The Fiscal Contract: States, Taxes, and Public Services," *World Politics* 57 (July 2005): 534–36. An early exposition of this approach is by M. Levi, *Of Rule and Revenue* (Berkeley: University of California Press, 1988). A similar view also informs some new work on tax compliance; see B. Torgler, M. Schaffner, and A. Macintyre, "Tax Compliance, Tax Morale, and Governance Quality," in *Developing Alternative Frameworks for Explaining Tax Compliance*, ed. J. Alm, J. Martínez-Vázquez, and B. Torgler (London: Routledge, 2010), 145–53, 160–67.
34. K. Breceda, J. Rigolini, and J. Saavedra, "Latin America and the Social Contract: Patterns of Social Spending and Taxation," *Population and Development Review* 35, no. 4 (2009): 734–35.
35. But see López and Perry, *Inequality*, 6–8.
36. W. Easterly and S. Fischer, "Inflation and the Poor," *Journal of Money, Credit, and Banking* 33, no. 2 (2001): 160–78.
37. S. B. Hager, "Public Debt, Ownership, and Power: The Political Economy of Distribution and Redistribution" (Ph.D. diss., York University, Toronto, 2013).
38. On the first point, see K. Cowan, E. Levy-Yeyati, U. Panizza, and F. Sturzenegger, *Sovereign Debt in the Americas: New Data and Stylized Facts*, Research Department Working Paper 577 (Washington, D.C.: Inter-American Development Bank, 2006). On the second point, see N. G. Mankiw, "The Savers-Spenders Theory of Fiscal Policy," *American Economic Review* 90, no. 2 (2000): 123.
39. International Monetary Fund, Press Release 12/445, Washington, 2012.
40. C. Garcimartín and S. Díaz de Sarralde, "Análisis del Sistema Impositivo de la República Dominicana," photocopy, August 2012; Ministerio de Hacienda, República Dominicana, "Gastos Tributarios en República Dominicana," September 2011.
41. N. Lustig, G. Gray Molina, S. Higgins, M. Jaramillo, W. Jiménez, V. Paz, C. Pereira, C. Pessino, J. Scott and E. Yañez, *The Impact of Taxes and Social Spending on Inequality in Argentina, Bolivia, Brazil, Mexico, and Peru: A Synthesis of Results*, Working Paper 331 (Washington, D.C.: Center for Global Development, 2012), 1.
42. V. Tanzi, *Taxation and Equitable Economic Development: A Historical Note*, Latin American Program of the Woodrow Wilson International Center for Scholars and Fedesarrollo, Washington, November 2014. http://www.wilsoncenter.org/sites/default/files/VitoTanzi_2014_final.pdf; abstract available at http://www.wilsoncenter.org/publication/Vito_Tanzi_Taxation-and-Development-A-Historical-Note.
43. J. R. Afonso, *A Economia Política da Reforma Tributária: O Caso Brasileiro*, Latin American Program of the Woodrow Wilson International Center for Scholars, Washington, September 2013, http://www.wilsoncenter.org/publication/ReformaTributariaBrasil.
44. Corbacho, Freites, and Lora, *More Than Revenue.* On informality and social insurance, see S. Levy, *Good Intentions, Bad Outcomes* (Washington, D.C.: Brookings Institution Press, 2008). On the dual income tax, see R. Bird and E. Zolt, "Dual

Income Taxation: A Promising Path to Tax Reform for Developing Countries," *World Development* 39 (2012): 1691–1703.

45. C. Elizondo, *Progresividad y eficacia del gasto público en México: Precondición para una política recaudatoria efectiva* (Washington, D.C.: Latin American Program of the Woodrow Wilson International Center for Scholars, 2014), http://www.wilsoncenter.org/publication/PoliticaFiscalMexico.
46. M. Ardanaz and C. Scartascini, "Inequality and Personal Income Taxation: The Origins and Effects of Legislative Malapportionment," *Comparative Political Studies*, April 2013.
47. T. Fairfield, "Business Power and Tax Reform: Taxing Income and Profits in Chile and Argentina," *Latin American Politics and Society* 52, no. 2 (2010): 37–71.
48. G. Ondetti, "Tax Burdens and Historical Legacies in Brazil and Mexico" paper presented at the Annual Meeting of the American Political Science Association, 2012, available at http://ssrn.com/abstract=2110920.
49. R. Bates, "A Political Scientist Looks at Tax Reform," in *Tax Reform in Developing Countries*, ed. M. Gillis (Durham, N.C.: Duke University Press, 1989), 486.
50. J. Gómez Sabaini, "Evolución y situación tributaria actual en América Latina: Una serie de temas para la discusión," in *Tributación en América Latina: En busca de una nueva agenda de reformas*, ed. O. Centrángolo and J. Gómez Sabaini (Santiago: Comisión Económica para América Latina y el Caribe, 2006), 111–12.
51. Bates, "Political Scientist Looks at Tax Reform," 483.
52. The literature on resource rents and governance is now huge. Two of the most relevant works are by M. Ross, *The Oil Curse: How Petroleum Wealth Shapes the Development of Nations* (Princeton, N.J.: Princeton University Press, 2012); and T. Dunning, *Crude Democracy: Natural Resource Wealth and Political Regimes* (Cambridge: Cambridge University Press, 2008).
53. M. Bergman, *Tax Evasion and the Rule of Law in Latin America: The Political Culture of Cheating and Compliance in Argentina and Chile* (University Park: Pennsylvania State University Press, 2009); B. Torgler, M. Schaffner, and A. Macintyre, "Tax Compliance, Tax Morale, and Governance Quality," in *Developing Alternative Frameworks for Explaining Tax Compliance*, ed. J. Alm, J. Martínez-Vázquez, and B. Torgler (London: Routledge, 2010), 145–53, 160–67.
54. J. Mahon, "Causes of Tax Reform in Latin America," *Latin America Research Review* 39 (2004): 1–29. On crisis and new administrations, see W. Ascher, "Risk, Politics, and Tax Reform: Lessons from Some Latin American Experiences," in *Tax Reform in Developing Countries*, ed. M. Gillis (Durham, N.C.: Duke University Press, 1989). Ascher adds two qualifications and one important observation: Crisis is useful if policymakers are credible and have good macroeconomic policies; new administrations are propitious if they won convincingly; and political opponents might (quietly) facilitate reform if they expect to win the next election and want the current administration to suffer the political cost (see 464-65).
55. See also T. Fairfield, *The Political Economy of Progressive Tax Reform in Chile* (Washington, D.C.: Latin American Program of the Woodrow Wilson International Center for Scholars, 2014), http://www.wilsoncenter.org/publication/TaxReformChile.

56. Mahon, "Causes."
57. D. Focanti, M. Hallerberg, and C. Scartascini, *Tax Reforms in Latin America in an Era of Democracy*, IDB Working Paper 457 (Washington, D.C.: Inter-American Development Bank, 2013).
58. The argument about the imperative of improving the quality of public spending is also central to the paper by Elizondo, *Progresividad y eficacia*.

CHAPTER 1

The Political Economy of Progressive Tax Reform in Chile

Tasha Fairfield

In 2009, the top 1 percent of adults in Chile earned 22 percent of national income.[1] But the income taxes they paid were modest; the average effective income tax rate was less than 16 percent, compared with 24 percent in the United States.[2] President Michelle Bachelet's high-profile 2014 tax reform aimed to change this situation. During the 2013 campaign, she announced plans to raise 3 percent of Chile's gross domestic product (GDP) by taxing the country's economic elites to finance public education reform. This tax proposal, which was sent to Congress shortly after Bachelet's inauguration, represented a dramatic break with Chile's experience over the past two decades of at most modest and usually marginal income tax reforms. This chapter examines why increasing income taxes proved so difficult under previous center-left administrations, how those governments passed incremental reforms despite the constraints they faced, and how the new political context in Chile following the wave of student protests in 2011 and 2012 created an opportunity for much more substantial progressive tax reform in 2014.

Significant political obstacles hindered progressive tax reform during the two decades following Chile's return to democracy in 1990. Strong political actors—organized business and parties on the political right (the Unión Demócratica Independiente, UDI; and the Renovación Nacional, RN)—defended the low-tax, neoliberal model implemented by the dictatorship of General Augusto Pinochet. Business had significant capacity to influence policy decisions, thanks to its strong cross-sectoral peak association, the Confederación de la Producción y el Comercio (CPC), which coordinated lobbying across sectors, and ties to the right parties, especially the UDI. In conjunction with Pinochet's designated senators, the right controlled enough senate seats to veto legislation during the 1990s. During the 2000s, the center-left Concertación coalition, which governed from 1990 to 2010, was able to replace several of Pinochet's designated senators with its own members. Nevertheless, the right and the left remained nearly tied in the Senate throughout the decade. After 2011, however, the student movement counterbalanced the power of business and the right.

The body of this chapter proceeds as follows. The first section describes Chile's tax system and identifies the main factors that have led to the undertaxation of highly concentrated income and profits; the second section explains the institutional context and the process of tax policymaking in Chile following democratization; the third section discusses the strategies that Chilean governments have used to implement incremental tax increases; and the fourth section examines cases in which they were applied with varying degrees of success. The fifth section turns to tax developments following the 2011–12 student protests. This section offers a preliminary analysis of Bachelet's 2014 reform, which was approved in the Chamber of Deputies in September following significant modifications introduced in the Senate a month earlier.

THE CHILEAN TAX SYSTEM

Like most Latin American countries, Chile relies heavily on indirect taxes (figure 1.1). The revenues raised by the value-added tax (VAT) equaled an average of 8.1 percent GDP during the period 1993–2005, constituting approximately 51 percent of total tax revenue. Meanwhile, income taxes generated an average of 4.0 percent of GDP. Though Chile's overall tax revenue is not low by Latin American standards, Chilean governments have faced periodic revenue needs (with the exception of the period 2006–9, when surging copper prices exogenously produced higher tax revenue). Because the VAT base is already quite broad and the rate is relatively high

Figure 1.1. Tax Revenue in Chile, 1993–2005

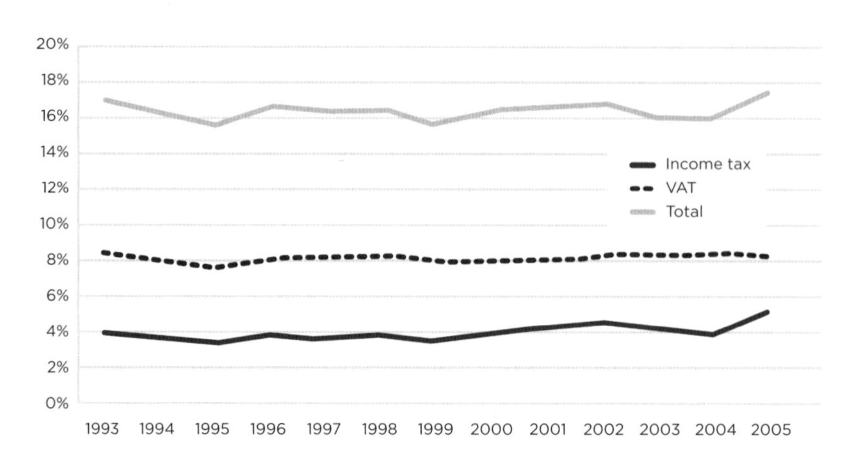

Source: Serie Ingresos Tributarios, www.sii.cl.

(18 percent from 1990 to 2003, and 19 percent thereafter), increasing the income taxes paid by upper-income individuals and big businesses has been an obvious option for increasing tax revenue.

Understanding the unique characteristics of Chile's income tax system is imperative for comprehending the nature of undertaxation of income and profits in Chile and the parameters of the tax reform problem. Chile has an integrated income tax system that ties together the corporate tax and the individual income tax. Businesses pay a corporate tax on their accrued profits. This corporate tax functions as a withholding against business owners' individual taxes. When a business distributes profits to its owners, these earnings enter into the owners' taxable income base, but the owners receive a credit for the corresponding corporate tax that the company already paid. This mechanism ensures that capital income is not double-taxed.

Individual income tax rates for wealthy Chileans are much higher than the corporate tax rate. As of 2013, the top marginal income tax rate was 40 percent, while the corporate tax rate was only 20 percent, one of the lowest in Latin America. This large gap in tax rates was intended to create incentives for businesses to reinvest their profits and thereby contribute to economic growth and development. However, the income tax system had a problematic, unintended consequence: It facilitated tax avoidance and evasion. Owners of businesses organized as partnerships, which are much more common than publicly traded corporations, found multiple ways to consume profits without declaring those profits as individual income (which would be subject to the much higher individual income tax rates). For example, a recreational vehicle for personal use could be registered to the firm rather than the owner, or the owner might simply omit distributed profits on his or her individual income tax declaration. It was very difficult for the tax agency to control income tax evasion for lack of adequate access to information that would allow the detection of undeclared distributed profits. In addition, independent professionals regularly formed "investment companies" to transform earnings that would otherwise be subject to high individual income tax rates into corporate income subject to the much lower tax rate. Wage earners were the only taxpayers who could not manipulate the income tax system to their advantage—their income taxes are automatically withheld by employers.

Ultimately, the large gap between the corporate and individual income tax rates did little to stimulate productive investment, and it was a source of substantial tax expenditures.[3] The tax agency calculates that the deferred taxation of business profits cost the state 0.9 percent of GDP in potential tax revenue in 2003.[4] Because capital income is highly concentrated in Chile, this special treatment of capital income also erodes the progressivity of income taxation.

Numerous additional special treatments and privileges for capital income, including low tax rates and exemptions for capital gains, further undermined the revenue capacity and progressivity of the income tax system. Total income tax expenditures (i.e., revenue that otherwise could have been collected) fluctuated between 3.1 percent and 4.4 percent of GDP from 2003 to 2008.[5]

This discussion illustrates that increasing the corporate tax rate and eliminating tax privileges for capital income are critical for increasing the revenue capacity and progressivity of Chile's income tax. The cases examined below, as well as Bachelet's much more radical reform proposal, are examples of such measures.

THE TAX REFORM POLICY PROCESS

Chile's stable institutional environment, along with its comparatively stable party system and highly organized and cohesive business sector, contributed to a consistent pattern of tax policymaking from 1990 to 2010 under successive Concertación governments. The Constitution grants the Chilean executive exclusive initiative on tax policy. The executive branch authorities in the Finance Ministry drafted reform initiatives, often consulting with legislators and leaders of business associations in order to assess the political feasibility of proposed tax policy changes. When the executive branch ascertained that a reform option would not enjoy sufficient support in Congress or would stimulate strong opposition from organized business, that option would be discarded. The anticipation of a veto by the right and Pinochet's appointed senators in Congress helped remove multiple income tax initiatives from the agenda during the 1990s. Governments also had incentives to avoid provoking conflict with business on taxation—a core concern of the largely Pinochet-aligned private sector—in the period following the transition to democracy. A pattern of informally institutionalized consultation with business associations on all matters of economic policymaking reinforced these incentives to avoid conflict with business in areas affecting its core interests,[6] so as not to disrupt productive cooperation on other issues.[7]

If the executive branch ascertained that a tax reform initiative had real prospects for enactment, a bill would be sent to Congress. The lower house would consider the reform first, followed by the Senate. Given that the center-right enjoyed greater representation in the Senate than in the lower house, thanks in part to electoral rules that are generally understood to favor the right, the most significant modifications to reform bills tended to arise from negotiations in the upper house. Although legislators can only vote to accept or reject measures in a tax reform bill—they cannot modify the text of a tax bill due to exclusive executive initiative—the executive regularly negotiated modifications to placate the right (and occasionally to maintain discipline within the governing coalition). Modifications were often necessary to ensure sufficient votes to pass legislation. In addition, Concertación governments tended to prefer securing at least some opposition votes in order to enhance the legitimacy and longevity of reforms; this style of policymaking rose out of the experience of key Concertación leaders during the 1973 coup and the subsequent dictatorship. For similar reasons, governments tended to underutilize strong constitutional executive powers.[8] Moreover, using veto powers constituted a "nuclear option" that in the future could undermine the executive's ability to negotiate reforms with the opposition.[9]

THE CONCERTACIÓN'S STRATEGY REPERTOIRE

The Concertación developed a repertoire of what I term "tax-side strategies" and "benefit-side strategies" to manage strong opposition from the business community and the right.[10] The former, which include attenuating impact and legitimating appeals, apply design-based and/or framing techniques. The latter—which include emphasizing fiscal discipline, compensation, and linking to social spending—aim to focus attention on the benefits that taxation will fund. These strategies are designed to mobilize popular support for and/or to mitigate elite resistance to reform. Several of these strategies have also served to consolidate support within the governing coalition itself; divisions between the more market-oriented wing of the coalition and its more statist, left-leaning wing occasionally threatened discipline on tax issues. In this section, I provide an overview of each strategy and explain the factors underpinning their potential for success as well as those factors that have occasionally limited their effectiveness. Some strategies have become less effective (if not less frequently employed) over time, while others have become increasingly potent due to the changing nature of electoral competition. In general, the Concertación has made use of multiple reform strategies when advancing any particular tax increase.

Attenuating Impact

This strategy involves gradualism, with the goal of minimizing opposition to reform by limiting its impact. Rather than attempting comprehensive reform, Concertación administrations pursued incremental reforms, gradually increasing tax rates and broadening tax bases when feasible, in accord with the early-1990s dictum of President Patricio Aylwin (1990–94) that reform should be undertaken "*en la medida de lo posible*" (in light of what is possible).[11]

Concertación administrations have used two reform design techniques to attenuate impact: phase-ins and "temporary" reforms. Phase-ins entail gradual implementation. For example, a tax-rate increase can be implemented in small increments over an interval of several years, or a base-broadening measure could be scheduled to take effect several years after its approval in Congress. Phase-ins give the business community a transition period in which to adjust investment plans or to finish projects that were already under way before the tax rules change. Consequently, phase-ins help to reduce business opposition and can neutralize concerns regarding a tax increase's potential impact on investment.

The second technique involves legislating a tax increase for a limited period of time, after which the pre-reform legislation will go back into effect. Variants of this technique were employed by President Eduardo Frei Montalva (1964–70) in the 1960s.[12] This technique was also used in Chile's well-known 1990 tax reform; initially designing the corporate tax increase as temporary helped to bring business and the right on board, and the Concertación was later able to make the tax increase permanent. In fact, every time a government legislated a temporary tax increase, the reform was later renewed or made permanent. Renegotiating reforms that have already been in effect for several years is often easier than passing the reform for the first time; governments have been able to argue convincingly that the tax increase in question did not hurt investment and that an abrupt loss of revenue would threaten fiscal discipline (below, see the discussion of emphasizing fiscal discipline).

While techniques that attenuate impact helped the Concertación legislate tax increases, business and the right became quite aware of this strategy over time and therefore tended to resist even incremental tax increases. A former general manager of the CPC explained business's position as follows: "What happened with many Concertación governments is that if you analyze a given law, or part of a law, on its own it does not have a big impact, but if you add up one law here and another six months later, and another and another, in the end, of course it has an impact."[13] Likewise, marketing reforms as "temporary" became less effective over time, given that business and the right came to anticipate that governments would try to make all such reforms permanent in the future—in essence, promises that tax increases would be temporary lost credibility.

Legitimating Appeals

Legitimating appeals aim to mobilize public support by drawing on widely espoused norms like equity, thereby pressuring politicians to accept reforms they might otherwise oppose. In Chile, Concertación governments deployed such appeals in an effort to draw the right's attention away from the interests of its core business constituency to focus instead on the broader electorate and the potential electoral costs of opposing tax increases.

Concertación governments applied two main types of legitimating appeals. The first type, vertical equity appeals, draws on the principle that taxation should be progressive. Equity appeals work best in conjunction with progressive reforms that clearly target economic elites rather than also affecting middle- or lower-income sectors. As in other countries, business and the right in Chile often framed tax increases as affecting small businesses or the middle class—usually, professionals who, although much better off than the average citizen, are not members of the truly wealthy elite. This argument is harder to make when tax increases narrowly and patently affect the wealthiest taxpayers.

Vertical equity appeals in Chile also served to align Concertación legislators behind executive tax proposals. On one hand, targeting tax increases at upper-income sectors helped to secure support from more conservative Christian Democrats within the governing coalition, who were often sensitive to arguments that tax increases would hurt to the middle class; during the 2000s, the Christian Democratic Party competed with the UDI to represent "middle-class" sectors.[14] The possibility that Christian Democrats and other legislators from the conservative wing of the Concertación might side with business and the right against the executive's tax proposals was a frequent concern for Finance Ministry technocrats. On the other hand, vertical equity appeals helped secure support from the left wing of the Concertación, which frequently complained that government policies were not sufficiently redistributive. To this end, the executive tried to use vertical equity appeals to promote even those tax increases that, strictly speaking, were regressive, such as the 2003 VAT increase.[15]

The second type of legitimating appeal draws on the principle of horizontal equity—individuals or firms earning similar incomes should pay similar taxes, even if the sources of their income are different. Eliminating sectoral tax incentives and broadening the income tax base to include exempt forms of capital income are examples of reforms that enhance horizontal equity. Cutting down on tax evasion also improves horizontal equity. Horizontal equity appeals can not only mobilize public support but may even generate support from business. For example, law-abiding firms tend to support reforms designed to control corporate tax evasion.[16] In theory, eliminating sectoral tax benefits can also generate support from business sectors that do not enjoy those benefits. In Chile, however, reforms to eliminate sector-specific tax benefits elicited at most tacit approval within the business sector, given strong business solidarity in opposition to tax increases. In several cases, the business community cohesively opposed reforms that sought to raise revenue from undertaxed sectors.

Legitimating appeals are most effective when political competition is strong and when major elections are approaching. Under these conditions, politicians tend to be most attuned to public opinion. However, research on political parties and representation has shown that multiple factors can break the logic of democratic accountability, such that politicians may escape electoral punishment even if their policy positions diverge from public opinion.[17] In Chile, the nature of the UDI's linkages to its electorate buffered the effect of legitimating appeals. Though the party attracts support from economic elites based on its economic policy positions, including low taxation, the party wins votes from low-income sectors through personalistic appeals and small-scale clientelism.[18] The UDI therefore has had leeway to maintain mass electoral support despite policy positions against redistribution.

Stressing Fiscal Discipline

Emphasizing fiscal discipline was a consistent feature of Chilean tax politics from 1990 to 2010. During the transition to democracy, organized business and the right worried that the Concertación would engage in irresponsible spending, which was deemed a major cause of the economic problems during the administration of President Salvador Allende (1970–73). Pointing out that higher tax revenue was essential for maintaining fiscal discipline—given increased demands on government resources in the context of democratization—was critical for passing the 1990 tax reform and making the corporate tax increase permanent in 1993.[19] After 2005, however, emphasizing fiscal discipline became a less effective strategy due to record fiscal surpluses associated with high copper prices. Copper revenue entered state coffers both through the state-owned mining company Codelco and through taxation of the booming private copper sector. Even governing-coalition politicians questioned the need to increase taxes to support new government expenditures in this context.

The Concertación almost always coupled an emphasis on fiscal discipline with either linking to social spending or elite compensation. In fact, linking tax increases to social spending requires either tacitly or explicitly making the case that expanded spending is acceptable only if new resources can be generated to finance it. The same observation holds in the case of forms of compensation for elites that entail fiscal costs, such as reducing other taxes.

Linking to Social Spending

Linking to social spending is a strategy for mobilizing public support and pressuring politicians to accept tax increases. Linking strategies help policy entrepreneurs place blame on legislators who vote against reform and can also create positive incentives for politicians to support reform by letting them share credit for providing popular benefits.

Linking tax increases to social spending has a long history in Chile. President Frei Montalva frequently employed this strategy in the 1960s.[20] Linking to spending played a key role in forging support for the 1990 tax reform and was employed in every tax increase after 1990, with only two exceptions.[21] Former officials from the Lagos administration and prior Concertación administrations consistently expressed the view that tax increases were feasible only when the executive could argue that a particular program(s) required funding. According to former president Ricardo Lagos, "The key to a tax reform is to link it to the destination of the funds.

I never wanted to discuss the tax reform, I discussed what I was going to do with the money."[22] Similarly, former finance minister Manuel Marfán maintained, "You debate the public policies and the financing in the same package. They form parts of a whole. . . . That is a very key element."[23]

The Concertación used three techniques for linking tax increases to spending. In some cases, links were based mostly on discourse. A second, stronger linking technique entailed formally including new spending programs with tax increases in the same legislative proposal, forcing both aspects to be debated at the same time and making the links more apparent, as described above by Marfán. Even tighter links could be created by making spending initiatives contingent on approval of the tax increase. This third technique was possible because the executive branch in Chile has the privilege of exclusive initiative on tax reforms—as noted above, only the executive can propose or amend a tax bill; while legislators can approve or reject measures in a tax bill, they cannot change the wording or the content of an article. Consequently, the executive could phrase a proposal such that if the tax increase were rejected, the spending program to be funded would not take effect. Contingency allows for the tightest possible linking to social spending in Chile, because earmarking is unconstitutional.

Linking to social spending could be an effective strategy for reducing opposition from the right, for two reasons. First, there tended to be more of a consensus between the left and the right in Chile on social spending than on taxation. The Pinochet regime pioneered targeted spending during the dictatorship, partly to generate a base of popular support,[24] and the Concertación subsequently adopted and expanded that model.[25] Second, right-party legislators can feel electoral pressure to support popular programs.[26] Especially in cases where the social program is viewed as—or can easily be framed as—highly justified on the basis of equity or morality, like pensions for the elderly poor, opposing a tax increase linked to social spending can be politically damaging. An UDI deputy commented, "It has an impact—the government's capacity to say 'no, those people do not want to improve the social projects and will not give money for that.' . . . It hurts us, the story that the government manages to tell."[27]

Business was also sensitive to the possibility that rejecting tax increases designed to fund social spending could damage its public image and foment demands for more extensive redistribution. Several business informants acknowledged that this strategy made it more difficult to oppose tax increases.[28] However, business and the right increasingly countered that social spending should be financed through improved efficiency, reallocation, privatization, or simply economic growth.

Compensation

These strategies provide benefits for elites who will bear the burden of tax increases. Compensation can take many forms, ranging from implementing policies that business advocates to cutting taxes other than those selected for increases. Concertación governments often created alternative investment incentives to replace tax benefits targeted for elimination, or simultaneously reduced inefficient taxes that business opposed. Governments sometimes compensated business with tax stability agreements. In 1993, the Aylwin administration was able to make the 1990 corporate tax increase permanent in exchange for cutting top personal income tax rates and informally agreeing not to increase direct taxes for the next four years. The Lagos administration offered mining companies benefits in the form of extended tax invariability clauses to mitigate opposition to the 2005 mining tax.[29]

Given the strength of business and the right, significant forms of compensation were usually necessary to reduce opposition to progressive tax increases in Chile. In contrast, Argentine governments were able to legislate more substantial tax increases in exchange for less expensive forms of compensation, given the organizational weakness and fragmentation of Argentina's business sector and the absence of a party with strong ties to economic elites in Congress.[30]

CASE STUDIES

This section discusses three case studies from the administration of President Ricardo Lagos (2001–5): the 2001 anti-evasion reform, the 2001 corporate tax increase, and the 2005 elimination of article 57 Bis, a tax subsidy for stock owners. These reforms were the most important initiatives to increase income tax revenue and/or equity after the 1990 tax reform, which increased the corporate tax rate from 10 percent to 15 percent. Equity appeals effectively minimized opposition from the right in the 2005 reform, given the high salience of inequality during the presidential campaign. By contrast, multiple strategies proved marginally effective in the 2001 reforms. The section ends with a brief analysis of income tax developments during the center-right Piñera administration's (2010–13) first year in office.

Anti-Evasion Reform

Equity appeals and strategic reform design helped the Lagos administration legislate the 2001 anti-evasion reform during a period of economic recession and strong contestation from business and the right. For political expediency, the government tried to raise revenue, mostly with measures to fight indirect tax evasion. However, the Finance Ministry also proposed restricting some income tax benefits that facilitated tax avoidance. These measures to broaden the income tax base were very modest in revenue yield, yet they were highly controversial. Though equity appeals did not prevent confrontations with business and the right, these strategies were nevertheless critical for legislating the reform.

The government used vertical and horizontal equity appeals in an effort to minimize business-right opposition. For example, President Lagos invoked vertical equity at a public meeting in September 2000, at which he announced that it was not fair for Chileans of modest means to pay 18 percent VAT on their purchases while those with more resources used loopholes to avoid paying their income taxes. He added: "There are bad Chileans who don't pay all their taxes. For that reason, I sent a proposal to the legislature aimed at ending tax evasion, so that all would pay their fair share in contributing to Chile's progress."[31] Meanwhile, the proposal text appealed to horizontal equity as follows: "Tax evasion represents a situation of great inequity, between those who fulfill their tax obligations and those who do not. Correcting this inequity is not only an ethical imperative; it is also indispensable to the proper functioning of a modern economy. . . . The fact that some companies fulfill their tax obligations creates a situation of disloyal competition vis-à-vis the rest of the private sector."[32] The government also applied equity appeals to the measures to broaden the income tax base, by characterizing the use of what business and the right considered legal tax benefits as tax avoidance. Portraying these tax measures as a way to clamp down on morally inappropriate behavior, instead of just an alternative way to raise revenue, aimed to discredit and undermine business opposition. The anti-evasion reform was also loosely linked to social spending, but this strategy played a secondary role, given the strong legitimacy of curtailing evasion.[33]

Although the government had to negotiate important concessions, the equity appeals helped navigate the package through Congress. Government informants asserted that the strategy put strong pressure on the right. The former Senate president asserted that the right found itself in an awkward position: "I definitely believe that they convinced themselves that their argument was not well founded. *[Interviewer: So in your opinion, the right was in a defensive position?]* "That's it; absolutely defensive. Anything that had even the slightest whiff of a higher tax rate or levy, they opposed. They looked for whatever kind of argument."[34] Similarly, an eminent Concertación senator asserted: "For the opposition, it was never easy to be strongly against the reductions in tax evasion. That had a basic legitimacy, and was a very significant part of the package. *[Interviewer] But the right argued it was a disguised tax reform, was that effective?* No, and finally they had to concede that this was reasonable."[35] In fact, two right-wing senators explained to the press that they had abstained instead of voting against the reform during the Finance Committee hearings in anticipation of damaging government recriminations: "If we hadn't done so, President Lagos would have said that the opposition was opposed to combating tax evasion."[36]

The 2001 Corporate Tax Increase

The 2001 corporate tax increase, an idea that took shape while the anti-evasion reform was under debate, was legislated with a different mix of strategies. Compensating economic elites in conjunction with emphasizing fiscal discipline were the central strategies in this case; equity appeals and phase-ins were employed as well.

The modest corporate tax increase from 15 percent to 17 percent was made feasible by simultaneously reducing personal income tax rates for individuals in the top income brackets—the bill proposed cutting the top marginal income tax rate from 45 percent to 40 percent, cutting the rate for the second-highest bracket from 35 percent to 32 percent, and creating an intermediate bracket with a rate of 37 percent. According to Finance Ministry calculations, this tax cut (along with additional modifications described below) exactly offset the revenue gains associated with the corporate tax increase, making the reform package revenue-neutral. However, the government anticipated that reducing the gap between the corporate and individual income tax rates would reduce incentives for tax avoidance and evasion, thereby leading to some revenue gain at the margins.

The individual income tax rate cuts compensated economic elites for the corporate tax increase. Business owners and independent professionals who did not engage in the types of avoidance and evasion described in the first section above would in fact receive a net income tax reduction, because the corporate tax is simply an advance payment on taxes owed when profits are distributed. Business owners and independent professionals who did engage in individual income tax avoidance and evasion would experience a very modest income tax increase, yet any other sources of income they earned would be taxed at the reduced individual income tax rates.

Although the individual income tax cuts contributed to reducing the gap with the corporate tax, which the Finance Ministry viewed as a major problem, an equally important function was to reduce resistance from business and the right to the corporate tax increase.[37] Former president Lagos described the tax cuts as a "candy" to placate these powerful actors.[38] As anticipated, business associations endorsed the personal income tax cuts as a move in the correct direction.[39] Right-wing politicians likewise condoned these measures.[40] Meanwhile, the government asserted that the personal income tax cuts were untenable without the corporate tax increase, given the importance of maintaining fiscal discipline and sustaining social programs for poor Chileans.

Equity appeals entered the debate in a different way from the anti-evasion reform: The government, and especially key Christian Democratic legislators, including Senator Alejandro Foxley, portrayed the individual income tax reductions as a tax cut for the "middle class." The logic was that wage earners, whose taxes are automatically withheld by employers, were the only taxpayers who could not find ways to avoid the high individual income tax rates, and in practice they therefore paid much higher effective tax rates than taxpayers with business income. The reform would therefore shift some of the effective tax burden from wage earners to business owners avoiding the individual income tax. The net effect of the reform would thus be mildly progressive, given that accrued profits greatly predominated over all other assets and income sources for taxpayers in the top brackets.

Of course, the few wage earners who would benefit from the tax cuts hardly belonged to any notion of the "middle class" grounded in Chile's objective income distribution. These taxpayers in fact belonged to roughly the top 1 percent of adults.[41] However, in comparison with Chile's far wealthier business magnates, these high-end wage earners fit with conceptualizations of the middle class employed by many Christian Democratic politicians seeking to court these constituencies, as well as right-coalition politicians and the taxpayers in question themselves. Something similar occurred in the Uruguayan case. Such subjective notions of the middle class have had important implications for tax reform elsewhere in Latin America as well.[42]

The government appealed to the broader universe of income taxpayers—also construed as members of the "middle class"—by increasing the taxable income threshold and by introducing a limited tax credit for mortgage payments. These measures appealed to business as well. The CPC endorsed the government's assertion that the mortgage tax credits would stimulate growth in the construction sector.[43]

In addition to compensating elites and framing the reform as enhancing vertical equity by reducing the burden on the middle class, the government gradually phased in the controversial corporate tax increase. The two-point increase was implemented in increments over a period of three years, such that the corporate tax rate would reach 17 percent only in 2004.

Negotiating the reform with the business community and the right proved difficult, despite the multiple strategies employed. Foxley described the process as "very complex and with a lot of conflict," and a prominent PDC senator described this mild corporate tax increase as the tax initiative that business and the right most strongly disliked during Lagos's administration.[44] Most of the RN and several of the designated senators voted in favor of the reform package as a whole, given their approval of the personal income tax cuts, but the UDI abstained to register their objection to increasing the corporate tax. The UDI voted en bloc to eliminate the corporate tax increase during the subsequent line-item vote.

Prospects for legislating the corporate tax increase would have been far worse if the personal income tax cuts had been omitted from the reform—transcripts of the Senate debate suggest that this compensation was critical for garnering support from among the ranks of the right-wing coalition and the designated senators. RN senators who voted against the UDI's motion to eliminate the corporate tax increase nevertheless spoke favorably of Chile's low corporate tax rate; the RN proposed its own motion to increase the corporate tax to 16 percent rather than 17 percent.[45] Designated senators who supported the reform package as a whole also expressed concerns over raising the corporate tax.

Eliminating 57 Bis

In 2005, the Lagos administration employed vertical equity appeals to help enact another reform to broaden the income tax base. This tax benefit, known as "57 Bis," which had been inherited from the dictatorship, was essentially a government subsidy for owners of new-issue stocks. The Concertación previously wanted to eliminate this tax benefit, but opposition from business and the right curtailed prospects for reform.

However, an opportunity for reform arose during the 2005 presidential campaign. UDI candidate Lavín blamed insufficient progress toward reducing poverty and inequality in Chile on the Concertación: "After 16 years of Concertación governments, there are a million and a half Chileans who live in overcrowded conditions, 190,000 people who live on 37,000 pesos (US$65.00) a month, and another 6 million Chileans who live on less than 2,500 pesos (US$4.40) a day."[46] President Lagos responded with the following public challenge: "The famous Article 57 Bis is still in force and signifies a tremendous source of inequality. . . . Instead of talking so much, how about if tomorrow we introduce a proposal for a new law and in less than 24 hours, we strike down Article 57 Bis?"[47] The vertical equity appeal was highly effective. Lavín quickly accepted the challenge, and the right followed his lead in the Senate. The bill received almost unanimous approval in Congress after only a brief debate. Whereas the anti-evasion reform spent almost a year in Congress, the 2005 reform was enacted in less than a month.

Because of the high-profile exchange between Lavín and Lagos and the salience of inequality during the presidential campaign, the anticipated political cost to the right of defending business interests was much higher than had been the case in 2000–2001, while the government was working to legislate the anti-evasion reform. If the right had decided to oppose the 2005 reform, it would have played into the government's hands by providing evidence that the right was hindering equity-enhancing reforms in Chile, and that Lavín could not command authority over the often unruly right-wing coalition. The right frequently countered government tax initiatives by warning of negative effects on the middle class; yet this approach was impossible because the 2005 reform narrowly affected economic elites. Tax agency data showed that only 0.5 percent of adults received 72 percent of the tax expenditures associated with 57 Bis. With the election close at hand, the right feared that voters would punish Lavín at the polls.[48]

Piñera's 2010 Corporate Tax Increase

Income tax politics took an unexpected turn in 2010, when newly elected right-wing coalition of President Sebastián Piñera (2010–14) temporarily increased the corporate tax to 20 percent. This reform emerged from an unusual conjuncture of factors. First, a massive earthquake created major, unanticipated revenue needs that made tax increases imperative in the view of many economists. Insiders concurred that the administration would not have considered tax increases if the earthquake had not occurred, in accord with Piñera's campaign platform and the preferences of organized business and the right. Second, Piñera experienced strong political pressure to signal that his administration would not be a government by and for big business. He was one of Chile's wealthiest businessmen, and the Concertación mounted a campaign to delegitimize his presidency on that basis. Leaders within the right-wing coalition judged that Piñera could have won the election by a wider margin if he had made more concerted efforts to alleviate concerns over potential conflicts of interest associated with his extensive business endeavors. These issues continued to plague the administration during its first months in office. Accordingly, government advisers hoped that increasing the corporate tax would signal Piñera's separation from the business world and regain public confidence.

Strategies pioneered by the Concertación helped the Piñera administration legislate the reform. Most important, the corporate tax increase was temporary. Moreover, the corporate tax increase was gradually phased *out*, in contrast to the usual Concertación practice of phasing *in* tax increases. The reform stipulated that the rate would fall from 20 percent to 18.5 percent in 2012, and would return to 17 percent in 2013. This reform design made the temporary nature of the tax increase more credible and helped win acquiescence from business and UDI legislators. In addition, the government included several forms of compensation, including a reduction in the stamp tax, which business associations had long lobbied to eliminate, and expanded tax credits for charitable donations.

TAX POLITICS FOLLOWING THE 2011–12 STUDENT PROTESTS: BACHELET'S 2014 REFORM

Despite the major political challenges associated with progressive taxation in Chile, subsequent developments created opportunities for much more substantial reform. The 2011 and 2012 student protests dramatically expanded the scope of debate on progressive taxation. Not only did the students' demands for major educational reform create massive new revenue needs, but the students also explicitly demanded that the government finance reform through progressive taxation. As politicians from both the left and the right struggled to improve their low approval ratings and respond to this new organized constituency of young people with significant disruptive capacity, a major debate on the structure of the tax system commenced. The student offensive compelled the Piñera administration to permanently raise the corporate tax to 20 percent, despite its clear prior intent that the 2010 increase would be temporary, in an effort to mitigate pressure for more radical reform.[49] The 2013 presidential campaign focused further attention on the issues of taxation and equity. The fact that the right had presided over an income tax increase emboldened politicians on the left to pursue more significant reform, and opposition candidates presented a variety of radical income tax reform proposals, in stark contrast to the incremental reforms of previous years.

President Michele Bachelet's 2014 tax initiative took shape in this new political context of social mobilization, discontent over inequality, and pressing revenue needs to finance expanded social spending—all of which initially relegated business concerns to the back burner. The new administration proposed increasing the corporate tax rate to 25 percent and, more important, eliminating the tax deferral for business income by mandating that all profits, whether distributed or reinvested, would enter the individual income tax base.[50] This major structural change would automatically eliminate the tax avoidance and evasion problems discussed above. In conjunction with a battery of new anti-evasion measures that previous Concertación governments had considered but never ventured to propose, these changes would significantly increase the taxes owed by the Chileans at the top of the income distribution.

The right-wing parties' 2013 electoral setbacks in Congress and business's defensive position in the context of civil society mobilization, which threatened social peace and potentially even the future of the neoliberal model, made this far-reaching reform politically feasible. The center-left coalition backing Bachelet (Nueva Mayoría, New Majority) secured a solid majority in the senate of twenty-one seats, while the right held on to only seventeen seats. In this context, business accepted the revenue target of 3 percent of GDP and significant modifications to income taxation as inevitable, while hoping to secure modifications to those components viewed as most problematic. Considering frequent prior business resistance to more minor tax increases, the government took business's recognition of the revenue target as legitimate to be a significant political accomplishment. The Bachelet administration went on to secure the bill's rapid approval in the lower house of Congress in May 2014.

Nevertheless, the Finance Ministry negotiated a compromise bill in the Senate to make the reform more palatable to business, the right, and concerned members of the government coalition. Most important, the system for taxing imputed profits (*renta atribuida*) was made voluntary. Taxpayers could instead opt into a new partially de-integrated income tax system with a slightly higher 27 percent corporate tax and a reduced credit of 65 percent against personal income taxes due when business owners received distributed profits.

Three interrelated factors contributed to the negotiated compromise: an intensive business campaign against the reform, dissent within the Nueva Mayoría, and growing concern over Chile's economic slowdown. Business strongly opposed the *renta atribuida* tax system, arguing that it would hurt growth and investment by creating incentives for business owners to withdraw their profits instead of reinvesting. The business associations emphasized these points in their presentations to the senate Finance Committee during the extensive hearings on the reform. The media reiterated these arguments; though favorable commentaries were published, negative coverage was more extensive and more prominently in the major newspapers.

Many economists associated with the center-left expressed similar concerns regarding the *renta atribuida* system and criticized the reform for not including new investment incentives to replace the preferential treatment of reinvested profits. Three former Concertación finance ministers were among those to publicly express concern regarding the tax reform's impact on investment. This dissent within the Concertación establishment reinforced business's arguments against the reform.

In light of these arguments, many Christian Democrats turned against the *renta atribuida* system. By early July, press reports suggested that the Finance Ministry recognized that it could not count on the Christian Democrats to vote in favor of this central article of the reform, thereby rendering the Nueva Mayoría's senate majority inoperable.[51] In this context, the Finance Ministry opted to rewrite the reform in direct negotiation with the members of the senate Finance Committee, including the RN and UDI representatives.

Chile's economic slowdown also appears to have contributed to the government's decision to compromise on the *renta atribuida* proposal. Whereas the government initially projected growth of 4.9 percent for

2014, the Central Bank released reports in mid-June projecting only 3 percent growth.[52] During the first stage of debate in the Senate, the Finance Ministry worked hard to allay concerns over the tax reform's impact on investment. Finance Minister Alberto Arenas presented evidence that investment in fixed assets is not sensitive to changes in business's reinvested profits funds.[53] However, by mid-July the finance minister's discourse had shifted from firm assertions that the tax reform would have no relevant effect on growth and investment to acknowledgment that ongoing debate on the reform was contributing to a climate of investment uncertainty.[54] Press accounts suggested that concerns over growth and investment motivated Bachelet to mandate a broadly negotiated agreement.[55]

An additional factor may also have contributed to the government's decision to compromise: tepid public support for the tax reform due to its technical complexity and an opposition campaign that the reform would hurt small business and the middle class. The government undertook noteworthy communication campaigns, including town hall meetings in which the finance minister himself answered questions from local audiences. Vertical equity appeals were prominent in government efforts to defend the reform; officials reiterated that it would affect only "*los más acomodados*" (the most comfortable).[56] However, the opposition maintained that the reform would have a much broader impact, and those assertions made a significant impact on public opinion. Widely publicized Cadem opinion polls showed support for the tax reform declining from 52 percent in April to a low of 33 percent at the end of June, while opposition rose from only 24 percent to 42 percent;[57] in early June, 68 percent believed that the tax reform would hurt the middle class.[58]

Although the government rewrote much of the bill during the negotiation process, the 2014 reform appears to be a major step toward increasing taxation of economic elites, particularly in comparison to prior initiatives during the fifteen years following the democratic transition. The corporate tax will increase by 7 percentage points with the new, partially de-integrated income tax, whereas previous governments had only ventured increments of 2 or 3 percentage points, and individuals will pay more tax on distributed profits given the reduced corporate tax credit. According to government calculations, the revenue target of 3 percent of GDP remains intact, and the majority of the revenue raised will still come from capital owners who occupy the top ranks of the income distribution. However, care must be taken to prevent new opportunities for tax avoidance and evasion that could arise due to the complexity of administering two parallel income tax systems, as well as the introduction of new tax benefits for small and medium-sized businesses that could potentially be abused by large businesses.[59]

CONCLUSION

The Concertación faced major obstacles to progressive income tax reform from 1990 to 2010, given the strength of business and the right; these powerful organized actors sought to keep income taxes low. However, skilled use of multiple reform strategies allowed governments to make some progress at the margins, particularly by restricting or eliminating tax benefits that disproportionately benefited big business and upper-income taxpayers. These strategies have been used elsewhere in Latin America and beyond to increase taxation of economic elites.[60] Where organized business and right-wing parties are weaker, these strategies have generally facilitated more significant reform.

The value of employing multiple reform strategies and pursuing incremental tax increases when opposition from societal actors and political parties is strong is a generalizable lesson emerging from the Chilean cases examined in this chapter. Reform strategies do not ensure success, yet the more strategies that can be simultaneously applied, the better the prospects. Consider Mexico, for example; linking to social spending has not been as effective as in Chile, in part due to citizens' perceptions that the state will not ensure that they receive the promised benefits, as noted in chapter 6.[61] In Mexico, initiatives to broaden the VAT base to include food and medicine have thus far failed. Yet combining progressive, highly elite-targeted income tax increases and vertical equity appeals with linking to social spending might garner greater public support, or at least acceptance—in the worst case, average citizens would be no worse off than at present. The obvious drawback, of course, is that upper-income groups would strongly oppose measures that aim to directly tax their income and wealth.

Meanwhile, Chile's 2014 reform provides some cause for optimism among those interested in promoting progressive taxation in Latin America. Economic elites do not always have strong enough political and economic power to block reforms they oppose, even if they are able to curtail radical structural changes. In this regard, pressure from organized social movements can be critical for creating political space for reform; astute "technopols" can take advantage of such opportunities.

NOTES

1. Parts of the analysis in this chapter draw on "Business Power and Tax Reform: Taxing Income and Profits in Chile and Argentina," by Tasha Fairfield, *Latin American Politics and Society* 52, no. 2 (2010): 37–71; and "Going Where the Money Is: Strategies for Taxing Economic Elites in Unequal Democracies," by Tasha Fairfield, *World Development* 47 (2013): 42–57. More extensive analysis of tax reform in Chile appears in *Private Wealth and Public Revenue in Latin America: Business Power and Tax Politics*, by Tasha Fairfield (New York: Cambridge University Press, 2015). Field research was supported by the Social Science Research Council and the International Center for Tax and Development. The author thanks Stephen Kaplan for helpful comments at the December 2012 Woodrow Wilson Center Workshop on the Political Economy of Tax Reform in Latin America.
2. Income shares are adjusted for underreported income; effective tax rates include personal and corporate income tax. For discussion, see Tasha Fairfield and Michel Jorratt, "Top Income Shares, Business Profits, and Effective Tax Rates in Contemporary Chile: New Evidence from Tax Return Data," ICTD Working Paper 17 (Brighton: Institute of Development Studies at the University of Sussex, 2014); updated version at http://eprints.lse.ac.uk/56016/.
3. Michel Jorratt, *La Tributación Directa en Chile*, Serie Macroeconomía del Desarrollo 92 (Santiago: CEPAL, 2009).
4. Servicio de Impuestos Internos, "Informe de Gasto Tributario," Santiago, 2004.
5. Michel Jorratt, "Gastos Tributarios y Evasión Tributaria en Chile," Working Paper, Centro de Estudios Públicos, Santiago, 2012.
6. Eduardo Silva, "Business Elites, the State, and Economic Change in Chile," in *Business and the State in Developing Countries*, ed. Sylvia Maxfield, and Ben Ross Schneider (Ithaca, N.Y.: Cornell University Press, 1997).
7. Fairfield, "Business Power."
8. Peter Siavelis, "Exaggerated Presidentialism and Moderate Presidents," in *Legislative Politics in Latin America*, ed. Scott Morgenstern and Benito Nacif (New York: Cambridge University Press, 2002).
9. Author's interview with Patricio Navia, Santiago, June 25, 2012. On the incentives for cooperation created by Chile's party system, see Gustavo Flores, "Statist vs.

Pro-Market: Explaining Leftist Governments' Economic Policies in Latin America," *Comparative Politics* 42, no. 4 (2010): 413–33.

10. For a more general theoretical treatment of these tax reform strategies, with applications to additional Latin American country cases, see Fairfield, "Going Where the Money Is."
11. Aylwin used this phrase with reference to his circumscribed pursuit of justice for military officials following the transition to democracy. "Aylwin reitera que investigará a fondo la violación de los derechos humanos en Chile," *El País*, January 2, 1991.
12. William Ascher, *Scheming for the Poor: The Politics of Redistribution in Latin America* (Cambridge, Mass.: Harvard University Press, 1984), 131.
13. Author's interview with a former business association staff member, Santiago, March 12, 2007.
14. Bernardo Navarette, "Un Centro Excéntrico: Cambio y Continuidad en la Democracia Cristiana, 1957–2005," *Política: Revista de Ciencia Política, Universidad de Chile* 45 (Spring 2005): 109–46; Carlos Huneeus, "A Highly Institutionalized Party: Christian Democracy in Chile," in *Christian Democracy in Latin America*, ed. Scott Mainwaring and Timothy Scully (Stanford, Calif.: Stanford University Press 2003), 122.
15. These appeals cited the fact that the bulk of tax revenue from the VAT originates from upper-income groups, given Chile's extreme inequality.
16. In Chile, business support for anti-evasion reforms varied depending on the measures proposed; e.g., business accepted higher fines for tax evasion but strongly opposed granting the tax agency greater auditing powers.
17. See, e.g.., Jacob Hacker and Paul Pierson, "Abandoning the Middle: The Bush Tax Cuts and the Limits of Democratic Control," *Perspectives on Politics* 3 (March 2005): 33–53; and Jacob S. Hacker, "Winner-Take-All-Politics: Public Policy, Political Organization, and the Precipitous Rise of Top Incomes in the United States," *Politics and Society* 38, no. 2 (2010): 152–204.
18. Juan Pablo Luna, "Segmented Party Voter Linkages in Latin America: The Case of the UDI," *Journal of Latin American Studies* 42, no. 2 (2010): 325–56.
19. Delia Boylan, "Taxation and Transition: The Politics of the 1990 Chilean Tax Reform," *Latin American Research Review* 31, no. 1 (1996): 7–31; Mario Marcel, "Políticas Públicas en Democracia: El Caso de la Reforma Tributaria de 1990 en Chile," *Estudios Cieplan* 45 (June 1997): 33–84; Kurt Weyland, "Growth with Equity in Chile's New Democracy?" *Latin American Research Review* 32, no. 1 (1997): 37–67.
20. Ascher, *Scheming*, 129–30n18.
21. Boylan, "Taxation," n25. The exceptions were the 2001 corporate tax increase, which was revenue-neutral due to an accompanying income tax rate cut, and the 2005 mining tax, which enjoyed strong public support based on nationalist sentiments.
22. Author's interview with former Chilean president Ricardo Lagos, Berkeley, Calif., September 20, 2006.
23. Author's interview with Manuel Marfán, former Chilean subsecretary of finance (1994–99) and finance minister (1999–2000), October 25, 2005.
24. Sebastián Etchemendy, *Models of Economic Liberalization* (New York: Cambridge University Press, 2011).

25. Rossana Castiglioni, *The Politics of Social Policy Change in Chile and Uruguay: Retrenchment versus Maintenance, 1973–1998* (New York: Routledge, 2005).
26. On electoral incentives motivating right-wing and left-wing parties to expand social programs, see Candelaria Garay, "Including Outsiders: Social Policy Expansion in Latin America" (manuscript).
27. Author's interview with UDI Deputy, Santiago, December 23, 2005.
28. Author's interviews with a former business association leader, Santiago, December 13, 2005; former business association staff member, 2007, n13.
29. A similar technique was used when the Piñera government increased the mining tax to help finance reconstruction following the massive 2010 earthquake.
30. Fairfield, *Private Wealth and Public Revenue.*
31. "Lagos pidió apoyo al proyecto contra la evasión," *El Mercurio*, September 10, 2000.
32. Mensaje de Proyecto 178-342, July 10, 2001.
33. Author's interviews with Lagos 2006, n22; and with Edgardo Boeninger, former minister of the General Secretariat of the Presidency and PDC senator (1998–2006), Santiago, November 14, 2005.
34. Author's interview with a Christian Democratic senator, Santiago, March 26, 2007.
35. Author's interview with Boeninger, 2005.
36. Senators Prat and Matthei, in "Avance trámite de evasión tributaria," *El Mercurio*, March 15, 2001.
37. Author's interview with a former finance minister, Santiago, March 25, 2005.
38. Author's interview with Lagos, 2006, n22.
39. Confederación de la Producción y del Comercio (CPC), "Observaciones de la CPC al Proyecto de Ley de Rebajo de Impuestos Personales y Compensaciones," Santiago, 2001.
40. See, e.g., "Diario de Sesiones del Senado de Chile," Legislature 244, Sesión 18a, August 7, 2001.
41. Claudio Agostini, Claudia Martínez, and Barbara Flores, "Distributional Effects of Eliminating the Differential Tax Treatment of Business and Personal Income in Chile," *CEPAL Review* 108 (2013): 175–201.
42. Andrés Rius, "The Uruguayan Tax Reform of 2006: Why Didn't It Fail?" Wilson Center Latin American Program, http://www.wilsoncenter.org/publication/Uruguay_Taxation_2013.
43. CPC, "Observaciones," n39.
44. Author's interviews with Alejandro Foxley, finance minister (1990–94) and PDC senator (1998–2006), Santiago, January 19, 2006; and with a Christian Democratic Senator 2007, n34.
45. This motion did not come to a vote, given that it violated exclusive executive initiative.
46. Quoted in "Iglesia pide que los votantes se informen," *La Tercera*, March 27, 2005.
47. Lagos, quoted in "Lagos reta a Alianza a derogar exención tributaria en 24 horas," *El Mercurio*, May 10, 2005.
48. *El Mercurio*, May 12, 13, 2005; author's interview with a UDI deputy, 2005, n27.
49. For further analysis of the Piñera tax reform, see Fairfield, *Private Wealth and Public Revenue.* For an integrated analysis of redistributive politics under the Piñera

administration (taxation and social spending), see Tasha Fairfield and Candelaria Garay, "The Politics of Redistribution in Unequal Democracies: Unexpected Reforms under the Right in Chile," paper given at Annual Meeting of the American Political Science Association, Chicago, August 29–September 1, 2013).

50. This change would eliminate the Taxable Profits Fund (FUT; i.e., retained profits pending personal income taxation), which gained notoriety during the presidential campaign. The bill also lowered the top personal income tax rate from 40 percent to 35 percent, given that including retained corporate profits in the income tax base dramatically increased the tax base at the top of the income distribution.
51. "El debut de la estrategia del segundo tiempo," *La Tercera*, July 13, 2014:
52. "Desaceleracion de la economía reduciría en US$2.370 millones los ingresos fiscales en 2014," *El Mercurio*, June 23, 2014.
53. Alberto Arenas, "La Reforma Tributaria que Chile Necesita," presentation as to the Senate Finance Committee, Santiago, June 2, 2014, 40–42. In fact, innovative new research on the 2003 US dividends tax cut suggests that even very large changes in capital income taxation have little effect on business's economic behavior. Danny Yagan, "Capital Tax Reform and the Real Economy: The Effects of the 2003 Dividend Tax Cut," Working Paper, 2014, http://eml.berkeley.edu/~yagan/DividendTax.pdf.
54. "Alberto Arenas: 'Dentro de los ruidos que han afectado las expectativas, también está el debate de la reforma tributaria,'" *La Tercera*, July 13, 2014.
55. "El debut."
56. Finance Ministry officials usually stated that the reform would affect only the 10 percent, although they also pointed out that the income tax changes would primarily affect only the top 1 percent. "Ejecutivo responde a empresarios y lanza video para defender reforma tributaria," *Diario Financiero*, April 29, 2014.
57. Cadem, "Track seminal de Opinion Pública," Estudio 30, Santiago, August 8, 2014.
58. Cadem, "Track semanl de Opinion Pública," Estudio 21, Santiago, June 9, 2014. The more established think tank June 9, 2014: reported that only 29 percent of Chileans thought the tax reform would worsen their economic situation, but that figure is still quite high considering that the reform was highly targeted at economic elites. Centro de Estudios Públicos, "Estudio Nacional de Opinión Pública No 71," Santiago, July 2014.
59. For an extensive critique of these and other potential problems with the reform, see "Claudio Agostini: 'El acuerdo tributario abre espacios de elusión mayores a los que había,'" *Mostrador*, July 10, 2014; and "Claudio Agostini: La escandalosa amnistía tributaria para evasores de altos ingresos," *Diario Financiero*, September 9, 2014.
60. Fairfield, "Going Where the Money Is."
61. Carlos Elizondo, "Progresividad y eficacia del gasto público en México: Precondición para una política recaudatoria efectiva," Latin American Program of the Woodrow Wilson International Center for Scholars, 2014, http://www.wilsoncenter.org/publication/PoliticaFiscalMexico.

Commentary on Chile: Bachelet's Tax Reform—Some Preliminary Thoughts

Francisco Rosende

Chile recently adopted an extensive reform of its tax system, with the goal of increasing its overall tax collections by 3 percent of gross domestic product (GDP).[1] In designing this reform, the authorities aimed to eliminate mechanisms that, in their judgment, lent themselves to tax evasion. Under the government's original bill, the resources generated by increasing tax rates and reforming the tax system would make it possible to substantially increase spending on education. This was consistent with the objective of significantly reducing inequality in income distribution in a relatively short period of time.

Any analysis of the recent Chilean tax reform should begin by referring to the system that was in place until a few months ago. That system originated in the mid-1980s, in the context of an acute external debt crisis. The crisis made it necessary to severely adjust domestic spending—as part of a program agreed upon with the International Monetary Fund—and set the stage for the implementation of policies that would make it possible to increase the Chilean economy's capacity for growth.[2] Essential aspects of this agenda included the application of a program to reduce import tariffs, the privatization of companies, and the design of a tax system focused more on spending than on income.

The 1984 tax reform provided individual and corporate savings incentives, in the form of "tax credits" for savings held in medium- and long-term bank deposits.[3] Credits were also available for acquisitions of stock in companies that were being privatized.

One interesting tool included in the structure of this tax system was the "Taxable Profits Fund" (Fondo de Utilidades Tributables, FUT), whose features are described here. First, however, it is important to underscore the essentially "integrated" nature of the tax system that was established. If a shareholder received dividends from corporate profits, any taxes on these dividends could be deducted from his or her total individual income tax, known as the "global income tax" or "surtax" (Impuesto Global Complementario).

The FUT was created in this context to offer an attractive savings option for shareholders. Once corporate taxes were paid on profits, shareholders could allocate any distributed profits to a taxable profits fund and postpone paying individual income taxes on those funds until they withdrew them from the FUT.[4] These funds could be reinvested in the same company or in other savings instruments.

This arrangement benefited corporate operations—at the time, companies were mired in debt and were finding it difficult to gain access to financing for their projects—and also stimulated reinvestment. At the same time, it offered a source of working capital based on undistributed profits, which were being reintegrated into the company through the FUT mechanism. This feature of the tax system was especially attractive for small and medium-sized companies, which usually face less favorable conditions for access to bank credit than larger companies.

Moreover, because this tax system made it possible to channel undistributed profits toward the acquisition of financial instruments—via the FUT mechanism—it helped to expand a financial market that was in its infancy.[5] It is estimated that at the end of 2013, resources in taxable profits funds amounted to about $250 billion, an amount comparable to the country's GDP and to its total savings.[6]

Although the Chilean economy went through a significant series of changes during the crisis of the mid-1980s, it seems reasonable to assume that the changes to its tax system would have the effect of increasing the savings rate as of the end of the 1980s. And sure enough, the savings rate, which had averaged just over 10 percent of GDP from 1960 through the mid-1980s, began to consistently exceed 20 percent starting in the late 1980s.

Furthermore, the low level of external debt that the Chilean economy has maintained since then is not unrelated to the incentive structure that characterized the tax system.[7] Indeed, the contrast in this aspect with many economies—both developed and emerging—is striking.

A TAX SHOCK

During the administration of President Sebastián Piñera—which preceded the current Bachelet government—a strong public debate took hold around the issue of inequality of income distribution and the need for a profound reform of the educational system to move toward a more egalitarian society. This was the case despite the fact that empirical studies were showing a progressive decline in income gaps among younger generations.[8] As a candidate, Michelle Bachelet laid out a goal of significantly increasing the share of resources devoted to public education, and making school and university free for broad sectors of Chilean society. That required raising tax revenues by 3 percentage points of GDP, as mentioned above.

It was with this aim in mind that Bachelet's campaign put together an economic strategy that included a series of adjustments to tax rates—an increase in corporate tax rates from 20 to 25 percent, along with the gradual elimination of the FUT, which was seen by economists affiliated with the candidate as a source of tax evasion for high-income groups. (As mentioned above, funds channeled through FUTs postponed the payment of taxes; thus, eliminating that mechanism would add funds to the fiscal coffers.) At the same time, the maximum income tax for individuals was lowered from 40 to 35 percent.[9]

An essential aspect of the debate on taxation is whether the FUT was a widely used mechanism for tax evasion or essentially an effective vehicle to promote savings. In my opinion, it was essentially the latter; but even if there was a reasonable suspicion of its misuse, it seemed unnecessary to eliminate it. In fact, specific aspects of its operations could have been corrected without altering its essence, as the economist and former presidential candidate Andrés Velasco suggested at one time. However, based on the stated objective of increasing tax revenues—and with the finance minister unjustifiably dismissing fears expressed by various economists that the government's proposed legislation and its elimination of the FUT would discourage savings and investment—the matter came before Congress.[10]

After quick approval by the lower chamber of Congress, where the administration has a majority, the bill moved to the Senate for the final steps. Even though the governing coalition also has a majority in that chamber, the analysis at this stage was more measured, in consideration of the well-founded fears and criticisms expressed by numerous economists and heads of trade associations. Thus, though the tax reform that was finally approved included profound changes in the tax system that had been in effect, it also introduced important changes to the government's original bill.

As has been indicated, the recent tax reform implemented in Chile includes numerous adjustments, ranging from taxes on capital gains associated with property sales to an increase in the taxes imposed on legal proceedings.[11] What stand out, for the most part, are the changes to corporate taxation, with significant changes made both to the tax structure and to tax rates.

First of all, the tax rate on corporate profits was raised from 20 to 25 percent over four years, as mentioned above.[12] The system of imposing taxes on the basis of income that is "withdrawn" or "received" by partners or shareholders in a company came to an end. Instead, a system based on "earned" or "attributed" income was established. This refers to the revenues to which a shareholder is entitled, even though he or she may not have received them. This did away with the FUT mechanism.

The change to the basis on which corporate profits are taxed sets forth two alternatives for how to treat corporate taxes:

1. An integrated system is maintained, by which the appropriate tax rate—25 percent, as of 2017—is imposed on payments, which continue to be used as credit against the global income tax on individuals, which includes all income and has its own rates.

2. The second is a partially integrated system, which raises the corporate tax rate to 27 percent. However, partners or shareholders can deduct 65 percent of what had already been paid via corporate taxes from their global income tax.

Considering that the maximum individual tax rate was established at 35 percent, it is conceivable that profits withdrawn from companies could end up being subject to a maximum tax rate of 44.4 percent.

One inescapable observation, in reviewing Chile's recent experience with tax policy, is the speed and magnitude of tax increases on corporate profits in recent years. We should keep in mind that until 2012, the rate was 17 percent; this was increased under the previous government to 20 percent, only to be revised upward again by the Bachelet administration.

It seems difficult to claim that there will be no adverse effect on investment and savings as a result of this tax reform. To get a sense of the importance of the adjustments made to the corporate tax burden, I must note that in the case of Chile, companies have few tax deductions. One illustration of the effect of deductions on tax revenues is the fact that with a corporate tax rate of 20 percent,[13] Chile collected 4.6 percent of its GDP in corporate taxes in 2012, whereas in the United States, with a tax rate of 40 percent, corporate tax revenues that same year were 2.6 percent of GDP.[14]

When the profitability of investments is affected, growth is most certainly affected, which in turn has an impact on fiscal revenues. This is something that was pointed out repeatedly by numerous economists in the context of the recent debate over the tax reform, but that was ultimately disregarded by the authorities.

Savings decisions will also be affected as a result of the tax reform. One reason is that opportunities for tax deductions for long-term savings are reduced significantly. Another is that taxes go up on the purchase of a home, which is usually an important source of savings for individuals.

In terms of companies, the larger ones can be expected to substitute the savings offered by the FUT for bank debt or bonds. The issue is more complex for medium-sized companies, which are treated differently under the reform, based on their annual sales. In any case, a reading of the many sections of the tax reform law shows how complex it is, in contrast to the system it replaced.

This complexity raises the risk that the agency in charge of administering the system—the Internal Tax Service—will have wide discretion, which will increase the disincentives to invest. In fact, some months after the reform was enacted, companies are waiting for the tax agency to issue a set of regulations and notes clarifying how the various components of the new law should be interpreted. As the noted economist Anne Krueger taught us many years ago, complex regulatory systems facilitate forms of privilege for sectors with the capacity to lobby or have political influence, which in this case could end up aggravating one of the problems the tax reform was attempting to solve.[15]

Finally, it is at least curious to note that while the economic authorities repeatedly talk about promoting entrepreneurship and innovation, in practice a tax system has been created that in relative terms penalizes the risk taking inherent to investment, with a maximum tax rate on the order of 44 percent—higher than the rate imposed on less risky activities, such as the maximum rate of 35 percent for a public or private employee. Moreover, it is simply illogical that the tax reform that was approved created a structure that discriminates against investment by Chilean residents; their maximum tax on profits is more than 44 percent, while foreign investors still have a rate of 35 percent. These are the curiosities of this tax shock that raise enormous doubts and fears regarding its consequences for the Chilean economy.

NOTES

1. My thanks to Verónica Miles and Rodrigo Cerda for their comments.
2. With respect to the policies followed during this period and the role that public finance management played in these policies, see H. Büchi, *La transformación económica de Chile: Del Estatismo a la Libertad Económica* (Bogotá: Grupo Editorial Norma, 1993).
3. "Tax credits" means deductions of taxes owed.
4. Taxes paid on profits are a first-category tax.
5. In any case, it is important to specify that the FUT was conceived as an accounting record and not a financial assets fund. Indeed, many of these funds are invested in the company itself and therefore are not liquid.
6. Chile's GDP was $276,971,000,000 in 2013.
7. In 2013, Chile's gross external debt was $130,724,000,000, equivalent to 47 percent of GDP.
8. In that regard, see C. Sapelli, *Chile ¿Más Equitativo? Una mirada distinta a la distribución del ingreso, la movilidad social y la pobreza en Chile* (Santiago: Ediciones Universidad Católica, 2011).
9. It is important to remember that a relatively small percentage of the population pays taxes at these rates.

10. On May 19, 2014, the newspaper *Pulso* quoted Finance Minister Albert Arenas as saying, "Those who raise the slogan that the Tax Reform will hurt investment are not speaking based on the numbers."
11. This was also known as the "stamp tax."
12. It increases to 21 percent in 2014, 22.5 percent in 2015, 24 percent in 2016, and 25 percent in 2017.
13. This example was offered by F. Larraín, "Positivo acuerdo....(aun) mal Proyecto," *La Tercera*, July 13, 2014.
14. For more on the relationship between tax rates and tax revenues, see A. Donoso, "Gasto Público y Tributación," in *Milton Friedman, La vigencia de sus contribuciones: Metodología, Teoría y Política Económica*, ed. R. Lüders and F. Rosende (Santiago: Ediciones Universidad Católica, 2015).
15. A. O. Krueger, *The Political Economy of Controls: Complexity*, NBER Working Paper 4351 (Cambridge, Mass.: National Bureau of Economic Research, 1993).

CHAPTER 2

The Uruguayan Tax Reform of 2006: Why Did It Not Fail?

Andrés Rius

This chapter seeks to identify the key factors that help explain Uruguay's success in passing and sustaining a comprehensive and progressive tax reform, following the electoral ascent of the left to majority government in 2005.[1] The key innovation and justification for the "progressive" qualifier was the (re-)introduction of a broad personal income tax with a significant nontaxable threshold and a schedule of increasing rates by income brackets. This allowed the reformers to rebalance the contribution of direct and indirect taxes without decreasing total revenue, taxing labor and capital rents more consistently.[2] The successful passage of such a major overhaul, including a substantial increase in the tax burden of the top income deciles, is a rare event in a region like Latin America, where economic inequalities are intertwined with power asymmetries, often blocking attempts at tax-based redistribution. Such rare events beg for investigation, with a view to expand our understanding and in search of lessons for future reformers.

The chapter explores the drivers of success and the resistance factors that could not prevent it. In the first section, the inefficiencies and inequities of a reactive style of policymaking are identified. The second section provides a minimal characterization of the reform and explains how the vicious cycle of the previous fifteen years could be broken. The literature's established hypotheses are considered, and their explanatory adequacy for the Uruguayan case is discussed. After exposing a fortunate conjunction of conditions favoring progressive reform, the chapter moves on to look in more detail at two sources of resistance that were somehow neutralized. The third section deals with the threat of a middle-class backlash and shows that the recorded dissatisfaction was in some sense inevitable, but it was not powerful nor real enough to impede progressive changes. In one of its key contributions, the chapter links resistance to the reforms to cognitive and perceptual biases that are increasingly present in the toolbox of fiscal political economists. The fourth section discusses why the economic elites and higher income strata could only mount a comparatively weak opposition, highlighting key features of their past and their current social configuration that constrain their power. The fifth and final section pulls all these strings together and draws out the implications of the case.

EQUITY IN TAXATION: POLITICAL WILL, OBSTACLES, AND EVENTUAL TRIUMPH

Starting in 1990, there were several partial modifications to Uruguay's tax code, typically in postelection years, when new administrations found themselves fighting stubborn fiscal imbalances that were sometimes exacerbated by a predecessor's preelection largesse.[3] Figure 2.1 offers a picture of this pattern. The gray boxes correspond to innovations aimed at boosting tax revenue, which usually were formalized in the five-year budget bill approved during an administration's first year in office. The 2001 episode is illustrative of the challenges faced by fiscally troubled governments, and the ingenuity forced on them to find none-too-visible taxes of high productivity.[4] Rather than identifying future needs and developing technically sound innovations, taking into account different long-term scenarios, the administration that was elected in 1999 opted for quick fixes to increase revenue, including adding a new sales tax applied in cascading fashion on top of the value-added tax (VAT)—almost a too-obvious raise in the prevailing VAT rates.

This pattern illustrates a *satisfycing* model of policymaking, with alternating "crisis" and "noncrisis" phases; the former are associated with emergency responses through broad policy packages; and the latter are associated with

Figure 2.1. Timeline of Tax Innovations, 1989–2005

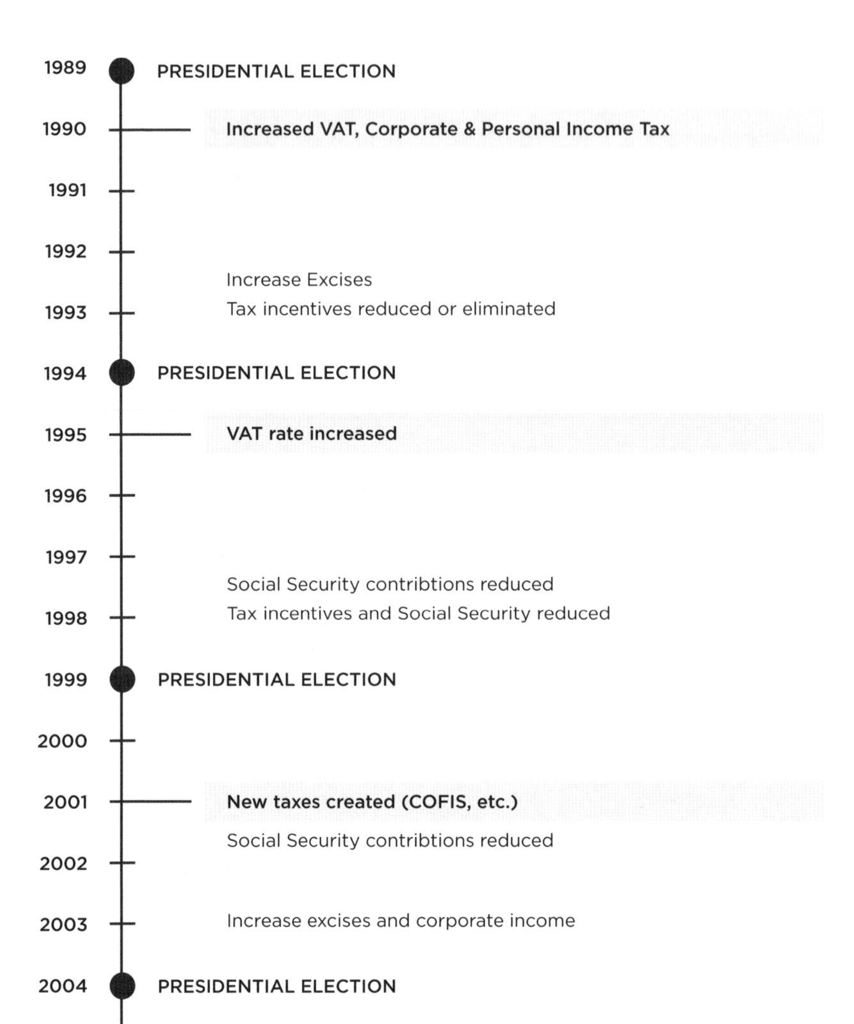

Source: The author, based on "La reforma del sistema tributario uruguayo desde la perspectiva de la eficiencia y la equidad," by Gustavo González-Amilivia, Dirección General Impositiva, Montevideo, mimeo, 2007; and Diego Focanti, Mark Hallerberg, and Carlos Scartascini, *Tax Reforms in Latin America in an Era of Democracy*, Working Paper IDB-WP-457 (Washington, D.C.: Inter-American Development Bank, 2013).

Table 2.1. Tax Revenue by Tax Base, 2002 (percentage of total revenue)

Element of Tax Base	Percent
Expenditures/consumption	40.1
Wages, labor income	37.5
Other rents	6.3
Capital: assets and transfers	12.3
International trade	1.6
Other	2.2
Total	100.0

Source: Figure 3 from "Estructura tributaria del Uruguay: Un enfoque descriptivo," by H. Vallarino, Asesoría Económica de la Dirección General Impositiva, Montevideo, mimeo, 2004, 4.

incremental, good-enough responses while the public's attention is focused on other, more urgent crises.[5] That would explain the limited regard for efficiency or equity effects in the tax innovations attempted by fiscally challenged governments.

The data given in table 2.1 reveal the drawbacks of this reactive style of policymaking. It can be observed there that the result of the tax innovations shown in figure 2.1 was a revenue structure heavily dependent on taxes on consumption and wages. Those two bases are known to have high productivity (particularly in a relatively "formal" economy such as Uruguay's), which made them appealing when deficit reduction was a high priority. Yet taxes on those bases may add to the overall regressive bent of the tax structure (e.g., by undertaxing capital vis-à-vis labor, or by allowing the benefits of VAT exemptions to "leak" to better-off segments).[6]

More than poor policy design, the trajectories of tax policy since 1990 reflect configurations of political and economic conditions conspiring against progressive reforms, and sometimes obstructing *any* significant fiscal innovation. Table 2.2 presents a battery of indicators reflecting the specific political and economic conditions prevailing at the time of the

Table 2.2. Political and Economic Conditions in the First Year of Four Administrations, 1990–2005

First Year of the New Administration	1990	1995	2000	2005
Party in executive office	Nacional	Colorado	Colorado	Frente Amplio
Share of popular vote in (t - 1), first round	38.9	32.3	32.8	50.5
Ideology	Right	Right	Right	Left
President in office	Lacalle	Sanguinetti	Batlle	Vázquez
President's party seats in House (total = 99) and Senate (total = 31)	39/13	32/11	33/10	52/17
Share of vote for president's sub-lema; or in primaries (1999, 2004)	58.1	76.3	54.9	100.0 (82.4)
President's approval rating (c. September of year t)	18	21	43	56
Economic cycle, phase	Stagflation	Ending recess	Recession	Expansion
Inflation (consumer prices variation %)	112	42	5	5
Year-on-year % change gross domestic product (GDP) at constant prices	0.3	-0.1	-1.4	6.6
Primary budget result as % GDP	1.5	-0.5	-1.4	2.7
Global budget result as % of GDP	-0.1	-1.9	-3.4	-1.6

Sources: (a) Corte Electoral, in Base de Datos, Facultad de Ciencias Sociales, Udelar, http://www.fcs.edu.uy/pagina.php?PagId=12299; (b) Philip Keefer, "The Database of Political Institutions," World Bank, http://econ.worldbank.org/WBSITE/EXTERNAL/EXTDEC/EXTRESEARCH/0,,contentMDK:20649465~pagePK:64214825~piPK:64214943~theSitePK:469382,00.html; (c) Banco de Datos FCS, Equipos-Mori, nacional, 08/1990, 09/1995, 07–09/2000, 09/2005.

inauguration of four consecutive administrations, ending with the one (2005–10) that led the successful progressive reform.

The table organizes the data in three panels: the first panel (the first three rows) describes the macro-political conditions. As the second row shows, the three administrations before Frente's took office with the direct electoral support of less than 40 percent of the vote, signaling a fragmented polity and serious governance challenges. The third row shows that those administrations' ideologies were unlikely to lead them to redistributive tax agendas.

In addition to naming the presidents, the second panel of table 2.2 (the second three rows) provides measures of the government's leverage: the number of seats expected to be controlled by the incumbent in the Senate and the House; the share of the party's vote that allowed the president to win the primaries (or alternative candidate-selection process); and the president's approval rating six months into the term. The third and last panel (the bottom four rows) highlights the difficulties on the economic front (as reflected by GDP growth, inflation, and fiscal balance) under each administration and until the remarkable upward turn at the beginning of the Frente's first term.

In view of the data, one could then be tempted to blame a perverse combination of *conjunctural factors* for the inability of three administrations to act more decisively in the fiscal sphere. Although conjunctural factors were no doubt important, their role in an explanation should not be exaggerated. Because many of those factors can actually run both ways (e.g., a *parliamentary majority* can be used to pass or to block a reform), overemphasizing conjunctural conditions may actually push back the need for an explanation rather than providing it (i.e., noticing an absolute majority in Parliament would not be enough, and one would need to explain how the political processes converged in a *progressive* majority in the 2004 election). This is of intrinsic interest; but investigating each and every driver, including their underlying and long-term determinants, is beyond the scope of the chapter.

What I actually do in the pages that follow is to discuss briefly some institutional and political factors, and then to go deeper into two complementary accounts that so far have been little studied. The investigated driving factors (and hypotheses) can be labeled institutions, instrumental powers, mass public opinion, and elites, respectively (the first two have been and are discussed in the remaining paragraphs of this section, and separate sections are devoted to each of the last two).

URUGUAY'S REFORM AND THE CONVENTIONAL WISDOM

The main features of the reform were the replacement of several *cedular* taxes (i.e., "a variety of taxes that burden some sources of income at different rates . . . exempting others"; Barreix and Roca)[7] with a new income tax on global income; the consolidation of sector-specific corporate income at a reduced tax rate (from 30 to 25 percent), matching the top marginal rate for personal incomes; the reduction of rates of the VAT and the suppression of the related sales tax, with the removal of exemptions for specific services; a revision of the net wealth tax (maintaining a high exemption threshold and a very low rate); and other minor innovations or corrections to the patchwork-like tax code. In general, the special treatments for economic sectors were abolished (e.g., in Uruguay's established pay-as-you-go pensions system, the employer's contributions were regarded as taxes, and there was a variety of rates for different industries reflecting concessions made to various lobbies over time). Overall, the reform reduced the participation of indirect taxes and increased that of direct taxes (although they have been at a very high two-to-one ratio since 2007), while significantly amending vertical and horizontal inequalities and putting the mechanisms in place for future fine-tuning of the instrument to goals through "parametric" adjustments.[8]

Conjunctures can be more or less limiting, or enabling, depending on configurations of *institutional factors*. For example, in countries with political/electoral regimes that tend to produce majority governments, the meager margins in the popular vote obtained by the three administrations since 1990 would have been less of an obstacle (yet, again, those tendencies by themselves could not have predicted if governments would be for or against progressive tax innovations).

Second, the right-of-center ideological orientation of the governments must be considered part of the explanation for the pre-2006 tax regime, in that the three governments were reluctant to consider redistribution as a legitimate goal of fiscal policies. Combined with the international intellectual climate and policy trends of the time, they created a favorable environment for a high reliance on indirect taxes for revenue and a minimization of the role of direct taxes in fiscal regimes. The configuration of conditions that made progressive reform viable included the reversal of these conditions just discussed and the favorable alignment of some others of longer duration.

In fact, Uruguay's progressive tax reform meets several conditions for success that have been identified in the literature. Specifically, it happened in a *relatively egalitarian society* (by Latin American standards) and was put forward by a *disciplined left-of-center party*, which obtained an absolute *majority in Parliament* and had a *clear blueprint*.[9] Notably, the reform was expected to be of help in addressing a "social debt" (*deuda social*) that the government felt the state had with the victims of the 2002 crisis. More strikingly, the fiscal position at the beginning of the term was such that *the Frente's government could credibly commit to not raising the overall tax burden*. Seated on a comfortable balance, the reformers had some leeway to design a more efficient and equitable tax regime, while *minimizing the number of "losers"* (i.e., those whose tax bill would be higher after the reform than it was before). The country's strong growth and stable macroeconomic environment had made it unnecessary to borrow from the international financial institutions. This meant that opponents could not attribute the reform to external pressures—an accusation that has often undermined reformers, especially those who come from the political left. Instead, the *reform could be credibly depicted as home-grown*.

That said, it was not obvious at the time why there was not a more serious and enduring challenge from those who thought that their tax bill was being increased. The next section begins to disentangle perceptions from realities, and the actors' powers. It is argued that the tax reform was doomed to have a hostile reception from large segments (possibly a majority) of the electorate self-identified with the "middle class." To make sense of the breadth of hostility toward a reform that was expected to benefit many, it is necessary to consider the literatures on behavioral economics and the behavioral political economy of fiscal policies. These characterize voters/consumers as possessing limited information-gathering and -processing capacities, and as unable to discern the net gains from complex reform packages. I argue that it is also crucial to consider biases in the self-perception of individuals' own place on the income scale, as demonstrated by several empirical studies. The section then investigates reasons why, despite the negative initial attitude, the implementation of the tax law could move forward without major upheaval. In this sense, the analysis adds a new factor to the list of those highlighted in this volume—specifically, the *political adeptness* of techno-political elites would be required to prevent a situation in which the fears of the "middle class" blocked the reforms, all in a world of imperfect information and bounded rationality.

The third section focuses on the response of the richest minorities. It aims to identify a set of main reasons why the sectors that actually experienced a substantial negative shock in disposable income did not mount a more determined opposition. Essentially, it points to the relative weakness of Uruguay's upper strata, which is most clearly seen when they are compared with their counterparts in the region's other countries. This section argues that Uruguay's economic elites are weaker in terms of their capacity to block adverse reforms because of their limited *instrumental power* related to *institutional factors* that evolved historically. In particular, I find that economic elites (1) are ideologically and organizationally divided; (2) have sparse social and familial interlinkages with the political elites, allowing the latter to enjoy greater autonomy; and (3) are constrained by the high institutionalization of political parties that curtails certain forms of influence. All these and related factors conspired against a powerful response of the "losers" and help account for the reform's high degree of compliance.

These hypotheses are not formally tested in this chapter, but their plausibility is examined in light of the relevant literature and available evidence. It is worth noting that, despite the role of structural or otherwise hard-to-change factors, there are levers for change, although perhaps fewer and less effective ones than is desirable, in some countries.

MASS PUBLIC OPINION: WHY THE MIDDLE CLASS COULD NOT BE WON BUT WAS NOT LOST

At the time of the public debate on the tax legislation, several actors from different quarters argued that the reform could affect the middle classes disproportionately (or be seen to have such an effect), creating the risk of political blockage or reversal.[10] These prospects troubled the reformers, who anticipated that any success was going to come about against public opinion that was based more on perception than on fact. Some numbers suggest that the reformers' concerns were justified, and configure a political economy paradox. These are crucial issues for would-be reformers: If they hope to succeed, they must learn how to overcome resistance. I show that some lessons from behavioral economics can shed light and help reformers decide what battles to fight, and how.

Table 2.3 presents ex-ante estimates of the net effects of the complete reform (including changes in direct and indirect taxes) on households' income, by deciles, based on static simulations run with 2004 data by Uruguay's highly competent economic analysis unit of the tax administration agency (Dirección General Impositiva, DGI). These types of exercises have become common with improvements in the availability of household surveys and processing power. Briefly, the "static" variety consists of going one by one through all individuals in a typical "living standards" or "employment and income" survey, imputing them—based on income, employment, and other socioeconomic data—the amount of money they would pay in taxes in the pre-reform regime and comparing it with the amount due under the terms of the reform. These pre- and post-reform figures for each individual can then be analyzed by groups (e.g., deciles) or larger categories.[11]

The first two columns of table 2.3 show that all but the top two deciles could expect a small reduction in their total tax bill, and only the top 10 percent of households were expected to experience a change in their disposable income large enough to be discernible (more on this below). Although there were prospective losers in all the deciles, they represented less than 10 percent of households in the first six deciles, and they were still an absolute minority up to the ninth one; only in the top decile was there an absolute

Table 2.3. The Tax Burden, Before and After Reform, and the Percentage of Winners and Losers, by Decile

Deciles of Households by Per Capita Income	Total Tax Burden, by Deciles		Percentage of Winners and Losers with Reform	
	Before Reform	After Reform	Winners	Losers
1	13.5	10.1	99.33	0.67
2	13.8	10.3	99.36	0.64
3	13.8	10.3	98.96	1.04
4	13.7	10.3	98.26	1.74
5	13.3	10.3	96.98	3.02
6	13.1	10.5	93.62	6.38
7	13.7	11.7	89.08	10.92
8	13.8	12.5	79.99	20.01
9	13.9	14.3	59.13	40.87
10	12.8	17.8	20.66	79.34
Entire population	13.4	13.3	83.54	16.46

Source: Gustavo González-Amilivia, "La reforma del sistema tributario uruguayo desde la perspectiva de la eficiencia y la equidad," Dirección General Impositiva, Montevideo, mimeo, 2007.

Table 2.4. Ex-Ante Effective Tax Rate for Personal Income Tax versus Its Predecessor

Deciles of Households, by Per Capita Income	Ex-Ante, Per Capita Effective Tax Rate (%)	
	IRP (pre-reform payroll tax)	IRPF (new, global income tax)
1	0.35	0.29
2	0.95	0.52
3	1.27	0.32
4	1.38	0.52
5	1.65	0.85
6	1.80	1.18
7	1.95	1.71
8	2.41	2.64
9	2.68	4.28
10	2.85	9.07

Source: Gustavo González-Amilivia, "La reforma del sistema tributario uruguayo desde la perspectiva de la eficiencia y la equidad," Dirección General Impositiva, Montevideo, mimeo, 2007.

majority of about 80 percent who could expect to pay more taxes after the reform than before. Overall, the whole reform would leave 85 percent of households better off than they were in the pre-reform situation.

Table 2.4 depicts similar expected outcomes from the introduction of the new personal income tax (Impuesto a la Renta de las Personas Físicas, IRPF), which replaced the pre-reform payroll tax (Impuesto a las Retribuciones Personales, IRP). It shows that, on average, effective rates could be expected to decline after the reform for households in the first seven deciles, and increase only for the top three. The paradox starts to take shape when these results are paired with public opinion data from the time, showing almost a majority of negative opinions about the main new tax. Table 2.5 presents such evidence in its simplest form.

The public opinion statistics clash with the distributive effects of the reform that showed the reform to have a lot more winners than losers, and even to be less burdensome than predecessor taxes for about 70 percent of households. Table 2.6 confirms that the paradox was not a result of misguided forecasts of effects, as the ex-post incidence studies show distributional patterns almost identical to the pre-reform simulations.

That is the paradoxical picture I try to unravel, for it may shed light on how to overcome attitudinal resistance to reforms. Such unraveling is made easier by insights from behavioral economics, and from an emerging behavioral political economy of fiscal policy.[12] Among the key tenets of those literatures, we find the following to be of particular explanatory value in the context:

1. People cannot calculate the direct and indirect effects on their own situation vis-à-vis complex policy innovations such as a comprehensive tax reform, so their decisions will be based on some combination of rules of thumb and heuristics that cannot be guaranteed to be bias-free.

2. Limited cognitive and calculation capacities, along with patterns of social interaction, make people vulnerable to perception biases, in particular regarding their relative social status.

Table 2.5. Opinion About the IRPF in Three National Surveys (percent)

Opinion:	November 2006	April 2007	September 2007
In favor	27	23	29
Neutral	11	12	12
Against	47	47	49
Don't know or did not answer	15	18	10
Total	100	100	100

Source: CIFRA, González Raga y Asociados, http://www.cifra.com.uy/novedades.php?idNoticia=17.

Table 2.6. Ex-Ante Effective Tax Rate for IRPF versus Ex-Post Net Gains from All Taxes on Income

Deciles of Households, by Per Capita Income	Ex-Ante, Per Capita Effective Tax Rate (%)	Ex-Post Direct Taxes over Market Income, as of 2009 (%)
	IRPF (encompassing income tax)	All taxes on incomes, excluding pension contribution
1	0.29	0.4
2	0.52	0.9
3	0.32	1.3
4	0.52	1.7
5	0.85	2.0
6	1.18	2.4
7	1.71	3.0
8	2.64	3.9
9	4.28	5.3
10	9.07	9.0

Sources: First column, Gustavo González-Amilivia, "La reforma del sistema tributario uruguayo desde la perspectiva de la eficiencia y la equidad," Dirección General Impositiva, Montevideo, mimeo, 2007; second column, Marisa Bucheli, Nora Lustig, Maximo Rossi, and Florencia Amabile, "Social Spending, Taxes, and Income Redistribution in Uruguay," SSRN eLibrary, 2012, table 5, third column.

3. Humans in their social setting dislike material losses more than they value identical gains; that is, they suffer from "loss aversion" (a case of the more general problem of "reference-dependent preferences").[13]

Applying those insights to our case, we can speculate that most voters/taxpayers were unable to put numbers to their expected gains and losses from the reform, even in households where the reform brought minor changes. It has been pointed out that voters often confuse marginal with average tax rates, and it does not seem preposterous to conclude that most Uruguayan taxpayers were unable to figure out the effects of all the taxes that were changed, created, or eliminated in 2006.[14] Moreover, if they had known and understood the calculations behind the data given in table 2.3, they might have been inclined not to spend time or money finding out the exact amount of their net gain or loss. They might have also defaulted to a preference for the status quo resulting from loss aversion and uncertain individual outcome—a preference that calculating agents would even maintain with knowledge of a positive expected payoff for a majority of households.[15]

Yet a second behavioral factor would seem to have had (and may be continue having) deeper consequences. At the time of the reform, it was not hard to run into taxpayers of varied socioeconomic statuses or occupation who would criticize the reform on the basis of its effect on their own circumstances; if the reform was not bringing a substantial reduction in their tax bill or, worse, if it would result in an increase, this was proof that the reform was going to harm the middle class, which would make the reformers incompetent or dishonest.[16]

Reformist players (particularly those at the helm of the Ministry of the Economy and Finance) also lamented being unable to convince the middle classes of the reform's benefits for them, and expected (at least until the 2009 elections) that this was going to cost them dearly in terms of electoral support. With the benefit of hindsight, one could argue that it was probably impossible for the government to win "the battle for the middle class," but that the outcomes do not really represent a defeat, and that they even offer lessons for other reforms seeking similar objectives.

Finding an explanation for the identified paradox could begin from a noteworthy empirical investigation conducted at the Universidad de la Plata in Argentina about people's biased self-placement on the income scale.[17] The study is based on a representative sample of the population of Gran Buenos Aires (i.e., the city's metropolitan region). This is useful because historically and up to the present time, there have been important cultural and socio-economic similarities between that region and Uruguay. We can therefore borrow some of their key insights.

The authors of the Gran Buenos Aires study interviewed about 1,100 individuals and asked them the following question: "There are roughly 10 million families in Argentina. Of those 10 million, how many do you think have an income lower than yours?" This question became their indicator for "subjective" self-placement on the income scale. The researchers also asked for information on actual income, getting interviewees to place their household in one of ten brackets of total income, defined by the actual thresholds among deciles from the latest national living standards surveys (which are supposed to be accurate and were unknown to the interviewees). This gave them the individuals' "objective" position on the income scale, to compare with the subjective or perceived position.

The results from this research reveal that there are quite large divergences between the subjective and objective positions on both extremes of the (objective) scale, with people generally believing that they are closer to the median than they really are (table 2.7). On average, for example, people belonging in the first decile tend to feel they are more than three deciles higher. The divergence decreases monotonically as one moves toward the median of actual incomes (i.e., top threshold of the fifth decile). From the other end, those in the top decile believe, on average, that they belong in the sixth or seventh decile, for an average perception bias of –3.15.

How do these results, along with the contributions from behavioral economics and public finance, help us to understand the success of Uruguay's 2006 tax reform? First, they suggest a context in which it was extremely unlikely that taxpayers could know the precise effects of the reform on their disposable income. The calculations necessary to estimate the effects of the reform required a capacity to understand legal and economic jargon, and to make complicated calculations. Although it probably helped to assuage concerns that the reform could be designed and credibly presented as revenue-neutral (as shown above), it is not a very strong assumption that most

Table 2.7. Objective and Perceived Decile by "Objective" Decile in a Survey of Residents of Gran Buenos Aires, by Cruces and Colleagues, 2011

"Objective" Deciles	Average Perceived Decile of Interviewees in the Respective Objective Decile	Average Bias
1	4.5	3.5
2	4.7	2.7
3	4.5	1.5
4	5.5	1.5
5	5.4	0.4
6	5.4	-0.6
7	5.7	-1.3
8	6.1	-1.9
9	6.3	-2.7
10	6.8	-3.2

Source: Guillermo Cruces, R. Pérez-Truglia, and M. Tetaz, *Biased Perceptions of Income Distribution and Preferences for Redistribution: Evidence from a Survey Experiment*, Discussion Paper 5699 (Bonn: Institute for the Study of Labor–IZA, 2011).

citizens/taxpayers could not undertake complex calculations to predict their own burden, let alone look for the required documentation and data. The minority who had the skills and inclination to run some of the calculations can safely be assumed to be heavily concentrated in the top income strata, and even that minority would have serious trouble discerning the *relative* burden for even a few income brackets; we are speaking, of course, about the capacities of individuals and not companies, which may have access to expert advice and could form informed predictions quickly.

Moreover, if they had not been reached by the messages from the government on the small expected effects for most taxpayers (i.e., estimates such as those given in table 2.3), many of the latter might have been suspicious of the source's intentions or could have removed the whole issue from their "agenda," given the low significance of the aggregate changes. For all the factors just mentioned, it is unlikely that all but a fraction of the top income earners would have some minimally precise idea about the expected changes in their tax bill.

Conversely, the high response rate in the Gran Buenos Aires study suggests that voters think they know their position on society's income scale, although—as we saw—they know it with substantial and systematic error. The combination of biased perceptions of relative income and rational inattention, calculation constraints, and complex innovations could mean (1) that wealthy voters recognize the increase in taxes they will face and deem it unfair because they see themselves as "middle class"; (2) that other voters at the top and near the middle of the scale are uncertain about effects and thus are not sure how to react or lean toward the status quo; and (3) poor voters cannot see that they will be exempt but consider themselves middle class and fear being taxed.[18]

With incomplete information, biased perceptions, and limited rationality in general, voters would need to make choices and form opinions in a world of uncertainty, particularly regarding their individual outcomes. Asked to support changes to tax policies that would result in greater transparency, efficiency, and fairness, those taxpayers might choose the status quo, fearing losses that are more acutely felt than similarly sized gains—even if they know that the majorities will be "winners," uncertainty about their individual outcome will throw them into a potentially opposing majority.

The Gran Buenos Aires study also shows that, on the basis of average responses, almost the whole population could be thought of as placing itself within plus or minus 3.5 deciles from the median, which is where the middle classes fall in recent academic research.[19] In other words, it is not only that the discourse about preserving and expanding the middle classes resonates well with the majority of public opinion; even when the likely consequences of the reforms are laid out in more "objective" terms, almost all the population believe themselves to be part of the unjustly taxed strata.

Hence, the "battle for the middle class" could not have been won by the reformist government. In the Uruguayan case, cognitive (computational) constraints, relative income/wealth perception biases, loss aversion, and some responses to these, such as following rules of thumb or choosing the status quo, would prevent the reformers from enjoying widespread support. That said, it does not seem right to describe the situation as a total defeat, for three main reasons. First, the responses of civil society and political actors to the reform were real and vocal for a while, but have quieted as time passed. The reform was indeed challenged in the courts by organizations of pension beneficiaries. The Supreme Court initially ruled that the application of the personal income tax to pensions was against the Constitution. However, with the scheduled replacement of one of its members, the majority opinion of the Court was to change. Because in Uruguay constitutional rulings only have effects for those who litigate, the government faced the prospect of having otherwise identical citizens facing different tax treatment, at least until everyone had sued. In addition, it was not prepared to absorb the loss of revenue that this setback implied. The government then got Parliament to pass new legislation substituting the IRPF on pensions with the newly created Impuesto de Asistencia a la Seguridad Social (IASS), with almost identical effects. The new tax was again formally challenged, but with its new composition, the Supreme Court ruled in 2009 that the new tax was admissible.

Opposition from organizations of pension beneficiaries led to the announcement of new efforts to amend the Constitution to prohibit *any* taxes on pensions. There were even threats of resorting to a referendum to repeal the laws, despite the fact that this kind of mechanism is not applicable to taxation-related laws. Interestingly enough, the majority of retirees were not among the worst hit by the tax reform (although many of them may be actually higher on the income scale than they believe they are). What they had that other segments did not have was cohesion and organizational resources, honed in prior battles (pay-as-you-go pensions were indexed to the average wage index in 1989, after a popular initiative ended with a victory at the polls) and the electoral power of a sizable constituency.

Second, the reform was not actively resisted by trade unions or other economically active groups when it started to have material effects in July 2007. This suggests that the expectations derived from the DGI's ex-ante simulations were largely validated and that the taxpayers could see the results reflected in their paychecks (but there is an additional behavioral interpretation, proposed below). The modest positive effects experienced by the majority of taxpayers might not have been enough to make them happier, but certainly did not cause those majorities to feel abused. Third and most important, had there been a deeper, cumulative resentment of excessive burdens or injustices contained in the new regime, it would have been much more difficult for the governing coalition to be reelected with an absolute majority again in 2009. In this sense, it is worth recalling that only a few months before the election, retirees were still fighting the tax(es) in the Supreme Court. Even this was not enough for any opposition candidate or party to make substantial gains on a platform emphasizing the reversal of the reforms.

There were four basic reasons "the battle for the middle class" that was impossible to win was not lost either. To the extent that these factors are relevant for other processes of reform, it is useful summarize them here:

1. As soon as the law was passed, the government, through the tax collection agency (DGI), undertook an aggressive national campaign, not only broadcasting slogans or abstract arguments but also setting up advisory services throughout the country that allowed taxpayers to find out exactly how much they were going to pay under the new regime. This was a direct and eventually effective response to the very specific challenges posed by a complex set of fiscal policy changes, addressing some of the cognitive limitations that behavioral economics emphasizes.

2. The economy was growing rapidly, and taxpayers are known to have difficulties discerning between sources of change in their aggregate financial position, especially when the latter results from variations in various components of different sizes that simultaneously change in opposite directions. It cannot be ruled out that rapid growth obscured the specific effects of the reform for at least some skeptics, and perhaps also for some of the taxpayers whose losses were modest. Strong growth may have misled some mildly losing taxpayers to perceive a net gain (or a neutral effect) from the reform.

3. Many taxpayers may have just concluded in July 2007 that the effects of the reform on their finances were simply not significant enough to worry about. The conclusion would not have been the result of complex calculations but rather reflect the observation that they were receiving a "more or less similar income" and that others would be experiencing the same; life went on without disruption for them and their employers/peers/clients. We do not know for sure what role it played, but consumers have been found to worry more about relative than absolute changes in actual or achievable consumption.[20] If the changes are small and are shared by many of a similar status, the comparisons people make when they assess their happiness might have served to avert or mitigate mass opposition.

4. It cannot be ruled out that some who felt a decline in their net income may have acquiesced to the reform based on considerations of fairness; experiments by behavioral economists have shown that fairness plays a more significant role in many individuals' decisions than it is generally acknowledged in mainstream microeconomics. The reform came after a left-of-center coalition won a national election for the first time in the country's history. Progressive redistribution was part of the Frente Amplio's platform, and they could not have received more than 50 percent of the vote without some support from relatively well-off voters (more on this below).

These explanations are congruent with the data presented above, even if they have not been empirically tested. If they appear plausible, they have distinct policy implications that are discussed in the last section. But first, let us consider the response to the reform from those who were certain to pay more taxes because of it.

THE UPPER STRATA: DIVIDED, DISORGANIZED, AND WEAK?

The success of the Frente Amplio government in passing the tax reform of 2006 raises the question of why it elicited only a weak response and no sustained opposition from the social segments that were most affected by it (i.e., those segments at the top of the income scale, whose tax burden increased with the reform). As mentioned above, Uruguay has a rich history of collective action to oppose economic reforms through institutional channels; as is shown below, that history was far from over at the time of the 2006 reform. Why, then, did the wealthy not try harder to stop the reform through the available political mechanisms?

Moreover, institutionalized collective action is not the only political alternative available to the wealthy. Typically, the upper classes can affect the policy process through various informal means (e.g., influencing the media to cast a negative shadow on the proposed reforms or the reformers themselves, threatening to withdraw support and financial contributions in the next election). If these means were tried, the force with which they operated was far from overwhelming.

As has been discussed, those negatively affected by the reform could be predicted to be a minority of the population (less than 20 percent), but they were far from just *any* minority.[21] As a group, those harmed by the reform had disproportionate *instrumental power*, manifest in a strong voice and multiple direct and indirect channels to influence the policymaking and political processes. In addition to their normal clout, they could have taken advantage of the widespread view that the reform was contrary to the interests of the middle classes, and thus they could have mobilized support from those self-identified as middle class.[22] Under these circumstances, it might have been possible to put together a winning coalition to defeat the reforms. In fact, Latin America's experience shows that, without the acquiescence of the richer segments, even limited progressive reforms usually stall or die (that has been the experience of Guatemala, Costa Rica, and Chile).[23] Why did the Uruguayan rich not react more emphatically and effectively?

One answer to this question could be that rapid economic growth also made the burden increases more palatable for the elites. However, one needs only to look at Argentina at the same time to remember that people, even well-off people whose incomes are growing rapidly (e.g., soybean producers), simply do not like to pay taxes or see them grow. To articulate a more nuanced answer to the question, I explore a set of hypotheses as well as some "soft" evidence regarding their plausibility, citing previous work to provide a comparative contrast.[24]

In the literature, the upper strata are assumed to have some way of influencing the fate of progressive reforms, but the foundations of such power, and how that power is specifically exerted, are often not spelled out. Also, in some studies, "business" as an actor is taken to be an encompassing and heterogeneous entity, including its visible organizations (e.g., industry-specific business associations) as well as the corporations and smaller firms that may or may not belong to and/or feel represented by them, and (mostly implicitly) also the households classified in the top percentiles of the wealth or income distributions. Although the previous section dealt essentially with households as mostly atomistic agents, I now turn to the political influence of "business," understood (and referred to) as *organized and formal pressure groups as well as more informal lobbying activity sponsored or undertaken by firms*. Thus, we reserve "upper classes," "economic elites," "upper segments of society," or "the rich," for *individuals and families with the greatest wealth and incomes*, who may or may not be active in business organizations or feel represented by them or by corporate leaders.

The reform of 2006 succeeded because Uruguay has an ideologically and organizationally divided *business* sector that failed to overcome the collective action challenges of confronting a majority government. The level of fragmentation of the organizations representative of the rich strata is thought to be a long-lasting feature of socioeconomic structure that is logically related to—although it does not require nor is determined solely by—a low density of personal and familial interlinkages between economic and political elites. The latter do contribute to the fact that (at least in normal times) economic and political elites are largely separate groupings, and to the fact that Uruguayan political parties and leaders enjoy relatively high autonomy from business interests. In addition, a highly institutionalized and inclusive party system prevented the upper strata from obstructing the reforms.[25] In broad terms, Uruguay provides an illuminating contrast to

Chile, where instrumental power is much more strongly felt despite similar levels of political party institutionalization.

The fragmentation of business elites in Uruguay has historical roots. The Uruguayan historian and political scientist Carlos Real de Azúa has portrayed the emergence of differentiated upper classes in the nineteenth century and their trajectory up until the late 1960s in terms that shed light on the possible causal channels that connect economic inequalities with elite behavior.[26] He identified factors that account for the lack of ideological cohesion among the elites, and the relative disconnect between the economic and political upper classes. Regarding the former, he highlighted a stronger Enlightenment influence among those Iberian colonizers who settled early on the eastern side of the Río de la Plata estuary. The weak influence of Catholicism would have distinguished the social milieu in Uruguay from that in neighboring regions (Real de Azúa mentions Argentina; I would add Chile)

Later immigration flows from diverse economic and cultural traditions, along with a relatively upwardly mobile society, weakened the impulse toward the unification of ideas and values, or to the elites' sense of belonging to a cohesive social category. Mobility, in turn, would have derived from the nature of the assets of the rich and the political turmoil that characterized the country for the half century after independence in 1830—internal and international armed conflicts periodically depleted "traditional" rural wealth (through their effect on stocks of cattle and other rural property), and the ascent of the local mercantile elites was checked since colonial times by the uneven competition between Montevideo and Buenos Aires as the major hub of regional trading networks.

Well into the twentieth century, the absence of a concentrated and ideologically unified supply of primary and secondary education for the elites, and the peculiar presence of the state and the middle classes in the hegemonic institution of tertiary education (the Universidad de la República), prevented the economic upper classes from acquiring ideological cohesion through shared socialization, which is a key asset in coordinating collective action.[27] Along with the lack of ideological unity, social dynamics did not promote a denser network of personal and familial ties, which could have united different segments of the upper classes more tightly. Religious, ideological, ethnic, and partisan cleavages cut across economic categories with similar or sometimes stronger force than material interest; these factors did not make intermarriage within a broader unified elite any easier. This other lack of cohesion among subsections of the economic elites had a direct impact on their capacity for coordination, particularly when most of the economic entities (companies, economic groups) are family owned and family run.

The emphasis on an account of Uruguay's upper classes written more than forty years ago might raise doubts as to whether the arguments retain their validity. However, there are at least two justifications for taking the historical explanation quite seriously. First, research on the social configuration and behavior of the Uruguayan elites has not been abundant lately, and the few studies available have not contradicted Real de Azúa's analysis.[28] Moreover, even if one recognizes that what has happened since 1969 must have had significant social effects, the nature of the factors highlighted by Real de Azúa are those that have lasting effects, with change coming only at almost a glacial pace.[29]

Even this sketchy characterization of the upper echelons of economic power could explain the absence of any cross-sector, second-level organization representative of broader business interests. And this was the case despite the existence of sector-level organizations of considerable influence. Perhaps the strongest are those representing big ranchers and smaller farmers and family agricultural businesses. They have long been organized in two historically distinct but frequently coalesced associations. Close to them in lobbying power comes the financial sector (in recent times represented exclusively by subsidiaries of foreign banks), and somewhere behind are the manufacturing and the mercantile sectors (with distinct organizations for the domestically oriented and export-oriented firms).[30] Attempts to aggregate and synthesize demands and to develop coordinated action by all these groups have not gone very far, except under exceptional circumstances (e.g., the transition from military rule to democracy in the 1980s). The large size of bipartite and tripartite bodies on the landscape of economic governance institutions (i.e., formal bargaining tables, without or with the government's active involvement) often reflects attempts to create enough seats to accommodate a plural business class whose members do not feel represented by a single or a few high-level organizations.[31] In brief, the nonexistence of a single confederation of the larger and economically most powerful business interests is not by itself the reason that explains weak resistance to the tax reform; instead, it symbolizes the lack of common views and the organizational power of the economic elites, making it harder to pose a serious threat to a determined reformist government with enough legislative backing.[32]

The other side of the coin of the division and disorganization discussed above is a political system that has exhibited high degrees of autonomy from economic powers. But this autonomy cannot be fully understood without highlighting the comparatively high degree of institutionalization of the party system, as well as the mixed social makeup of the major political forces. In fact, Uruguayan parties record some of the greatest longevity and vote share stability in Latin America.[33] They have been characterized as fractionalized, but not to a level that different from parties in other stable democracies, and they are capable of acting in a reasonably disciplined manner when either in control of the executive branch or in the opposition.[34]

In terms of their electoral (and financial) supports, none of the parties can be identified clearly as the party of the wealthy (much as no party can be credibly identified as the party of the working classes). In this context, business organizations—and sometimes even trade unions—have been careful not to be seen as too closely aligned with the positions of a single political organization. Regardless of their frankness or cynicism, in the 2004 election there had to be segments of the upper classes prepared to endorse the policy platform put together by the left, so they were aware of the impending tax changes and took their potential adverse outcomes as the price to pay for other valued policies expected from the new government. In the language of financial analysts, many wealthier segments had already "discounted" the tax reforms when they occurred. Second, the multiclass nature of the parties made it harder for any opposition faction to raise the flag of an anti-reform agenda that could easily be construed as the agenda of the rich and alienate centrist middle-class voters.[35]

A final combination of factors regarding the political representation of the richer strata involves the degree of party institutionalization and the effectiveness of campaign financing as a tool of instrumental power. In fact, the country lacks effective regulation of political financing to curb at least the most blatant forms of goodwill buying; but confronted with institutionalized multiclass parties that tend to have heterogeneous agendas, it has become customary among the wealthy to hedge their bets (rather than betting to win) by spreading their contributions among several contenders.[36] Perhaps inadvertently, this has weakened another channel through which the wealthy could have exercised veto power.

This is a far cry from situations where actual or promised contributions suffice to motivate legislators to leave their political party and set up another political force from scratch, hoping to compete for greater prizes in the next election (to some extent, this describes a frequent phenomenon in places such as Guatemala). In Uruguay, the political and party system has had long-lasting features that are detrimental to the influence that the better-off might want to have on policies. This provides parties with the necessary electoral backing but also with the degree of independence to introduce innovations that in other contexts would have died in Parliament or earlier. This does not mean that business is a passive "taker" of policies in Uruguay, but the most decisive force is reserved for narrower but potentially more rewarding fights, as I now show.

A recent effort to reinforce tax progressivity occurred a few years after the 2006 reform. An analysis of what happened may confirm previous speculation on the role of ideological and organizational cohesion in addressing collective action challenges. On November 29, 2011, Parliament approved the law that created the tax on the concentrated ownership of rural land (Impuesto a la Concentración de Inmuebles Rurales, ICIR).[37] This tax was to be paid by individuals, households, or companies owning more than 2,000 hectares (in productivity-adjusted units), and it was calculated as a fixed yearly amount per hectare (in inflation-adjusted accounting units), increasing through four brackets of the total area owned.[38] The proceeds were to be administered by local governments at the first level of decentralization (*intendencias municipales*) and were to be earmarked for investments in maintenance and/or new additions to the road network, which was seen to have suffered the most from the explosive growth of agriculture in recent years.

Although land assets are already taxed both at the municipal level (*contribución inmobiliaria*) and at the national level (*impuesto al patrimonio*), the

ICIR was meant to discourage the *concentration* of land ownership. Such concentration appeared to be occurring in parallel with the boom in agricultural commodity exports and the establishment of large pulp and paper plants, processes fueled by acquisitions by corporations, investment funds, and Argentine and Brazilian agribusiness groups. Unlike other countries in Latin America, Uruguay does not face pressure from a forcibly displaced and/or a large and rapidly growing rural population, and some economic analysts doubt that the concentration that might have occurred is all negative.[39] However, the political left had historically questioned the uneven distribution of landownership and sees its further concentration as as much a driver of population expulsion as a way for rich families and organized investors to capture greater rents from natural resources. From a technical point of view, the tax was designed to add to the progressive aspect of the Uruguay's direct tax structure; but its proceeds were to be earmarked for rural infrastructure largely enjoyed by those paying the tax (which made the tax politically more palatable but economically less progressive).

Unlike the Impuesto a la Renta de Actividades Económicas (IRAE) and the IRPF, the ICIR targeted the assets of one segment of the upper strata. Even considering that there have been changes in the ownership structures of Uruguay's productive land, the traditional large landholders, and the more recently arrived foreign entrepreneurs and companies, clearly shared an interest in stopping the ICIR from being implemented.[40] Among the affected is a subsegment of the economic elites—medium-sized and large landholders—who had a history of lobbying the public sector on measures that would have a negative impact on their profits. As mentioned above, big ranchers and cattle growers, occasionally joined by other farmers' organizations, have for more than a century organized themselves in two major sector associations, each with a long tradition of unified thought and action. Although the Asociación Rural has traditionally represented wealthier *estancieros* (ranchers), its actions have often been coordinated with the less elitist Federación Rural whenever there have been policy changes that they perceived as potential threats.

The reactions against the ICIR did not take much time to emerge. Some of the responses are illustrative of the new makeup of the rural interests: three of the early lawsuits were brought by large companies that had diverse and nontraditional investments in which land has a variety of functions.[41] Soon after its approval in Parliament, more traditional *ruralistas* set up a basic organizational structure to demand a Supreme Court ruling on the constitutionality of the new tax. The two organizations encouraged and provided legal support to individuals willing to sue the government. As of November 20, 2012, the Federación Rural was actively advising its members to comply with the regulations but to file lawsuits, while organizing public events with legal experts to question the legitimacy of the tax and issuing public statements attacking it.[42] The Supreme Court ruled late in 2012 that the tax was incompatible with the Constitution, because it contravenes the local governments' fiscal autonomy (by taxing a base constitutionally reserved for the latter). The government has since then been considering ways to replace it with a similar tax that does not conflict with constitutional principles.

The rapid and emphatic reaction to the tax from the *ruralistas* and their organizations marked a clear difference from what had happened earlier following the approval of the 2006 tax reform. In no small measure, the greater cohesion of the smaller affected group and its representative organizations helped account for that difference, supporting the hypothesis about the role of cohesion in bringing about veto capacity. Those who have explored the role of family and marriage in the formation and evolution of economic groups in Uruguay have found evidence of such a role, but anecdotal evidence suggests that on this dimension Uruguayan elites are also less "cohesive" than those in neighboring countries such as Chile.[43] Nonetheless, intramarrying is probably greater within homogeneous groups—such as, for example, *ruralistas* versus, for example, retail shop owners or industrialists. That could be related to the greater apparent cohesion of the *ruralistas* vis-a-vis other sectors, when they are or see themselves as targeted by fiscal innovations. The mobilization of the *ruralistas* in 2012, compared with the acquiescence of larger affected groups in 2006, would seem to speak of a denser network of personal-business relationships among traditional (old wealth) landowners than in larger segments of the economic structure.

Finally, the ICIR generated criticisms from parties of the opposition, but the political system has largely avoided getting drawn into a debate that could be easily portrayed as one between a greedy government and a small group of wealthy ranchers. This "cold" relationship is not what one expects to see during precampaigning and fund-raising times, but is not surprising in other times when parties and their interlocutors have broad, heterogeneous agendas.

IMPLICATIONS OF THE URUGUAYAN CASE

This chapter has reviewed a number of the factors that help explain why Uruguay's progressive and comprehensive tax reform of 2006 did not fail, despite the discomfort of elites and the flawed perceptions and expectations of a large constituency self-described as middle class. Some of the factors thought to account for the widespread acquiescence can be considered historical accidents, and several others point to social, political, and economic structures that cannot be easily changed by deliberate political action (at least not in the short term). This analysis provides valuable insights for those attempting progressive tax reforms in similar contexts.

A first conclusion is that the bounded rationality of taxpayers and policymakers demands that reformers carefully use their political capital and communications capacities in order to achieve success. For example, where individuals have difficulties computing the net effects of complex reforms, signals become quite important. It will be easier for voters to believe that a government is committed to fair taxes and that it is honest when it reports predicted outcomes, if the government is fighting tax evasion at all levels, no matter how powerful or visible the offenders.[44] Commitment to perceived tax fairness is important for gaining support or at least for diminishing resistance.

The successful experience of progressive reform in Uruguay shows that perception biases make some battles unwinnable, but this does not mean that they should not be fought or that honest and competent analyses do not matter at all to the public. Informing taxpayers in very personal (and accessible) ways about the effects of the new law on their purchasing capacity appears to have been a most valuable investment in generating a climate that encouraged compliance. In an extension of their survey, the authors of the Gran Buenos Aires study informed a subsample of their subjects of their real position on the national income scale, while the rest were not given such information. Interestingly, those who discovered that they held a position lower than they thought they held were more favorable to redistributive policies than those who were not offered the additional information. This speaks to the value of information, even if many choose not to listen and/or doubt the purposes of a government that provides it.

Information is also important because there are taxpayers that pay and accept taxes out of a sense of fairness and duty.[45] Moreover, if consumers care more about relative than absolute consumption, then being able to make sense of comparisons with their reference group or relevant role models is quite important.[46] A reform that has carefully addressed issues of horizontal equity should then be more easily accepted if taxpayers know the expected equity outcomes, as opposed to if they cannot.

The strengths and weaknesses of the upper classes, despite deep historical roots, can still be influenced by reformers. For instance, the fact that the opposition parties were reluctant to mount a more direct attack on the reform because of their socially diverse makeup could suggest that forming a diverse reform coalition that includes well-known, economically successful individuals and organizations may help neutralize discourses that construe it as something that is socially divisive or an obstacle to economic success.

Another factor contributing to the success of the reform seems to have been the absence of a unified opposing voice from the highest tiers of the wealth scale. The structural factor was somehow exploited strategically by the government, when setting up an early "public consultation" on the principles of the tax reform (which was undertaken despite the fact that it was not required by legislation). The reformers could claim that the mechanism allowed for a transparent discussion of general principles, forcing those expecting special treatment to justify it publicly.[47] This was not enough to fully isolate the reformers from the pressure of large and small interest groups, but these groups were somewhat weakened by the transparency principle established by the government and the creation of a parallel track for the negotiation of fiscal incentives.

The reform of the Investment Promotion Regime was timed and specifically conceived to (further) weaken the resistance of opposition segments of business, but its effects were no doubt helped by a booming economy, and the balanced budget that made it sufficient to introduce revenue-neutral taxes, and indeed allowed for a drop in the corporate income tax rate. In fact, during the public consultation, some argued their case by claiming that jobs were at stake or that growth or export income would be compromised. These arguments did not mix well with the discussion of personal taxes and with considerations of fairness and equity. The approach of the government was then to split the negotiations in two, focusing each one on a segment of the issues and guiding principles; while efficiency and equity were key issues in the discussion of the 2006 law, the promotion of investments was negotiated separately and materialized in the 2007 decree that reorganized the whole regime of fiscal incentives. This splitting of issues allowed the second negotiating table to discuss "conditionality" for the benefits granted. It can be reasonably assumed that separate tables, transparency, and universalism work best with a divided business sector, but they should not be prematurely discarded with more cohesive elites.

The discussion above demonstrates that recognizing the real capacities of human actors and their political organizations, and examining the sociopolitical channels that translate inequalities in wealth and incomes into effective powers in the policy arena, can open a broad window on an agenda that is most profitably explored through systematic comparative analysis. Viewed through a comparative lens, the Uruguayan case suggests that success stories can be greatly illuminating even if they do not provide straightforward recipes.

As for the sustainability of the reforms, the seven years since their implementation have largely confirmed the revenue-generating and equity outcomes that were predicted by reform supporters; and the second government of the Frente Amplio (2010–March 2015) was able to deliver on its early promises to fine-tune the IRPF and keep reducing VAT rates (albeit slowly). In 2014, in the midst of the electoral campaign for the second general election since the reforms were approved, the main campaign promises of the opposition have referred to changes to the IRPF's rate schedule (and the IASS's, as far as it affects retirement/pension incomes), and possibly for some form of capital incomes (landowners' earnings from residential leases); all these measures appear aimed at the desires of a fraction of the middle class, with predictable regressive effects.[48] Even the Frente Amplio appears to have entered the game of schedule revisions, although in its case the proposed changes seem to mostly restore the effects of income taxes to a previous distribution of income now superseded by the economy's strong growth since 2007. The Frente Amplio's proposals do not involve rate reductions, except for the VAT. In the longer term, the Colorado party seems intent on getting rid of the IASS and IRPF, while the Blanco party (with a better chance of becoming a government) speaks more cautiously of gradual adjustments.

The failure of José Mujica's administration to maintain the tax on land-ownership concentration has to be interpreted as partial confirmation that the 2006 reform benefited from a divided business sector that lacked the means to solve difficult collective action problems. Instead, the *ruralistas*' greater cohesion, organization, and ideological affinity were capable of bringing down the concentration tax. The government's own internal disagreements may have helped produce that outcome, at least if technical mistakes are interpreted as a reflection of a hastily designed proposal that did not go through sufficient internal review within the party.

Although the structural weakness of the economic elites and upper strata—and their democratic convictions—cannot be easily replicated elsewhere, the Uruguayan case suggests that progressive reforms are more likely to succeed if a broad and diverse social coalition can be built to support them, one that includes some visibly successful individuals and business organizations; and if the personal and corporate income design issues can be handled separately from economic stimulus measures.

NOTES

1. The author acknowledges with gratitude the valuable comments of Juan P. Jiménez, Felipe Monestier, the editors of this volume, and participants in the workshop "The Political Economy of Tax Reform in Latin America," held at the Woodrow Wilson Center in Washington on December 11, 2012. Guillermo Cruces and Gustavo González-Amilivia generously shared data. None of them is responsible for anything said or implied here.
2. The reform in the broadest sense also includes a rationalization of the tax code (i.e., the elimination of distortionary low-productivity taxes) and the continued

strengthening of the tax collection agency. See Gustavo González-Amilivia, "La reforma del sistema tributario uruguayo desde la perspectiva de la eficiencia y la equidad," Dirección General Impositiva, Montevideo, mimeo, 2007.

3. Diego Aboal, Fernando Lorenzo, and Gabriel Oddone, "La economía política de los déficits fiscales en Uruguay," in *Economía política en Uruguay*, ed. Diego Aboal and Juan A. Moraes (Montevideo: Trilce, 2003), 21–45.
4. "Visible" is meant here as the opposite of "prone to fiscal illusion." On "fiscal illusion," see R. Sausgruber and J. R. Tyran, "Testing the Mill Hypothesis of Fiscal Illusion," *Public Choice* 122, nos. 1–2 (2005): 39–68. The "Mill Hypothesis" states that the burden from indirect taxes will be underestimated because those taxes are less visible or transparent than direct taxes. See also D. Heald, "Fiscal Transparency: Concepts, Measurement and UK Practice," *Public Administration* 81, no. 4 (2003): 723–59.
5. On the "satisfycing" model of policymaking, see Paul Mosley *The Making of Economic Policy* (London: Palgrave Macmillan, 1984).
6. Juan C. Gómez-Sabaini, "Cohesión Social, Equidad y Tributación: Análisis y Perspectivas Para América Latina," Serie políticas sociales, número 127 (Santiago: CEPAL, 2006). For Uruguay before the reforms, see I. Perazzo, C. Robino, and A. Vigna, *Sistema impositivo y distribución del ingreso en el Uruguay*, Trabajo de investigación monográfico para la Licenciatura en Economía, FCEA, Universidad de la República, Montevideo, 2002.
7. A. Barreix and J. Roca, "Uruguay," in *Tax Systems and Tax Reforms in Latin America*, Working Paper 587, ed. L. Bernardi, A. Barreix, A, Marenzi, and P. Profeta (Pavia: Società Italiana di Economia Pubblica, Dipartimento di Economia Pubblica e Territoriale, Università di Pavia, 2007).
8. The reformers (mainly those at the helm of the Ministerio de Economía y Finanzas, the senior managers of the tax authority, and external advisers) introduced this perspective through the so-called dynamic fiscal responsibility approach (*enfoque dinámico de responsabilidad fiscal*), which involved delaying technically sound expansionary measures until future assessments could demonstrate that their revenue effect was neutral or better (interviews with undersecretary of finance and senior economic adviser at the time, recorded in 2011.
9. After more than three decades of competing unsuccessfully for the presidency but growing steadily in support, the Frente Amplio, a coalition of parties and organizations from the centre-left to the left of the political spectrum, was led by Tabaré Vázquez to a national victory in 2004. The coalition got slightly over 50 percent of the vote in the first round, avoiding a runoff election and securing simple majorities in each house of Parliament. Uruguay's quasi-presidential regime ensured that the Frente could move economic legislation forward without any support from the opposition, although this required a high level of discipline of its elected representatives, and the latter involved not minor internal negotiations given the coalition/party's political makeup.
10. For interviews with key actors and observers, see Andrés Rius, *La reforma tributaria uruguaya de 2006: Algunas consideraciones de economía política y comportamental*, Serie Macroeconomía del Desarrollo 125 (Santiago: CEPAL, 2012).

11. The simulations are called "static" when they do not attempt to reflect behavioral changes that individuals might consider in response to the tax reform (e.g., whether they would want to work more hours or take more paid or unpaid leave, etc.).
12. Daniel Kahneman, *Thinking, Fast and Slow* (New York: Macmillan, 2011); Richard H. Thaler and Cass R. Sunstein, *Nudge: Improving Decisions about Health, Wealth, and Happiness* (New Haven, Conn.: Yale University Press; 2008); J. Slemrod, *Old George Orwell Got It Backward: Some Thoughts on Behavioral Tax Economics*, Working Paper 2777 (Munich: Center for Economic and Social Studies, 2009); W. J. Congdon, J. R. Kling, and S. Mullainathan, *Policy and Choice: Public Finance through the Lens of Behavioral Economics* (Washington, D.C.: Brookings Institution Press, 2011).
13. Congdon, Kling, and Mullainathan, *Policy and Choice*, 35.
14. Slemrod, *Old George Orwell.*
15. Raquel Fernández and Dani Rodrik "Resistance to Reform: Status-Quo Bias in the Presence of Individual-Specific Uncertainty," *American Economic Review* 81, no. 5 (1991): 1146–55, provides an early and elegant formalization of this scenario where the status quo bias results simply from individuals' uncertainty about their own specific outcome, even when all the other parameters are common knowledge and the reform is expected to have more winners than losers.
16. Those observations were usually built loosely on impressions, with no attempt to ground them on a logical analysis of changes resulting from the reform.
17. Guillermo Cruces, R. Pérez-Truglia, and M. Tetaz, *Biased Perceptions of Income Distribution and Preferences for Redistribution: Evidence from a Survey Experiment*, Discussion Paper 5699 (Bonn: Institute for the Study of Labor–IZA, 2011).
18. Assuming that voters know the estimated net effects of the reforms for different deciles, and maintain the biased perceptions of their place in the income scale, the conclusions could be drastically changed: if a top income earner knows the effective tax rate for each decile, but sees herself as belonging to the middle class, she will expect no or minor losses with the reform, and might support it. However, those cognitive and calculative capacities are seriously questioned by the evidence from behavioral economics, and particularly for the segment of that literature that applies the concepts to fiscal policies. Thaler and Sunstein, *Nudge*; Congdon, Kling, and Mullainathan, *Policy and Choice.* I thank Jim Mahon for directing my attention to this point.
19. See, e.g., the literature reviewed by Martín Hopenhayn, "Clases Medias en América Latina: Sujeto Difuso en Busca de Definición," in *Clases Medias y Desarrollo en América Latina*, ed. Alicia Bárcena and Narcís Serra (Barcelona: CIDOB–CEPAL, 2010), 11–38.
20. James Duesenberry, *Income, Saving and the Theory of Consumer Behavior* (Cambridge, Mass.: Harvard University Press, 1949); Carol Graham, "The Economics of Happiness," *World Economics* 6, no. 3 (2005): 41–55; Robert H. Frank, *Falling Behind: How Rising Inequality Harms the Middle Class* (Berkeley: University of California Press, 2007).
21. The estimates available of winners and losers come from ex-ante simulations, because there are no panel data or other retrospective records to actually identify unambiguously those that faced an increased vs. a reduced tax burden. The ex-ante simulations gain

validity from comparing them with results of ex-post incidence analyses, e.g., Marisa Bucheli, Nora Lustig, Maximo Rossi, and Florencia Amabile, "Social Spending, Taxes, and Income Redistribution in Uruguay," SSRN eLibrary, 2012.

22. The top quintile or decile cannot be assumed to be a socially homogeneous group (see below, on the use of "rich" vs. "business"). Most consequential for our purposes is the uneven distribution within those groups of political resources and accurate information. Specifically, the hypotheses discussed below are compatible with the evidence from Cruces et al. if it is assumed that the smaller, core subgroup of *business leaders* or economic elites know with a narrow confidence interval their tax burden in different scenarios, but the rich in general do not. The arguments still require perception biases about relative standing, but are consistent with different interpretations of them (in particular, whether they come from miscalculation, cultural appeal, or civic attachments; I thank Jim Mahon for suggesting this possibility.
23. See Gómez-Sabaini, "Cohesión Social"; Tasha Fairfield, "Business Power and Tax Reform: Taxing Income and Profits in Chile and Argentina," *Latin American Politics and Society* 52, no. 2 (2010): 37–71; and ICEFI, *La política fiscal de Centroamérica en tiempos de crisis* (Guatemala City: Instituto Centroamericano de Estudios Fiscales, 2012).
24. See Fairfield, "Business Power"; James Mahon, "Causes of Tax Reforms in Latin America, 1977–95," *Latin America Research Review* 39, no. 1 (2004): 3–30; Cynthia Arnson and Marcelo Bergman, *Taxation and Equality in Latin America* (Washington, D.C.: Woodrow Wilson International Center for Scholars, 2012), and Rius, *La reforma tributaria.*
25. More generally, it is possible to hypothesize but not prove that, rather than causing the political phenomena, the more permanent levels of economic inequality (e.g., those that are revealed by averages and relatively stable positions in cross-country rankings) actually *result* from (also long-lasting) characteristics of the upper sectors and the political system (e.g., their ideological cohesion, the depth of the linkages between economic and political elites, and the relative autonomy of institutionalized and catchall parties).
26. Carlos Real de Azúa, *La Clase Dirigente*, Serie Nuestra Tierra 34 (Montevideo: Nuestra Tierra, 1969).
27. Real de Azúa explicitly compares the relatively loose authority and influence of Uruguay's secondary and tertiary institutions with that of the British "public schools" or the "Ivy League" universities in the United States." Real de Azúa, *La Clase Dirigente*, 40.
28. Among these, Stolovich and colleagues could be thought to detect a greater concentration of power and more powerful elites, but that is largely because the approach is Marxist; it will be shown below that their observations can explain a counterexample to the 2006 tax reform. See Luis Stolovich, Juan Manuel Rodríguez, and Luis Bértola, *El Poder Económico en el Uruguay Actual* (Montevideo: Centro Uruguay Independiente, 1987). Also see Cristina Zurbriggen, "Estado, empresarios y redes rentistas durante el proceso sustitutivo de importaciones en Uruguay: El path dependence de las reformas actuales" (doctoral diss., Universidad Eberhard–Karls de Tübingen, Alemania, 2005), and the works cited there, by Carlos Filgueira, Gerardo Caetano, and Jorge Lanzaro, mostly coincide with Real de Azúa on the limited power of business over the policy process, and the relative autonomy of the political elites. A classical contrasting view to Real de Azúa's, but one that needs qualifications from

a comparative perspective and that is based on weaker evidence, is that of another "founding father" of Uruguayan sociology: Aldo Solari, "Las Clases Sociales y su Gravitación en la Estructura Política y Social del Uruguay," *Revista Mexicana de Sociología* 18, no. 2 (1956): 257.

29. Nothing from this paragraph should be taken to mean that it would be unenlightening to initiate or deepen research on these matters. It is probably the case that new economic groups have emerged that coexist with the old. E.g., that seems to be the case in the agriculture and livestock industry. Yet the persistence of the old (and very old, by the country's relatively short history) can be gauged from the relative influence they still enjoy (see below).
30. Emerging crucial actors in the business sector in Uruguay are the large multinationals responsible for recent major investments (e.g., in the pulp and paper industry), but their tax burden is *negotiated* with the government within the framework of a highly discretionary investment promotion regime that allows them to claim almost a full freeze of their tax status at the time of signing the investment contract. Many of the recent foreign direct investments are based on tax-free zones, something that makes them relatively uninterested in the business taxation issues raised by the 2006 reform (although the reform and the investment promotion regime are not disconnected policies; nor is their "political economy").
31. That is the case, e.g., of the Consejo Superior Tripartito (Tri-Partite Superior Council), which has government, unions, and business representatives to oversee tripartite collective contract negotiations and has six seats for the each of the "social" actors (a single national labor confederation occupies the six seats for workers), to accommodate the diversity of views from the private sector on matters of "industrial relations."
32. Indeed, some could argue that the reform benefited the business sector by reducing the tax on corporate incomes (from 30 percent of the pre-reform IRA and IRIC to the 25 percent of the new IRAE). However, this would miss the point as the consolidated 25 percent rate was then "tied" to the marginal rate on the top IRPF bracket, to prevent tax arbitrage, and was then linked for the longer term to the debate on progressivity and the fair level of redistribution.
33. Michael Coppedge, "Latin American Parties: Political Darwinism in the Lost Decade," in *Political Parties and Democracy*, ed. L. Diamond and R. Gunther (Baltimore: Johns Hopkins University Press, 2001), 173–205; Juan Pablo Luna, "Frente Amplio and the Crafting of a Social Democratic Alternative in Uruguay," *Latin American Politics and Society* 49, no. 4 (2007): 1–30.
34. Luis E. González, *Political Structures and Democracy in Uruguay* (Notre Dame, Ind.: University of Notre Dame Press, 1991).
35. Ibid., González established the catchall nature of all the major parties, a point that was not trivial for the Frente Amplio at the time but that has only been more evident with the Frente's progression to majority in three consecutive elections.
36. See Kevin Casas-Zamora, "State Funding and Campaign Financing Practices in Uruguay," *Cuadernos del CLAEH* 1, no. se. (Montevideo), 2006.
37. Law Number 18,876. It took the government twelve months to issue the decree that lays down the specific rules for the administration of the tax, which is symptomatic of internal disagreements that exist over this tax among members of the left-of-center

coalition; see, e.g., *Brecha Digital*, September 7, 2012, http://brecha.com.uy/index.php/politica-uruguaya/515-teoria-de-la-interpretacion.

38. The owners of (productivity-adjusted) 2,000 to 5,000 hectares must pay 67 unidades indexadas (UIs) per hectare; those owning 5,000 to 10,000 must pay 100 UIs; and those owning more than 10,000 will pay 135 UIs per hectare. On September 30, 2012, the UI was 2,4570, and the US$ was 20.988 pesos per US$, so the amounts per hectare were equivalent to US$7.84; US$11.70; and US$15.80, respectively. The law defines a set of family ties and firm linkages that make the group a taxable entity, to prevent the avoidance of the tax through nominal proprietorship.
39. E. Errea, J. Peyrou, J., Secco, J., and G. Souto, *Transformaciones en el Agro Uruguayo: Nuevas Instituciones y Modelos de Organización Empresarial* (Montevideo: UCUDAL, 2011).
40. The incentives for collective action were not identical; however, some foreign investors have their land covered by major industrial investment projects that have negotiated tax exemptions derived from specific clauses of the investment promotion regime. Those exemptions are contained in investor-government contracts that were thought to protect the firms from policy innovations, something that eventually happened.
41. The first lawsuit was filed by one of the largest rice-producing companies, which owns land for its plantations. The second came from the Chilean-Nordic consortium Montes del Plata, which has been hoarding land for the tree plantations that will feed its large pulp and paper project in the western part of the country. The third litigant was a group best known for running the ferries system between Argentina and Uruguay but which also owns a large dairy company. The second and third lawsuits were later dropped by the complainants, which happened to have multiple and major dealings with the government for their various business dealings.
42. See "Federación Rural recomienda impugnar impuesto a la tierra," *El País* (Montevideo), March 20, 2012, http://www.elpais.com.uy/121120/ultmo-676895/ultimomomento/federacion-rural-recomienda-impugnar-impuesto-a-la-tierra/; and "Con el campo: Para el Uruguay," http://www.federacionrural.org.uy/.
43. Luis Stolovich, Juan Manuel Rodríguez, and Luis Bértola, *El Poder Económico en el Uruguay Actual* (Montevideo: Centro Uruguay Independiente, 1987).
44. This precisely has been the situation since 2004, a time when the tax collection agency was institutionally strengthened and a proactive CEO pursued a proactive strategy that did put it in conflict with visible, large companies. The Frente Amplio kept the CEO in his job, but he eventually resigned to signal political disagreement with the reform of 2006; he was a militant of the Colorado Party, if still a relatively independent one.
45. S. Bowles and H. Gintis, *A Cooperative Species: Human Reciprocity and Its Evolution* (Princeton, N.J.: Princeton University Press, 2011).
46. Duesenberry *Income, Saving and the Theory*; Frank, *Falling Behind*.
47. The source here is the author's interviews with senior officials on the reform team at the Ministry of Finance, March 2012.
48. The data in this sentence and the rest of the paragraph are from M. Brum and G. Alves, "Ni es lo mismo, ni es igual: La política tributaria y el impuesto a la renta," http://matiasbrum.com/2014/09/ni-es-lo-mismo-ni-es-igual-la-politica-tributaria-y-el-impuesto-la-renta/.

CHAPTER 3

The Political Economy of Colombia's 2012 and 2014 Fiscal Reforms

Gustavo A. Flores-Macías

Colombia's 2012 fiscal reform (Ley 1607 de 2012, December 26) was different from most others in the country and elsewhere in Latin America in that it did not respond to the need to generate additional revenue in the short to medium terms. Instead, the reform's main objective was to rebalance the fiscal burden—both horizontally (across different types of activities) and vertically (related to different levels of income)—in order to promote progressivity and formal employment, which in turn were expected to lead to accelerated growth. Among the main factors behind the 2012 reform were the government's legislative majority and its ability to frame the reform in terms of revenue neutrality and employment generation. This strategy allayed concerns about an increased fiscal burden, turned labor-intensive industries into clear winners from the reform, and made the reform's fight against informality a common cause among the business sectors.[1]

In the final days of 2014, however, Colombia was again embroiled in a debate over the need for fiscal reform, for the second time in less than two years. Due to declining oil revenue, the government's promise to increase spending in education and infrastructure, and the scheduled sunsetting of two important sources of tax revenue, President Juan Manuel Santos's administration found itself with a projected fiscal gap of about 2.4 percent of gross domestic product (GDP). Constrained by a fiscal rule and facing potential expenditures associated with the conclusion of the peace process, the government introduced a revenue-generating reform aimed mainly at preserving the taxes on wealth and financial transactions. As of this writing, in November 2014, the proposed reform was modest; rather than adopting structural reforms or improving progressivity, it focused on the continuation of taxes set to expire.

This chapter outlines the main features of the 2012 reform, discusses key factors that contributed to its adoption, and provides lessons derived from this experience. Additionally, it introduces the contours of the 2014 reform, its main drivers, and potential outcomes based on information available at the time of writing.

COLOMBIA'S 2012 REFORM: ADDRESSING INEQUALITY, UNEMPLOYMENT, AND EVASION

Three main objectives of Colombia's 2012 fiscal reform are worth highlighting from a political economy perspective. The first and perhaps most important objective was to reduce the inequalities generated by the tax code. The second was to promote the generation of employment and discourage informality. The third was to reduce the levels of tax evasion. Each is discussed in turn in the following paragraphs.

Reducing Inequality

A key objective of the 2012 reform was to reduce inequality in the tax system. Colombia is the seventh most unequal country in the world, based on the Gini coefficient—a measure of the income distribution ranging from 0 to 1.[2] Although fiscal policy can be a useful tool to address income inequality, in Colombia its contribution to ameliorating inequality has been very limited. Whereas for countries that belong to the Organization for Economic Cooperation and Development (OECD), the difference in Gini coefficients before and after taxes and transfers is considerable, in Colombia this difference is negligible. As figure 3.1 suggests, fiscal policy in Colombia—and other Latin American countries—does not contribute much to the redistribution of income and is far from the effect seen in most OECD countries.

Figure 3.1. Gini Coefficient Before and After Taxes and Transfers, Selected Countries

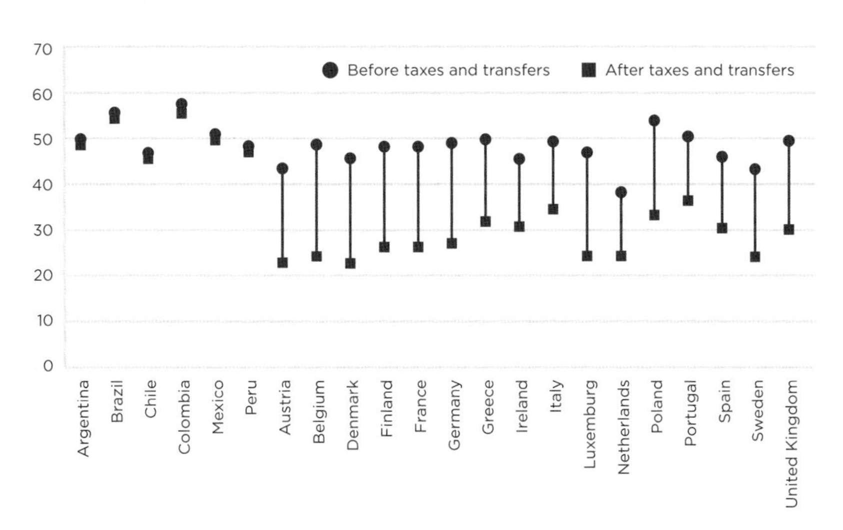

Source: Ministerio de Hacienda, Exposición de motivos del proyecto de ley 1607 de 2012, October 2012.

An important factor contributing to the ineffectiveness of fiscal policy as a redistribution tool is the lack of progressivity in the income tax. For example, those salaried workers with the lowest levels of taxable income would pay a higher effective rate than those with higher levels because the latter would be required to file a tax return and could take advantage of deductions. Higher-income groups also enjoyed a greater number of deductions, exceptions, and other prerogatives. Further, salaried income tends to be subject to tax withholding at the source, whereas higher incomes from capital are not subject to withholding and thus are conducive to higher evasion rates. As a result, those at the highest income levels would often pay less than 1 percent of their annual income.[3]

To make the system more progressive, the reform introduced the National Minimum Alternative Tax (Impuesto Mínimo Alternativo Nacional, IMAN), a presumptive tax that taxpayers must calculate and that establishes a tax floor once all exceptions and deductions have been taken into account. The IMAN was intended to prevent the sectors with the highest levels of income from drastically reducing their tax burden due to fiscal prerogatives. This would also bring a dose of horizontal equity, reducing the differences in effective taxes paid for taxpayers with similar income levels. Therefore, the IMAN sought to improve the progressivity of income taxes—with rates ranging from 0 to 27 percent—while providing a floor for fiscal revenue. In particular, those making less than CO$3.35 million (US$1,706 per month) are not required to pay income tax, and taxpayers would have the option of paying instead the Simple Minimum Alternative Tax (Impuesto Mínimo Alternativo Simple, IMAS)—a slightly higher but definitive and more easily calculated presumptive tax. The government expected the reform to decrease the country's Gini coefficient by 2 points, from 0.57 to 0.55.

Encouraging Formal Employment

A second major objective of the reform was to address informality by encouraging the generation of formal employment. Informality is a problem because it prevents firms from becoming more productive and people from realizing their employment potential and accessing employment benefits, both of which in turn hinder growth and development.[4] It also reduces the government's fiscal intake, which affects the quantity and quality of the public goods provided by the government. Figure 3.2 illustrates the extent of informal employment.

The government identified an excessive burden on corporations as one of the main factors contributing to informality. This rests on the premise that payroll-related costs are the main impediment to scaling up and consolidating a business in the formal sector. These costs are problematic for employment generation because they disproportionately affect those companies with the largest number of formal employees by increasing variable costs.[5]

Before the reform, nonwage costs corresponded to 51 percent of a worker's salary, of which about a fifth was taxes and the rest was expenses related mainly to health care, pensions, and holidays.[6] These nonwage taxes, dubbed *parafiscales* in Colombia, had been the main source of funding for the country's National Apprenticeship Service (Servicio Nacional

Figure 3.2. Informal Workers as a Share of Total Employment, Thirteen Urban Centers

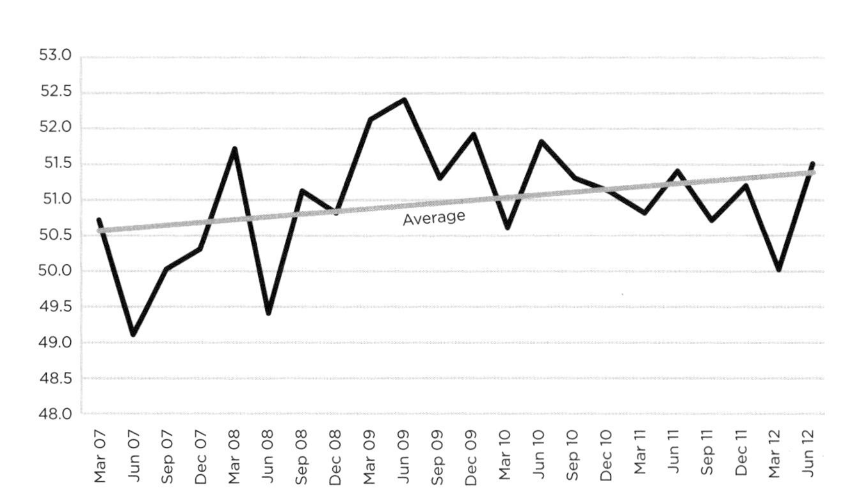

Source: Ministerio de Hacienda, Exposición de motivos del proyecto de ley 1607 de 2012, October 2012.

de Aprendizaje, SENA)—a government agency in charge of devising programs for workers' educational development—and the Colombian Institute for Family Welfare (Instituto Colombiano de Bienestar Familiar, ICBF)—a branch of the Ministry of Social Protection whose mission is to provide social protection to the family in general and children in particular. To alleviate the payroll-related burden on corporations with employees whose salary is up to ten times the statutory minimum wage, the reform eliminated part of the fiscal burden from the *impuestos parafiscales*—the tax of 13.5 percent on payrolls associated with benefits from the ICBF (3 percent), SENA (2 percent), and the Sistema de Salud (Health Care System) (8.5 percent), which cover the entire population.

In order to maintain funding for these benefits, the reform created the Income Tax for Equity (Impuesto Sobre la Renta para la Equidad, CREE), which is levied on net corporate income at a rate of 9 percent for the first three years—until 2015—and subsequently at a rate of 8 percent. The extra percentage point adopted until 2015 is earmarked for higher education (40 percent), health care (30 percent), and agriculture (30 percent). However, the introduction of the CREE was generally offset by a decrease in the corporate income tax from 33 to 25 percent. This way, the total corporate income tax burden on business remained at 33 percent, as it was before, but the reduction of the burden from *parafiscales* was important for stimulating the generation of formal employment.

In particular, the reform partially decoupled the payroll tax from the benefits provided by the ICBF, SENA, and Sistema de Salud, so that the decision to employ an individual would be less affected by this fiscal consideration. Instead, these benefits would be partially funded by all corporations based on their taxable income through the CREE. The government expected this reduction in 13.5 percentage points in non-salary-related costs (*costos no salariales*) to translate into an 11 percent increase in formal employment (between 400,000 and 1 million new jobs in the formal sector) and a 10 to 15 percent increase in the relative size of the formal sector.[7]

Curbing Tax Evasion

The 2012 reform also took steps to discourage evasion by simplifying the tax code and consolidating existing value-added tax (VAT) rates. For example, it limited corporations' ability to deduct interest payments on liabilities that exceed three times the value of their liquid assets. This was intended to dissuade companies from setting up "ghost" debt structures, often carried out by sister companies abroad, that allow them to deduct several times the company's worth. The reform also identified a list of countries as fiscal havens and required that all transactions taking place with any party in these countries be reported and subject to the transfer pricing regime. This was meant to discourage the practice of reporting transactions with entities in fiscal havens below market prices, in order to avoid paying taxes in Colombia and then selling at market prices in the fiscal haven in order to receive a lower tax bill.[8]

Additionally, the reform simplified the VAT—which in Colombia has been characterized as having low productivity and contributing to horizontal inequity. It consolidated the seven existing rates of 0, 1.6, 10, 16, 20, 25, and 35 percent into three: a generalized standard rate of 16 percent for most goods and services; a reduced rate of 5 percent for some goods, such as prepaid medicine and many agricultural products; and 0 percent for exempt goods and services, such as education. This should simplify the administrative burden for taxpayers and aid efficiency in oversight and collection for Colombia's tax collection agency—the Dirección de Impuestos y Aduanas Nacionales.

The new law also created an excise tax on the consumption of certain goods. This tax was intended to compensate for the forgone tax revenue from reducing some of the higher VAT rates and to discourage the consumption of certain goods because of negative externalities. Examples of goods subject to this tax are automobiles (8 percent, if the price is less than US$30,000, and 16 percent otherwise) and cellular communications (4 percent). Moreover, the reform also replaced the VAT on restaurants with an 8 percent consumption tax in order to simplify tax compliance—because the consumption tax is less administratively complex than the VAT—and to discourage informality.[9]

In short, the 2012 reform presented a series of measures meant to address important shortcomings of the Colombian tax system. Rather than increasing fiscal revenue as the main objective—as the previous reform in 2010 had done—this reform had progressivity, employment generation, and simplification of the tax burden as guiding principles.[10]

THE DRIVERS OF COLOMBIA'S 2012 REFORM: STRUCTURAL, POLITICAL, AND CONJUNCTURAL FACTORS

Colombia's 2012 reform took place in the midst of a favorable economic context and the aftermath of a series of successful revenue-generating reforms, both of which are central factors to understand the revenue neutrality and redistributive nature of the measure. Although at the cost of concessions to different interest groups in order to make the changes politically palatable, reforms throughout the previous decade—in 2003, 2006, and 2010, among others—had addressed the need to cover budgetary gaps.[11] Given the increase in public spending since 1991 as a result of the government's obligations set forth in the new Constitution and the urgency of financing the security apparatus, previous fiscal reforms had steadily increased fiscal revenue over time.[12]

The adoption of these reforms, as well as the gradual improvement of security conditions since 2002, contributed to increasing Colombia's appeal to foreign investors and improving economic conditions. In particular, the consistent ability to raise fiscal revenue and the transparency brought about by important measures in the fiscal realm—for example, the adoption of the Fiscal Transparency and Responsibility Law and the Medium-Term Fiscal Framework (Law 819 of 2003) and the quantitative fiscal rule (Law 1473 of 2011)—translated into increased investor confidence and led credit-rating agencies to grant investment grade to the Colombian government's debt for the first time since 1999. Buoyed by these factors, and with the help of a hydrocarbons and mining boom, the economy grew by 6.6 percent in 2011, 4.05 percent in 2012, and 4.26 in 2013, a performance much better than the regional average of 4.3 percent, 2.9 percent, and 2.5 percent, respectively.[13] In this context, the government considered these conditions ideal for pushing for an ambitious reorganization of the tax system.

However, though the string of successful reforms in previous years and the auspicious economic context might explain the objectives of the reform, they are less helpful in accounting for the prerogatives that the final text granted to some and took from others in the process of pursing its main objectives. Despite the period of relative economic stability and good performance, the approved reform was fairly different in scope from the one originally proposed by the Santos administration. When President Santos and his finance minister, Juan Carlos Echeverry, first announced the government's proposal for a fiscal reform early in 2012, they characterized it as one that would "make the rich and tax evaders cry."[14] Complicating the prospects for the reform, however, a leaked draft of the proposal galvanized opposition even before Minister Echeverry formally presented the initiative to Congress.

Above all, the government's initial proposal sought to carry out a comprehensive structural fiscal reform, dubbed ELISSA—for *equidad, limpieza, sencillez, seducción y adaptación internacional*, which roughly translates as equity, transparency, simplicity, appeal, and adaptation to international standards. The proposal was ambitious in its attempt to reorganize and simplify the tax code, aiming to reduce the number of the code's articles by a fourth, from 1,200 to 900.[15] It also introduced several changes that were similar to those ultimately approved by Congress as part of Law 1607 of 2012. These included reducing the general corporate income tax rate—from 33 to 27 percent, in the original proposal—introducing the presumptive IMAN for individuals and corporations, simplifying the VAT to a general 16 percent rate, and adopting a consumption tax on luxury goods.[16]

However, several important aspects of the proposal were modified or eliminated because of opposition among different interest groups and legislators in Congress. For example, the plan to introduce a 4 percent tax on dividends faced strong antagonism from the business community. Leading the effort against the measure were the Consejo Gremial—a semiformal union of the country's most important business associations[17]—as well as the Asociación Nacional de Empresarios de Colombia (ANDI; National Business Association of Colombia) and the National Association of Brokerage Firms.[18] In a letter addressed to Congress, Consejo Gremial president Rafael Mejía stated that the dividends tax would unfairly "constitute double taxation, first on corporations and again on shareholders."[19] Similarly, the plan to limit deductions related to housing and voluntary contributions toward pensions for salaried workers encountered significant opposition in Congress because it would have disproportionately affected salaried workers compared with those deriving income mainly from capital gains.[20] The plan to tax pensions among the wealthiest sectors, excluding those up to CO$13 million (US$6,600), was opposed by both business groups and legislators, because the measure would have mostly affected the pensions of top business executives, members of Congress, and court justices.[21]

Whereas these considerations were mainly opposed by the business sector, the most prominent aspect facing generalized opposition was the proposal to adopt a 5 percent VAT for basic consumption items such as rice, milk, and meat and for some agricultural products, while seeking to compensate the lowest income sectors with food vouchers or other benefits. In line with other Latin American countries' experiences, in Colombia this proposal encountered severe criticism from many fronts. For example, the president of Colombia's Cattle Ranchers' Association characterized the measure as absurd because it would increase the cost of living and push many into the informal sector.[22] Echoing this view, Simón Gaviria, the leader of the Liberal Party (Partido Liberal), stated that the measure would have a negative impact on the lower and middle sectors, which would run counter to the spirit of the reform to make paying taxes more equitable. Therefore, he warned that his party would oppose the reform if this measure were included. Upon the generalized negative reaction against the 5 percent VAT, President Santos himself withdrew his support for the measure due to the political cost the measure could bring in subsequent elections.

Adding to the friction between the government and the different sectors of society generated by the initial proposal, the government was emerging out of a period of strained relations with Congress. When President Santos was first elected, he put together a heterogeneous coalition comprising the main parties in Colombia, including the Social Party for National Unity (Partido de la U), the Conservative Party, the Liberal Party, and the Radical Change Party. This legislative coalition, dubbed the Coalition for National Unity, enjoyed a comfortable majority in Congress, having won about 80 percent of the seats in the legislature. In particular, Santos's own party, Partido de la U, was the main political force, with about 28 percent of the senators and 28 percent of representatives, followed by the main coalition partner, the Conservative Party, with 22 percent of senators and 23 percent of representatives. However, the coalition also represented a diversity of actors and interests, including the Liberal Party—which had been in the opposition during President Álvaro Uribe's administration—and the General Labor Confederation (Confederación General del Trabajo) and other labor groups supporting Santos's vice president, labor leader Angelino Garzón.

The government coalition was tested when President Santos had vetoed a controversial constitutional reform to the justice system in the previous months on the grounds that it included unacceptable privileges for legislators and former government officials.[23] The confrontation had soured executive-legislative relations to the point where some legislators were seeking to impeach the president, with several legislators—both outside and within the coalition—feeling that the government was responsible for leaving Congress to fix a poorly drafted and highly controversial justice reform.[24] In this context, the Santos government opted for postponing the fiscal reform.[25]

The government's window to introduce meaningful reforms was closing as President Santos entered the second half of his first four-year term. Pushing for a fiscal reform in 2013 would be harder because of the proximity of parties' primaries in anticipation of the 2014 elections. A few months later, however, the new finance minister, Mauricio Cárdenas, modified the reform proposal to give it a less ambitious scope. Instead of structural reform, the aim would be to make the tax burden more equitable and to promote formal employment. After formally presenting the revised proposal to the legislature in October, Congress and different interest groups voiced concerns about the new text. Rather than having the discussion take place in the legislature, the government then withdrew the proposal to take into account this dissent and reintroduce the text with modifications. Table 3.1 summarizes the 2012 fiscal reform proposals.

This revised proposal also met opposition in Congress. Among the opposition sectors, union representatives in general and the Alternative Democratic Pole (Partido Polo Democrático, PDA) in particular criticized the reform for favoring corporations and the wealthy and running contrary to the lower and middle classes. For example, PDA senator Jorge Robledo argued that the reduction of the income tax from 33 to 25 percent translated into a benefit of CO$8 billion (US$4.1 million) for big business.[26] The PDA also denounced the elimination of the taxes on dividends and on pensions on the wealthy as evidence that the government and its legislative coalition in Congress were bowing down to the interests of the affluent. Overall, the PDA argued that, even though President Santos had reiterated that the middle class would not be affected, the 2012 reform was less about equity and more about favoring growth among certain sectors.

Conversely, the government argued that the reduction of the fiscal burden on corporations was essential to generating formal employment and increasing growth. Highlighting the national unemployment rate, which hovered above 10 percent in 2012, the government expressed concern about the negative consequences of the steady appreciation of the Colombian peso because of the influx of hard currency related to mining activity. The main

Table 3.1. The 2012 Fiscal Reform Proposals

Echeverry's Reform	Cárdenas's Reform
Structural reform that reduced the number of articles in the tax code by 25%, from 1,200 to 900.	Mini reform that introduced a law with 102 articles.
Objective: equity, transparency, simplicity, appeal, international standards	Objectives: equity, formal employment
Reduction of corporate income tax from 33 to 27%	Reduction of corporate income tax from 33 to 25%, but offset by new CREE tax
Eliminate exceptions	Exceptions remained unchanged
VAT on basic consumption goods	No VAT on basic consumption goods, but creates consumption tax
Tax on dividends	Discarded tax on dividends
No change to the price of gasoline	Changes to the price of gasoline and diesel

Source: Based on information from Observatorio Legislativo, *Reforma Tributaria*, boletín de seguimiento 209, Instituto de Ciencia Política, November 2012.

worry was that the appreciation of the peso could in turn lead to the further loss of competitiveness of the tradable sector at the expense of the non-tradable sector, which would push even more workers into the informal sector. As the government put it, "One of the most worrisome aspects for the prospects of employment generation is the decreasing share of GDP of labor intensive sectors, such as agriculture and industry."[27] For this reason, the government sought to compensate the sectors most affected by the peso's appreciation—the exporting sectors—by generating what it called an "internal devaluation," which would be achieved by reducing domestic costs associated with hiring.[28]

Additionally, the decision to decouple the funding of benefits provided by the ICBF, SENA, and Sistema de Salud and payroll taxes in order to encourage the formalization of employment—though compensating for the forgone tax revenue with the CREE—resulted in the shifting of the tax burden from labor-intensive to capital-intensive sectors. This was a welcome change for labor-intensive industries—including retail, agriculture, fisheries, construction, textiles, wholesale, and transportation—which were expected to see a decrease in the fiscal burden related to their employees by as much as 4 percentage points. Not surprisingly, some of the main advocates of this measure were representatives of the manufacturers of automobiles and auto parts, as well as of the flower growers' industry. As Augusto Solano, head of the Colombian Association of Flower Growers (Asocolflores) estimated, the measure could represent an 18 percent decrease in production costs.[29] Similarly, as Luis Carlos Villegas, then president of ANDI, concluded, "The reform is equitable and well thought out. It incorporates many of the fiscal proposals that the private sector has been advancing for decades. It could generate between 850,000 and 1 million formal jobs in the first year."[30] Conversely, capital-intensive industries such as mining, utilities, and financial services would now bear more of the burden. In the case of mining the increase in the fiscal burden was estimated at 22 percent greater as a result of the CREE. In the words of Carlos Zuluaga, president of ACESCO (Colombia's Steelmakers' Association), "the consequences of several aspects of the reform are unpredictable."[31] This perspective was shared by COLMINEROS (Colombia's Miners' Association), which expressed concern that the fiscal reform would hurt the sector's competitiveness.[32]

This switch in the burden to favor the labor-intensive sectors was generally well received in the legislature because changes favoring the generation of labor were perceived as translating into votes. Outside Congress, the measure generated some debate, however. In the words of Juan Mauricio Ramírez, vice president of the think tank Fedesarrollo, "Growth by itself does not generate formal employment. The reform makes sense because the ICBF, SENA, and Sistema de Salud will be financed less by small and medium-sized businesses and more by the mining and banking sectors—by companies such as Bavaria, Ecopetrol, Pacific, Comcel (Claro), Cerrejón, and banks such as Bancolombia and Banco de Bogotá." In the view of Argentina's former minister of finance, Domingo Cavallo, who served as an adviser to the government, "this change by itself makes the reform worth it."[33] Others were skeptical, such as the economist and banker Mauricio Cabrera, who argued that the decrease in costs would translate into greater profits rather than more employment, because the elasticity of the demand for labor is very low.[34] In his view, this would be a drop in the bucket compared with the real drivers of informality and the considerable currency appreciation of the last decade.[35] Yet others agreed with the reform but lamented the earmarking of the CREE, which responded to the need to maximize the political feasibility of reform.[36]

Some of the criticism against the reform for favoring the affluent sectors also came from within the government coalition in Congress. Some legislators from the Liberal Party expressed concerns about specific aspects of the government's plan disproportionately affecting the lower and middle classes. For example, Partido Liberal senator Camilo Sánchez denounced the proposal to adopt a consumption tax on restaurants serving low-income sectors, particularly those providing low-income breakfasts—known in Colombia as *corrientazo*.[37] Similarly, Liberal Party leader Simon Gaviria pointed out that the government's proposal to introduce the IMAN would result in an effective rate increase of up to 45 percent for those taxpayers making monthly incomes between CO$3.36 million and CO$6 million (between US$1,700 and US$3,100).[38] Another criticism of the IMAN was that it would make filing taxes even more complicated, which ran counter to the simplifying impetus of the reform. Moreover, Radical Change Party senator Daira Galvis expressed skepticism that reducing the tax burden on corporations would translate into formal employment.[39]

In response, Finance Minister Cárdenas dismissed the characterization that the reform disproportionately affected the lower and middle sectors. He pointed instead to the reform's protection of these sectors by setting a threshold of about CO$3.5 million (about US$1,750) to start withholding at the source and commended Congress "for protecting the interests of the Colombians in the lowest income levels."[40]

Culminating a special legislative period convened by President Santos, on December 21, 2012, Congress overwhelmingly approved the fiscal reform. Fifty-two senators voted in favor and only 6 voted against. In the lower chamber, 104 representatives gave their support, whereas 10 registered their opposition to the law. Upon the approval of the law, Finance Minister Cárdenas stated that "the reform will allow Colombia to stop being one of the most unequal countries in the hemisphere, since it will bring more equity and formal employment." He added that, in spite of the net loss in yearly revenue of about CO$500 billion to CO$700 billion (between US$280 million and US$400 million) that would result from the changes the legislature made to the government's initiative,[41] the reform was nonetheless a considerable step forward.[42]

On balance, both the least and the most affluent sectors saw their interests protected in the final version of the reform, but the middle class was the least favored by it. This is because the working sectors' interests were championed in the legislature by the PDA, and the rich were well organized to make their voices heard and enjoyed representation across the government's coalition. Conversely, the middle classes were at a disadvantage because they have a more diverse set of interests and are less able than economic elites to evaluate the impact of the reform. For these reasons, the middle sectors were unable to find a champion that would push back on their behalf. Moreover, the middle sectors are more likely to have their salary income withheld without many of the compensatory mechanisms benefiting the poor.[43]

LESSONS FROM THE 2012 REFORM

Overall, the 2012 law represents a pragmatic approach to fiscal reform. It was gradual and not particularly ambitious, but it was politically feasible and allowed for smaller and consistent steps in the desired direction. Naturally, the reform fell short of achieving many changes the government had initially deemed desirable. Ideally, the reform would have also increased fiscal revenue to finance both mounting commitments related to education and infrastructure—as President Santos had promised during his campaign—and the potentially successful conclusion of the peace process, which was likely to be financially very onerous. These resources could have come from the elimination of the special tax zones (*zonas francas*), the adoption of taxes on pensions of the wealthy and on dividends, and the reduction of the myriad exceptions to the VAT that constitute a patchwork of fiscal prerogatives for different interest groups.

Similarly, the reform could have applied the IMAN across the board, regardless of whether the taxpayer was a salaried worker, while eliminating additional deductions that benefit the wealthy. It could have attempted to get rid of distortionary taxes, such as the wealth tax and the tax on financial transactions, which, respectively, discourage savings and investment and the use of formal financial institutions.[44] The reform could also have attempted to establish a CREE without unnecessarily constraining the destination of its revenue with the earmarking for the ICBF, SENA, and Sistema de Salud.

However, Minister Echeverry's failed attempt at comprehensive reform showed that a truly structural fiscal reform is bound to encounter significant opposition from a number of fronts. In the absence of a major crisis that forces the main political forces to agree on a grand fiscal bargain, this approach risks sacrificing any progress altogether. Instead, the success of Law 1607 of 2012 was mainly due to the pursuit of more limited reform, pitched not as a game changer but as a necessary, limited step in a longer series of adjustments.

In addition to the government's strategy of understating the nature of the reform and setting expectations low in its revised formulation, three main factors proved important in securing its approval in Congress. First, the government was able to deactivate opposition and even gain supporters among the working sectors and their representatives in Congress by emphasizing the revenue neutrality of the reform and the generation of employment. The first feature conveyed the sense among the population that the government did not intend to exert a greater fiscal burden on society, regardless of whether specific sectors inevitably lost from the reform or whether a revenue-generating reform would likely be required in the near future.[45] The second made the promise of greater employment an appealing banner for legislators to embrace before their constituents.

A second important factor relates to the government's ability to identify labor-intensive industries as the clear winners from the reform. This numerous group proved instrumental in the government's building of a coalition of allied forces by providing both a lobbying arm in Congress and contributing to winning over public opinion. Conversely, capital-intensive industries such as mining and banking—which were among the losers of the reform—tend to be less favorably viewed by the public and less able to translate their opposition into public pressure on legislators. The stated objective of the reform to address informality also gave the business community in general a stake in the proposed changes.

A third strategy that contributed to the success of the reform was the government's decision to withdraw the initial reform proposal after encountering opposition among legislators once Minister Cárdenas's initiative was formally introduced in Congress. Rather than risking that the different political forces make significant changes to the initiative, the government adjusted the text to incorporate dissenting views while maintaining the general coherence of the proposal with an emphasis on revenue neutrality. Avoiding piecemeal discussion of the proposal contributed to the approval of a final text that was fairly close to the one the government had presented after taking into account legislators' opinions.

Notwithstanding these strategic successes, a fundamental underlying factor facilitating the adoption of the reform was the existence of a majority in Congress behind the president's initiative. Despite the rift between President Santos and the legislature over judicial reforms to the Constitution a few months before the discussion of the fiscal reform, the president's legislative majority played a decisive role for the reform's approval. Although not every vote from the Partido de la U, Conservative Party, Liberal Party, and Radical Change Party was guaranteed, there was relatively little uncertainty as to whether the Coalition for National Unity would ultimately garner enough votes to adopt a fiscal reform along the general lines of what Minister Cardenas's proposal had outlined.[46]

FROM REVENUE NEUTRALITY TO REVENUE GENERATION: THE 2014 FISCAL REFORM

Almost two years after the adoption of the 2012 reform, the government's Medium-Term Fiscal Framework projections pointed to a budget gap of about 2.4 percent of GDP.[47] This estimate was based on the expected decline in oil production, the phasing out of the tax on financial transactions (from CO$4 per 1,000 pesos to CO$2 per 1,000 pesos beginning in 2015) mandated by Law 1410 of 2010, and the sunsetting of the wealth tax originally intended to pay for the government's security efforts.[48] The forgone income from these two taxes accounts for about 55 percent of the projected fiscal gap—1.3 percent of GDP. Whereas oil production had increased in

Colombia until it reached a peak of 1.1 million barrels per day in 2012,[49] it is expected to decline to well under 1 million barrels per day, along with greater production costs.[50] Combined with a lower expected price of the Colombian basket, this will represent lower revenue for government coffers.[51] Guerrilla attacks during the first half of 2014 on the country's oil infrastructure only magnified the problem.[52]

On the expenditures side, although not explicitly considered in the fiscal framework's projections, government spending is likely to surpass expected levels because of the financial burden related to President Santos's campaign promise to increase investment in education and infrastructure, and because of potential commitments resulting from the peace negotiations with the Revolutionary Armed Forces of Colombia (Fuerzas Armadas Revolucionarias de Colombia) in Havana.[53] However, the bulk of the spending that exceeded projections came from the government's operating costs, which increased by 12 percent from the previous year. Additionally, expenditures related to pensions grew faster than expected. The government's reduction of investment expenditures by 5.5 percent was not enough to compensate for the increase in spending.[54]

The government's policy options are constrained by the "fiscal rule" adopted in 2011 (Law 1473 of 2011). Conceived as a mechanism to avoid procyclical fiscal policies, the Law's Article 5 establishes that structural expenditures may not exceed structural revenue by more than the preestablished goal set for the structural balance. The rule establishes a limit for the structural deficit of 1 percent of GDP by 2022, and a transitional period with more moderate ceilings—2.3 percent by 2014, 1.9 percent by 2018, and 1 percent by 2022 and beyond. Given that the estimated fiscal gap amounted to about 17 percent of expenditures and exceeded the deficit allowed by the fiscal rule, the government was faced with two main revenue-generating options to cover this gap. The first was to push for a comprehensive revenue-generating fiscal reform—despite President Santos's opposing this during his reelection campaign. The second was to postpone the expiration of the wealth tax and the phasing out of the financial transactions tax to address the country's short-term financial needs.

The government first floated a reform to renew the wealth tax and postpone the phasing out of the financial transactions tax for another four years.

This early proposal intended to raise the maximum marginal rate for the wealth tax from 1.5 to 2.25 percent and establish a progressive tiered rate. In particular, the wealth threshold to pay the tax would decrease from CO$1 billion to CO$750 million (from about US$500,000 to US$380,000). The marginal rates would be 0.4 percent for wealth between CO$750 million and CO$3 billion (US$380,000 to US$1.5 million); 1.1 percent for wealth between CO$3 billion and CO$5 billion (US$1.5 million to US$2.5 million); 2 percent for wealth between CO$5 billion and CO$8 billion (US$2.5 million to $4 million); and 2.25 percent for larger amounts.[55]

Even before the government formally presented the initiative to Congress, however, several sectors expressed dissatisfaction at this early stage. For example, the president of the National Federation of Merchants (Federación Nacional de Comerciantes), Guillermo Botero Nieto, complained that "there have been considerable updates on property value carried out in the registry since 2011, and the renewal of the wealth tax would have an impact on the productive sector in a sudden way."[56] He also urged the government to reduce current spending, particularly on the bureaucracy, and opposed preserving the tax on financial transactions because it runs against the push for incorporating businesses into the formal banking sector. Similarly, the head of the chocolate maker Grupo Nutresa expressed frustration that the government would resort to more taxing of the same narrow base with every reform and urged the government to instead expand the base. Along the same lines, Carlos Eduardo Botero, head of the Institute for Exports and Fashion (Indexmoda), exhorted the government to put an end to the black market and informal trade rather than raising taxes.[57]

Many of these opposing views interpreted the need for additional revenue as a failure of the 2012 reform. They pointed to the steady decrease in the yearly rate of growth in fiscal revenue, from 25 percent in 2011 and 15 percent in 2012 to 7 percent growth in 2013, and attributed this decline to the reduction in the corporate tax rate from 33 to 25 percent.[58] Among the most salient critics was the current head of ANDI, Bruce MacMaster, who criticized the government's proposal for failing to address more long-term fiscal problems, including the causes of declining oil revenue.[59]

This opposition was not shared by all business sectors, however. Supporters among the business associations included Julián Domínguez Rivera, leader of the Confederation of Chambers of Commerce (Confecamaras), and Arturo Gutiérrez de Píñerez, the head of the gas company Gases de Occidente, who argued that these taxes are a continuation of the fiscal burden to which Colombians are accustomed, and are therefore not problematic. In their view, what is important is that the government continue to invest in education. However, they also argued that the government would need to do a good job of cracking down on tax evasion and not generating any more taxes.[60]

Others even advanced their own alternative proposals. For instance, Colombia's Exporters Association (Analdex) proposed maintaining the wealth tax without changes to the base or rate, because the real appreciation of real estate would bring even more revenue to the government. It also advocated maintaining the financial transactions tax. Further, its main proposal was to raise the generalized VAT rate from 16 to 17 percent, which it argued would prevent having to carry out yet another reform in a year or two, because revenue from oil and mining is likely to continue to decrease.[61] This proposal was similar to the one advanced by the Association of Financial Institutions (Asociación Nacional de Instituciones Financieras), which favored phasing out the tax on financial transactions but suggested instead increasing the VAT rate by 1 percentage point for two years, and by 2 percentage points, to 18 percent, starting in 2017.

Some of these views were echoed in Congress, with several legislators expressing concern about the government's early plan. For instance, María del Rosario Guerra, senator from the Democratic Center—a right-of-center party formed in 2013 by former president Uribe and that became the main alternative to Santos in the 2014 presidential race—pointed out that "the approval of expenditures without securing ways of financing is worrisome, particularly when the president never spoke of raising taxes during his campaign. I see a lot of improvising."[62] Others, such as Green Party senator Antonio Navarro, favored eliminating deductions for mining companies and adopting a 5 percent tax on dividends. [63] The Alternative Democratic Pole, through statements by Senator Jorge Enrique Robledo and Representative Alirio Uribe, condemned the government's tendency to tighten the belt on labor and the middle class while reducing the tax burden for corporations in previous reforms and strongly rejected any attempt to raise the VAT to 18 percent.[64] In this regard, even the president's own party sounded a note of caution. As Senator José David Name, president of the Senate, stated, "Colombia cannot keep burdening the middle class with more taxes."[65]

In light of this opposition, Minister Cárdenas indicated that his preference would be to make permanent the tax on financial transactions and the wealth tax in order to sustain current levels of investment in education and poverty reduction.[66] Although improving on these levels will require finding additional resources in the future, beyond what the preservation of these two taxes could bring, the Santos administration's final proposal excluded both the dividend tax—which had been a contentious point in the 2012 reform—and an increase in the VAT to minimize animosity toward the reform among economic elites and their allies in Congress.

Instead, the final text of the initiative presented to Congress in October 2014 focused on three main issues: (1) adopting a wealth tax for another four years, (2) postponing the phasing out of the tax on financial transactions, and (3) and creating a surcharge for the CREE.[67] First, the wealth tax—whose name in Spanish was modified from Impuesto al Patrimonio to Impuesto a la Riqueza—differed from the government's early proposal in that the rates were less steep and the threshold to pay the tax remained unchanged at CO$1 billion (about US$500,000). Table 3.2 shows the different marginal tax rates and corresponding taxes associated with each level of taxable wealth. The government expects that 52,000 individuals and 32,000 corporations would be required to pay the tax.[68]

Table 3.2. Proposed Wealth Tax in the 2014 Fiscal Reform

Wealth (CO$)	Marginal Rate (%)	Tax (CO$)
< 2 billion	0.20	(Taxable base) x 0.2%
Between 2 billion and 3 billion	0.35	[(Taxable base - 2 billion) x 0.35%] + 4 million
Between 3 billion and 5 billion	0.75	[(Taxable base - 3 billion) x 0.75%] + 7.5 million
Over 5 billion	1.50	[(Taxable base - 5 billion) x 1.5%] + 22.5 million

Source: Proyecto de Reforma Tributaria, Ley 134 de 2014.

Second, the financial transactions tax would remain at CO$4 x 1,000 until 2018, instead of it being phased out in 2015, as originally scheduled. It would now be phased out—becoming CO$3 x 1,000 in 2019, CO$2 x 1,000 in 2020, CO$1 x 1,000 in 2021, and disappearing in 2022. Third, the CREE would remain at 9 percent permanently, instead of decreasing to 8 percent in 2015 as scheduled. There would also be a 3 percent surcharge on the CREE for taxable corporate income over CO$1 billion (about US$500,000). The government estimates that 6,000 corporations would be affected by the surcharge.

Although the formal presentation of the government's initiative elicited statements from ANDI and the oil sector (Asociación Colombiana del Petróleo) calling the reform a setback for small and medium-sized businesses and hindering the oil sector's contribution to Colombia's economy, Congress will likely approve a version that is not far from the government's proposed reform.[69] This is because, in spite of the weakening of the government's coalition and the strengthening of the Centro Democrático in the 2014 legislative elections, President Santos still enjoys a majority in Congress. Additionally, whereas the benefits of progressivity and horizontal equity in the 2012 reform will only be felt in the medium to long runs, there is some preliminary evidence that the government's efforts have begun to pay off: Employment generation appears to be on the right track following the 2012 reform, with the unemployment rate reaching 9.9 percent of the country's labor force in 2013—the lowest in twelve years.[70] These factors, combined with the modest scope of the reform, are conducive to its approval without much complication for the government. However, the reform's limited scope might end up being a double-edged sword, because the government is likely to find itself having to revisit the plan for a more ambitious revenue-generating reform in the near future, especially if the peace process comes to fruition.

EPILOGUE

As this book went to print in December 2014, the Colombian Congress approved a new fiscal reform law (Law 1739). The final text of the legislation differed from the government's proposal in several ways. One important change was that individuals and corporations are treated differently with respect to the wealth tax. Individuals will pay roughly what the government had proposed, with a tiered rate starting at 0.18 percent on income over CO$2 billion (about US$1 million) and a top rate of 1.5 percent on income over CO$5 billion (US$2.5 million) for the 2015-18 period. But corporations will pay the tax for only three years and at lower rates: the top marginal rates are 1.15 percent in 2015, 1.0 percent in 2016, and 0.4 percent in 2017 for incomes over CO$5 billion (US$2.5 million). Moreover, the CREE will remain as proposed—at 9 percent—but the threshold for the CREE surcharge for the 2015-18 period will be on taxable corporate income over CO$800 million (about US$400,000), with rates of 5 percent in 2015, 6 percent in 2016, 8 percent in 2017, and 9 percent in 2018. The tax on financial transactions remained unchanged.[71]

These changes reflected an intense negotiation between the government and business sectors on the eve of the reform's approval. Due to intense pressure from Colombia's main private sector groups, the government conceded a reduction in the wealth tax in exchange for higher corporate taxes through the CREE surcharge in order to cover the projected fiscal gap. The government also committed to pursuing a comprehensive fiscal reform in the future; the final text of the law mandated that a commission be established to evaluate the existing fiscal system and make recommendations.

On balance, the 2014 reform contributed to the progressivity of the system by introducing relatively high thresholds and tiered marginal rates for the wealth tax and the CREE surcharge. It also contributed to closing the projected fiscal imbalance while maintaining existing expenditures on social programs and infrastructure. However, it postponed the elimination of distortionary taxes that discourage financial transactions and savings and missed an opportunity to introduce more ambitious changes to address the decline in oil revenue. The 2014 reform's limited scope, the continued drop in oil prices (by the end of 2014 oil prices were half of what they were mid-year), and the potential successful conclusion of the peace negotiations will likely set the stage for a more ambitious reform in the near future.

NOTES

1. For a discussion of strategies for fiscal extraction see Tasha Fairfield, "Going Where the Money Is: Strategies for Taxing Economic Elites in Unequal Democracies," *World Development* 47 (July 2013).
2. Ministry of Finance, "Exposición de motivos del proyecto de ley 1607 de 2012," October 2012.
3. Ibid.
4. Matías Buso, María Victoria Fazio, and Santiago Levy, *Informal and Unproductive: The Productivity Costs of Excessive Informality in Mexico*, IDB Working Paper 341 (Washington, D.C.: Inter-American Development Bank, 2012).
5. "Reforma Tributaria," *Revista Dinero*, October 12, 2012.
6. Gustavo Hernández, "Payroll Taxes and the Labor Market: A Computable General Equilibrium Analysis," *Latin American Journal of Economics* 49, no. 1 (May 2012).
7. Although some studies challenged the government's estimates regarding employment generation, preliminary data for 2013 point to an 8.6 percent increase in formal employment and a 2.9 percent decrease in informality. See "El empleo formal crece tras la reforma tributaria," *Portafolio*, March 18, 2014; and Stefano Farné and David Arturo Rodríguez, *Bajar los impuestos al trabajo genera empleo? Ley 1607 de 2012 de Reforma Tributaria en Colombia*, Cuadernos de Trabajo 14 (Barranquilla: Universidad Externado de Colombia, 2013).
8. "Law 1607 of 2012," *Official Gazette*.
9. Roberto Steiner and Juan Camilo Medellín, "Perspectivas Fiscales 2014–2018: Elementos para una nueva reforma tributaria," *Cuadernos Fedesarrollo* 52, April 2014.
10. "Law 1430 of 2010," *Congressional Gazette*, December 29, 2010.
11. See, e.g., Gustavo Flores-Macias, "Financing Security through Elite Taxation: The Case of Colombia's Democratic Security Taxes," *Studies in Comparative International Development*, Online First 2013.
12. Sergio Clavijo, Alejandro Vera, and Nelson Vera, "Estructura fiscal de Colombia y ajustes requeridos (2012–2020)," Centro de Estudios Económicos de ANIF and Fedesarrollo, March 2013.
13. World Development Indicators, Online Resource 2014, World Bank, Washington, http://data.worldbank.org/data-catalog/world-development-indicators.
14. "Reforma Tributaria hará chillar a los ricos," *Revista Dinero*, April 27, 2012.
15. Observatorio Legislativo, "Reforma Tributaria," *Boletin de Seguimiento 209*, November, 2012.
16. Natalia Salazar, *Political Economy of Tax Reforms: The Case of Colombia*, Woodrow Wilson Update on the Americas, October 2013, 17.
17. Angelika Rettberg, "Business vs. Business? Grupos and Organized Business in Colombia," *Latin American Politics and Society* 47, no. 1 (April 2005).
18. In comparative perspective, Colombia's peak business associations are among the best organized and most influential in Latin America, comparable to those in Mexico and Chile. See Ben Schneider, *Business Politics and the State in Twentieth-Century Latin America* (New York: Cambridge University Press, 2004).

19. Letter from the Consejo Gremial President, Rafael Mejía, to Congress, December 14, 2012, available at http://www.portafolio.co/sites/portafolio.co/files/CARTA%20 CONSEJO%20GREMIAL.pdf.
20. "Filtración inoportuna de la reforma tributaria," *Semana*, May 12, 2012.
21. Ibid.
22. "La reforma que proponen los académicos y los empresarios," *El Universal*, October 19, 2011.
23. "Santos devuelve al Congreso la reforma a la justicia," *Semana*, June 21, 2012.
24. "Los congresistas que votaron en contra de la reforma a la justicia," *El Espectador*, June 21, 2012.
25. Observatorio Legislativo, "Reforma Tributaria," *Boletín de Seguimiento 209*, November 2012.
26. Polo Democrático Alternativo, "Reforma Tributaria le ahorró 8 billones a los más ricos: Robledo," Press Release, December 21, 2012.
27. Ministry of Finance, *Exposicion de motivos de propuesta de reforma fiscal 2012*, October 2012.
28. *Revista Dinero*, "Reforma Tributaria," October 12, 2012.
29. Ibid.
30. "Empresarios afirman que reforma tributaria es equitativa," *Portafolios*, October 25, 2012.
31. Ibid.
32. "Mineros en desacuerdo con reforma tributaria," *El Nuevo Siglo*, October 22, 2012.
33. "Reforma Tributaria*," Revista Dinero*, October 12, 2012.
34. Ibid.
35. According to the government's estimates, the reform would address the currency appreciation associated with Dutch disease by alleviating business' fiscal burden, which would be equivalent to a10 percent depreciation. Ministry of Finance, *Exposicion de motivos de propuesta de reforma fiscal 2012*, October 2012.
36. Steiner and Juan Medellín, "Perspectivas Fiscales 2014–2018."
37. Observatorio Legislativo, "Reforma Tributaria," *Boletin de Seguimiento 209*, November, 2012.
38. "Reforma tributaria afecta clase media," *El Nuevo Siglo*, December 11, 2012.
39. "La Reforma Tributaria hay que hundirla: Senador Robledo," *El Universal*, October 26, 2012.
40. "Congreso aprobó reforma tributaria y quedó lista para ser ley," *El Tiempo*, December 21, 2012.
41. The net loss will be a result of Congress's lowering of the gasoline tax and the changes to the VAT.
42. "Congreso de Colombia aprueba reforma tributaria, introduce cambios," Reuters, December 20, 2012.
43. Salazar, *Political Economy*.
44. Ibid.
45. The 2014 revenue-generating fiscal reform, which was intended to cover a budgetary gap projected in the government's medium-term fiscal framework, is discussed in the next section.
46. On July 9, 2014, the Constitutional Court rejected a challenge based on procedural allegations to the 2012 fiscal reform and declared valid Law 1607 of 2012.

47. "El Marco Fiscal de Mediano Plazo confirma la necesidad de reforma tributaria," *Revista Portafolio*, June 17, 2014.
48. Law 1430 of 2010, *Official Gazette*.
49. "Colombia ya produce más de un millón de barriles de petróleo al día: Santos," *El País–Colombia*, December 30, 2012.
50. Although Colombia's oil company, Ecopetrol, had targeted 819,000 barrels per day in 2014, the mid-year estimate put production at a considerably lower 770,000. "Oil Majors Lodge Bids for Colombia Exploration Rights," *Financial Times*, July 24, 2014.
51. "El Marco Fiscal confirma la necesidad de reforma tributaria," *Revista Portafolio*, June 17, 2014.
52. "Colombia Proposes Increasing Capital Gains Tax to 2.25%," *Reuters*, September 8, 2014.
53. Leonardo Villar and David Forero, "Escenarios alternativos y necesidades de recursos para el cuatrienio," *Cuadernos Fedesarrollo* 52 (April 2014).
54. "El Marco Fiscal confirma la necesidad de reforma tributaria," *Revista Portafolio*, June 17, 2014.
55. "Colombia proposes increasing tax on wealth to 2.25 percent," *Reuters*, September 9, 2014.
56. "Reforma tributaria divide opinión de empresarios," *El Tiempo*, September 5, 2014.
57. "Industria le pone peros a la reforma tributaria," *El Pais–Colombia*, August 16, 2014.
58. Dirección de Impuestos y Aduanas Nacionales, *Recaudo Anual por Tipo de Impuesto 1970–2014*, November 20, 2014.
59. "Proposed 4-Year Tax Hike Won't Cover Colombia's $6.5 Billion Budget Gap," *Colombia Reports*, September 8, 2014; Fedesarrollo and Latin American Program, *Relatoría sobre el debate: Hacia una nueva reforma tributaria*, 2014, http://www.wilsoncenter.org/publication/ColombiaRelatoria2014
60. "Reforma tributaria divide opinión de empresarios," *El Tiempo*, September 5, 2014
61. "Exportadores piden a Santos estabilidad tributaria y proponen modelo de reforma," *El País–Colombia*, September 11, 2014.
62. "Reforma tributaria: En qué consiste y quiénes serán los más afectados," *El Tiempo*, September 13, 2014, http://www.eltiempo.com/archivo/documento/CMS-14530038; see also, Fedesarrollo and Latin American Program, *Relatoría sobre el debate: Hacia una nueva reforma tributaria.*
63. "Reforma tributaria."
64. Polo Democrático Alternativo, "El Polo no aprobará más impuestos contra los sectores populares y la clase media," press release on the Alternative Democratic Pole's position on a potential fiscal reform, September 10, 2014.
65. "Reforma tributaria."
66. *El Tiempo*, "Reforma Tributaria Divide Opinión de Empresarios," September 5, 2014.
67. Ministry of Finance, *Proyecto de Reforma Tributaria*, Ley 134 de 2014, October 4, 2014.
68. "El gobierno radicó la propuesta de reforma tributaria," *Portafolio*, October 3, 2014.
69. *Portafolio*, "El gobierno radicó la propuesta de reforma tributaria," October 3, 2014.
70. "Colombian Unemployment Lowest in 12 years, Rural Unemployment Still High," *Colombia Reports*, November 1, 2013.
71. It remained at CO$4 x 1000 for the 2015–18 period and phasing out at CO$3 x 1000 in 2019, CO$2 x 1000 in 2020, CO$1 x1000 in 2021, and no tax by 2022.

CHAPTER 4

Institutions, Inequality, and Taxes in Guatemala

Maynor Cabrera and Aaron Schneider

Levels of taxation in Guatemala are among the lowest in Latin America despite frequent reforms. These reforms have raised only marginal revenues, have failed to significantly alter the tax structure, and have reproduced a highly unequal distribution of wealth. Instead of contributing to revenue-raising efforts, at least some of those who hold wealth would appear prefer to use their power to exercise a veto over state building, opting for a weak state that is resource poor. As a result, the state possesses insufficient resources to support sustainable and equitable development and it can address neither widespread social exclusion nor the criminality that infects both state and society. This chapter investigates taxation as an expression of the capacity of the state, and demonstrates the structural and institutional difficulties of building progressive tax capacity in the Guatemalan context.

To understand tax capacity in Guatemala since the end of the civil war in 1996, the chapter proceeds as follows. First, we explore the determinants of tax capacity with reference to the economic and political-institutional conditions of the country. Subsequently, we explore episodes of tax reform with particular attention to their impact on tax capacity. For each episode, we analyze the political and institutional context that opened opportunities for reform but at the same time limited the possibility of change. We end with an exploration of the 2012 reforms, which are notable for the political and institutional context that produced them, but with a limited impact on tax capacity and equity.

THE POLITICAL ECONOMY OF REFORM

Guatemala collects among the lowest tax levels in Latin America, and the revenues it does collect are gathered inefficiently, with regressive effects on distribution, and suffer frequent changes. The tax administration suffers from politicization and bureaucratic weakness, providing impunity to those who evade or avoid their tax obligations. Evasion is further exacerbated by the poor use of funds collected, as corruption and inefficiency in expenditures weakens tax morale. The result is a tax system that produces revenues insufficient to finance the state, which remains in a condition of recurring fiscal crisis.

According to various statistical measures of tax burden, Guatemala collects among the lowest amount of revenues in Latin America.[1] To explain the country's low level of taxes, we focus on its high rates of poverty and inequality, as well as its fragmented political elite operating in institutions that block efforts to reach a consensus and facilitate efforts to veto significant change.

Guatemala has high rates of poverty. In 1989, in the midst of civil war, 63 percent of the population was below the poverty line. Two decades later, the poverty rate has barely fallen, at 51 percent in 2006 and rising to 53.7 percent according to the latest household survey (National Household Survey–Encovi, for its acronym in Spanish), in 2011. Though 18 percent of the population lived in extreme poverty in 1989, the proportion had fallen only to 16 percent in 2000, 15 percent in 2006, and 13.3 percent in 2011.

Within the poverty statistics can be found some of the historic dimensions of exclusion that characterize Guatemalan society. Extreme poverty in the urban sector affected 3 percent of households in 2000 and 5 percent in 2006, while the incidence of poverty in the rural sector was several times higher, holding steady at 24 percent in 2000 and 2006. These patterns of poverty coincide with inequality, which is among the highest in the world. In 2002, the poorest 10 percent of the population received 0.8 percent of national income while the richest 10 percent received 44.2 percent, a ratio of 33 to 1.[2]

These social inequalities interact with distortions in the political system to block efforts to build state capacity. Though the large popular sector might provide a social base to support an expansion in progressive tax capacity, its political influence is limited by conditions of poverty, inequality, and the legacy of repression, fragmentation, and weakness that is the residue of the civil war and the policies of previous systems.

Although economic elites are dominant and could potentially advance their own state-building project, they remain economically and socially fragmented, divided among multiple cleavages—including export-oriented versus domestic market-oriented, urban-rural, regional, emerging interests, traditional, oligarchic, and occasionally illicit actors organized into rival groups of familial and oligopolistic firms. Rival elite factions are organized enough to secure themselves political space, but they muster cohesion only sufficient to block efforts by any one faction to expand state capacity and establish dominance. Instead, they prefer to keep the state weak and therefore incapable of confronting poverty and inequality.[3]

This pattern of fragmentation and mutually canceling vetoes is reflected in political institutions that fail to coordinate interests and channel them to the state. First, the party system is fragmented and volatile, indicating a political elite with limited roots in society and a limited capacity to manage internal divisions.[4] Second, these party system characteristics operate within a Congress governed by internal rules that promote personalistic leadership, frequent backbench defections, and incentives for particularistic benefits targeting local allies instead of the pursuit of universal policies. Third, the Constitutional Court, with supreme power over constitutional issues such as taxation, is both porous to the interests of economic elites and has ample powers to overturn any tax reform. Finally, though pacted processes of societal consultation offer some access to popular sectors in support of tax capacity, economic elites have been equally adept at using social pacts to insert their own preferences in proposals for tax reform.

With respect to the party system, two indicators offer a useful snapshot. The first is the number of effective parties, an indicator developed by Lakso and Taagepera calculated as the inverse of the sum of the proportions of seats (or votes) squared.[5] Table 4.1 presents the number of effective parties in the last five elections. After two elections with fewer than three parties, the effective number of parties has since jumped above four, remaining at an elevated level to this day.

Table 4.1. Guatemala's Party System

Election	Effective Parties	Volatility
1995	2.53	72.5
1999	2.35	35
2003	4.64	69.5
2007	5.05	67
2011	4.14	66

Source: Authors' calculations, based on data from the Supreme Electoral Tribunal.

Table 4.1 also presents an indicator of volatility developed by Pederson.[6] This indicator is the sum of the absolute value of changes in seats for each party from election to election divided by two. It provides a measure of the instability of the party system. In four of the last five elections, volatility was higher than 65, indicating that almost half the 158-member Congress is replaced with each election.[7]

The level of volatility also suggests the role of parties as personalistic vehicles. Parties reach an apex in congressional representation in the year they win the presidency—especially the Party of National Advancement (Partido de Avanzada Nacional, PAN) in 1995, the Guatemalan Republican Front (Frente Republicano Guatemalteco, FRG) in 1999, and the Grand National Alliance (Gran Alianza Nacional, GANA) in 2003—but their fortunes rapidly dissipate afterward, especially if they have failed to elect a successor. After elections in which this has happened, the parties of the president have generally become insignificant or have disappeared entirely, with only, National Unity of Hope (Unidad Nacional de la Esperanza, UNE), being able to maintain a reasonable level of representation in 2011 after having governed in 2007. However, this level of support came only through an electoral alliance with its former opposition, GANA.

The role of personalistic leaders, called caudillos in reference to traditional military strongmen, is further encouraged by internal legislative rules.[8] Party leaders assign members to commissions, control the individual budgets of congressional offices, and can approve or block resources dedicated to the constituencies of individual politicians. Leadership dominance produces discipline in voting, with backbenchers loyally voting the party line, as indicated by the Rice index, which measures the level of discipline or defection of party members as a percentage. The Rice index for the largest parties is consistently between 0.98 and 1.00.[9]

What the Rice index does not capture, however, is the fact that this loyalty is temporary—the same deputies who toe the party line in votes defect to other parties to secure benefits for their constituents or to position themselves for victories in future elections. In Guatemala, party-switching is so common it has been given a name, *transfuguismo*, loosely translated as cross-fleeing. During the UNE government from 2008 to 2011, for example, almost two-thirds of Congress switched parties (100 out of 158 members). If the Pederson index is applied to the beginning and end of this particular Congress, volatility is 57, suggesting that politicians change their party between elections almost as fast as voters change their preferences from election to election.

The personalistic practice of leadership and the limited loyalty of members to each party combine with institutions that further encourage particularism, rather than universalism, in legislative decisions. One example can be found in budget processes, in which the Finance Commission assigns resources to specific projects by introducing amendments to the executive budget proposal. Members of the commission use their power of amendment to target resources to their electoral constituencies, campaign contributors, and other clients. These resources include tax incentives and spending projects.

Another key institution is the Constitutional Court, which was established by the 1985 Constitution with significant oversight powers for taxation legislation, a strict reading of limits on tax powers, and porous access by opponents of tax reform.[10] Article 243 of the Constitution prohibits confiscatory taxes or multiple taxations of the same source, something that the Court has interpreted in a narrow sense to constrain the type of taxes that could be applied. Other articles refer to principles of legality, nonretroactivity, and the protection against self-incrimination, interpreted in ways that limit the power of the tax administration to monitor and capture the resources of private actors that prefer not to disclose their finances.

The members of the Constitutional Court serve five-year terms, and include five magistrates and the same number of replacements, with one each appointed by the executive, legislative, and judicial branches as well as the Bar Association and Board of the National University. With ample discretion over how and when to interpret the Constitution, the Court has been a key battlefield in decisions about the amount of resources available to each government. Over twenty years, the Court received slightly over 100 demands to halt or water down tax reforms and approved 85 of the cases.[11]

Finally, it is important to consider fiscal pacts as an important institution in Guatemala. Pacts are rooted in theories of consensus within the political process and were formalized in the peace accords for the Guatemalan civil war that were signed in 1996. When Latin America faced fiscal adjustment during the 1990s, the UN Economic Commission for Latin America and the Caribbean articulated a view in favor of social consensus, via

> fiscal pacts, understood as a basic sociopolitical agreement that legitimates the role of the state and the scale and scope of government responsibilities in the economic and social spheres, can be analyzed within five fundamental aspects: consolidate the ongoing fiscal adjustment, raise the productivity of public administration, provide greater transparency in public finance, and promote equity and development of democratic institutions.[12]

The Guatemalan peace accords of 1996 were overseen by the Commission of Accompaniment of the Peace Accords, which included members of civil society and the private sector. As the peace agreement included a commitment to raise taxes to 12 percent of gross domestic product (GDP), the strategy of pacting was extended to fiscal policy through the creation of the Preparatory Commission of the Fiscal Pact (CPPF) in March 1999. The CPPF was charged with the task of elaborating a proposal for tax reform that would be technically sound and legitimated by the social actors included in the process of reaching the pact.[13]

For various reasons discussed below, the Fiscal Pact reached in 2000 went unfulfilled, yet each government that has since followed has repeated the effort to create a social and/or political pact to support tax reform. Each government has failed to reach its goal. There were various reasons—in one case, social actors pressured to dilute reform proposals; in other instances, roundtables were abandoned, removing their legitimacy. The only significant reform passed in the last twenty years, in 2012, was one in which there was virtually no attempt at a fiscal pact. That reform passed in the first days of the new government; it was essentially the same proposal advanced by the previous government; and it passed with the help of both opposition parties and the private sector.

To understand the successes and failures of fiscal reform in Guatemala, the analysis in following pages emphasizes the institutions and practices outlined here: parties, Congress, the Constitutional Court, and fiscal pacts. The discussion also examines the impact of reforms, with particular attention to the impact on tax capacity and distributive impact. Tax reform is emblematic of broader political trends—actors opposed to efforts to build state capacity find multiple opportunities to block change. Finally, despite the most significant reform of the past two decades passed in 2012, the tax system continues to exacerbate inequalities and fails to generate the resources necessary to meet social needs.

FISCAL REFORMS, 1990–2014

Despite the commitments of the peace accords and multiple reform efforts, tax revenues have increased only marginally and with limited sustainability. From 1995 to 2002, the tax burden increased from 8.8 to 11.9 percent of GDP, and ever since has fluctuated around these levels. There was a decrease to 11.2 percent in 2005, an increase to 12.1 percent in 2007, and a fall again to 10.3 percent in 2009. The difficulty in sustaining revenues at or above the 12 percent target demonstrates the fragility of reforms, especially in the face of Constitutional Court rulings enforcing strict constitutional interpretations of the limits on state power to raise revenues.

Despite instability and relatively low levels of reform, there have been some advances in tax revenues (table 4.2). During the 1990s, the largest increase occurred in indirect taxes, mostly coming from the value-added tax (VAT), as trade and customs duties decreased as a result of trade liberalization and free trade agreements, as well as decreases in specific-value excise taxes, in real terms, through inflation.[14]

Table 4.2. Tax Revenues by Base, 1991–2013 (percentage of GDP)

Tax	1991-95	1996-2000	2001-5	2006-10	2011-13
Direct	1.7	2.4	3.0	3.2	3.5
Income and profits—corporate and personal	1.6	1.5	1.9	2.4	2.8
Income, other	0.0	0.9	1.2	0.8	0.7
Property	0.1	0.0	0.0	0.0	0.0
Indirect	6.8	7.9	8.6	8.0	7.3
VAT	2.9	4.4	5.4	5.3	5.2
Customs and import duties	2.0	1.4	1.4	0.9	0.6
Excise	1.3	1.6	1.4	1.3	1.0
Other indirect	0.5	0.4	0.5	0.5	0.5

Source: Authors' calculations, based on Ministry of Public Finance data.

Since 2004, there has been a slight increase in the weight of direct taxes. Still, the low proportion of revenues from the personal income tax, the practically nonexistent property tax, and the high dependence on the VAT preserve an overall regressive impact of the tax system. The tax system has limited redistributive capacity due to both its low level and a slight regressivity in incidence.[15] Although not immediately evident from the table, another important form of inequity in the tax system is horizontal, in the form of differential rates paid by otherwise similar economic actors operating in different sectors. The cause of horizontal inequality is the proliferation of tax exemptions, putatively intended to attract foreign investment and encourage domestic investment, but with a limited impact, except perhaps to increase employment in privileged sectors.[16] To explain these ongoing patterns of low capacity, regressivity, and horizontal inequity, along with the limited changes that have occurred, the following sections explore episodes of reform.

THE PEACE ACCORDS, 1996–99

The first government after the peace accords advanced a few reforms but fell short of a comprehensive overhaul or the goals set in the 1996 peace agreement. In 1996, the government raised the rate of the VAT from 7 to 10 percent, and in 1997 it advanced a minimum income tax, labeled the Tax on Commercial and Agro-Pecuniary Firms (IEMA), closed some tax loopholes, and lowered the highest bracket for the income tax from 30 to 25 percent. Still, the government was unable to pass a proposed property tax (Impuesto Único Sobre Inmuebles), and it chose to leave the remainder of the fiscal reform agenda to the CPPF, which invited broad participation but had no mandate to advance reforms until the next government entering in 2000. These results can be traced to political conditions characterized by limited political capital and a right-wing alliance that provided political and ideological support for certain reforms but not others.

Conditions just after the peace accords provided a degree of political capital to the government, as the accords included a commitment to raise revenues and offered a generally positive scenario to advance tax reform. The two biggest parties in Congress, the governing PAN and the FRG, were able to work together, in part due to a shared right-wing history and ideology. While the FRG, led by ex-general and ex-president Efraín Ríos Montt, was more closely associated with the military, PAN was more closely associated with the business elite. The leaders of the two parties counted on strong personal networks, that of Álvaro Arzú (PAN) in urban areas and that of Ríos Montt (FRG) in the countryside. PAN held 34.3 percent of congressional seats, and the FRG 20 percent.

The first reform, to raise the VAT, had been agreed to by PAN and the FRG on the condition that the peace accord was signed by January 1996. The second reform, which reduced the income tax rate, was opposed by the main business association—the Coordinating Committee of Agricultural, Commercial, Industrial, and Financial Associations (Comité de Asociaciones Agrícolas, Comerciales, Industriales y Financieras, CACIF)—because it included a temporary minimum tax and closed certain tax incentives, including some for the importing of capital goods and inputs.[17] Still, their opposition was relatively mild, as the reforms followed the generally probusiness Washington Consensus ideology advanced by the government, which was shared by CACIF, and articulated by a neoliberal-oriented think tank, the National Center of Economic Investigation (Centro de Investigaciones Económicas Nacionales).

Still, the failure of the property tax proposal showed the limits to the right-wing alliance in support of reforms. A property tax conflicted with the conservative base of PAN and the FRG, as well as libertarian ideologies within segments of the private sector, and it was introduced when the political capital surrounding the peace accords had already faded. As the next elections approached, party defections in Congress increased the FRG's share of seats to 41.2 percent while PAN's share fell to 28.8 percent, and the private sector began to hedge its bets on who would form the next government. The reform was withdrawn when it was met with a disinformation campaign in the press, and Arzú turned his attention to the more drawn-out fiscal pact process that would only be implemented by the next government.

THE FISCAL PACT, 2000–2003

The period that bridged the formation of the Fiscal Pact Commission and subsequent reforms increased the VAT to 12 percent, raised the maximum tax rate on personal income to 31 percent, and adjusted the rates on the rest of the personal income tax brackets. Reforms increased the minimum tax (IEMA) from 1.25 to 2.25 percent on total sales and from 2.5 to 3.25 percent on net assets.

Despite these increases, there were a number of setbacks. The attempt to reduce the credit allowed on personal income tax based on VAT contributions was declared unconstitutional, as was an attempt to raise excise taxes on alcoholic drinks. In fact, the 2000–3 period was the one in which the highest number of complaints were filed with the Constitutional Court with respect to taxation. As a result, though reforms raised revenues to historically high levels, Court decisions overturned the IEMA, the changes to the VAT rates, and the drinks excise. Further, the reform failed to overturn an already high number of exemptions and deductions to the personal income tax; nor did it prevent the introduction of additional new exemptions in subsequent years.

The failure to meet the goals of the peace agreement with respect to tax had led Arzú to form the Commission for the Accompaniment to the Peace Agreement (Comisión de Acompañamiento de los Acuerdos de Paz, CAAP). Multiple sectors participated in the CAAP, including businesspeople, academics, and civil society organizations, producing a reform proposal that appeared to have broad support. Still, Congress failed to adopt the proposal in unified form, preferring to address each portion separately, allowing opponents to pick off one after another item. Those portions that were passed were overturned in the Constitutional Court, favoring complaints submitted by CACIF and by individual factions within the business community, such as beverage-bottling firms and even the Ombudsman's Office for Human Rights.

As a result, tax capacity failed to reach the goals set in the peace agreement. The government also failed to implement the proposals drafted by the Fiscal Pact Committee, including not only tax but also fiscal balance, tax administration, spending, debt, and accountability. This failure was driven mostly by the confrontation between the government and the private sector. Though business associations had participated in the CAAP, they withdrew at the last moment, preferring to block implementation and abandoning the government. The CAAP had also failed to take into account political party representatives, leaving the party of the government, the FRG, to attempt to build a congressional coalition in support of reform by presenting tax proposals one at a time. This drew out the process, which was further delayed as reforms were met with challenges in the Constitutional Court. Rather than use its political capital to win these cases in the Court, the FRG government concentrated its judicial efforts on securing approval for the presidential candidacy of Ríos Montt, who was barred for having been dictator during the civil war. Though they won Court approval for his candidacy, they lost most of the tax reform cases (along with the elections).

There were forty-four complaints filed against the twenty-seven tax laws passed by the government, and the Court overturned sixteen of them. The judicial process was affected by a private-sector media campaign, along with the partisan dynamics of the period. To favor the FRG, the Court delayed its decision on the IEMA until December 23, 2003, the very end of the government. By then, the FRG had lost the presidential elections, and the Court's decision essentially denied resources to the incoming government, which was led by Oscar Berger of GANA.

PATCHING FISCAL HOLES, 2004–7

The GANA government immediately faced fiscal pressure as a result of the outgoing Court decisions, which overturned the IEMA and cut revenues by approximately one-tenth.[18] The FRG had also left a series of spending commitments, such as payments to the Civil Defense Patrols.[19] In response, the government convened a Technical Commission on the Fiscal Pact (Comisión Técnica del Pacto Fiscal, CTPF) to design a reform proposal that could balance accounts. The main goal was to repair the damage to the tax system that resulted from the Court decisions of previous years. To start, the government introduced an Extraordinary and Temporary Tax in Support of the Peace Agreement (IETAAP, Decree 19-2004), a temporary tax on net assets and total income. In addition, the government introduced a new Distribution of Beverages Tax (Decree 21-2004) to restore the one overturned.

In the face of opposition, the government declined to introduce any other reforms until 2006, as it approached the end of its mandate, when it advanced only a law titled Legal Disposition to Strengthen Tax Administration (Decree 20-2006). This law gradually introduced retentions of VAT payments at the source, new regulations on fiscal credits through bank transactions, a new registry of firms, and other measures to cut evasion.

GANA was a coalition of relatively new parties, including the National Solidarity Party (Partido Solidaridad Nacional, formed in 2002), the Reform Movement (Movimiento Reformador, formed in 1995), and the Patriotic Party (Partido Patriota, PP, formed in 2002). Its presidential candidate, Óscar Berger, required a runoff to win the presidency, and the government coalition of only 47 of 158 deputies was further depleted when the PP left within six months of Berger's inauguration. In the face of congressional weakness, the formation of the CTPF was an attempt to build support as well as to divert debate to a forum led by the Ministry of Finance in direct consultation with social actors. The CTPF immediately faced conflicting social pressures, because the civil society Collective of Social Organizations (COS) opposed changes to the income tax that would hit those with incomes lower than 2000 quetzales per month (approximately $260), and CACIF opposed any increase in the income tax whatsoever. To avoid repeating the mistake of the 2000 Fiscal Pact, from which partisan representatives were excluded, Congress staged a number of public audiences with social actors, including narrow interests such as the beverage industry, which submitted its own proposal directly to Congress. To secure congressional support, Berger entered conversations directly with Ríos Montt, trading fiscal reform for targeted projects in the constituencies of specific deputies. In the end, the government was able to secure only a temporary tax similar to the IEMA, limited specifically to the period of GANA, titled the Extraordinary and Temporary Tax in Support of the Peace Agreement (Impuesto Extraordinario y Temporal en Apoyo a los Acuerdos de Paz, IETAAP).[20]

FISCAL STASIS, 2008–11

With the IETAAP time-limited to the term of Berger, Congress granted a one year extension to the incoming government until December 2008. To extend the revenues, a new law created the Solidarity Tax (Impuesto de Solidaridad, ISO) of 1 percent of gross sales or net assets, with an option to credit the ISO toward the trimestral income tax payments, this time without a time limit (Decree 78-2008).

UNE had won the presidency behind the candidacy of Álvaro Colom, the same candidate who had lost to Óscar Berger in 2003. By winning in the second election round against PP candidate Otto Pérez Molina, Colom repeated a number of party system patterns. First, the election demonstrated that majorities were fleeting in the fragmented party system. Candidates who lost in the second round of one election won the presidency four years later but were unable to elect a successor. Colom differed only in that he hailed from the center-left, without the military or business links that had characterized all the other presidents since the civil war.

Despite Colom's victory, his mandate was weak, with only 28.3 percent of the electorate supporting him in the first round and a UNE share of Congress at only fifty-one deputies, 32 percent of the total. Even this limited level of congressional support rapidly decayed, as a scandal in the use of legislative funds was exposed by the financial crash of 2008 and a murdered lawyer, Rodrigo Rosenberg, left a video falsely blaming Colom and his wife for his murder. To confront this weakness, the government invited representatives of the private sector to cabinet positions and offered policy and material incentives to partisan allies in Congress.

Although the Colom government was relatively weak in legislative terms, it was armed with a reform proposal designed in 2006 at the initiative of the international community and the National Peace Accords Commission. They had convened the Promoting Group for Fiscal Dialogue and had devised proposals to introduce a dual-rate income tax, make the IETAAP permanent, replace customs duties on vehicles with a tax on registration, introduce norms for transfer prices, rationalize tax incentives, and tighten regulations on the VAT and customs.[21] The UNE government began with these proposals and added taxes on dividends and increases in the general income tax system from 5 to 7 percent, but made few legislative advances.

First, conflicts emerged between the UNE government and members of the Promoting Group for Fiscal Dialogue, which had been appointed by the previous government and included representatives of the business elite and chambers of commerce. Further divisions opened within the Colom government, with some ministers opposing the reform. With the weakening of the UNE representation in Congress, members of the government's base—for example, deputies with car import businesses—came out against the reforms or pressed for privileges favoring personal interests,. The UNE government sought allies among the GANA delegation, but there were few legislative victories. The opposition made use of filibusters and other delays, including long testimonies by ministers, blocking the legislative agenda on taxes, along with legislative action on debt. When the government opted to advance a smaller reform, the *reformita*, of limited scope and time, even this was blocked by lobbying internal to the cabinet against taxes on communications, and this eventually led to the resignation of the minister of finance, in 2010.

EARLY BUT LIMITED SUCCESS, 2012–15

Everything seemed to change with the next government, that of the PP and its candidate, Otto Pérez Molina—who had been a general during the civil war with support from those close to the military—attracted the support of the business community against the potential candidacy of the outgoing UNE government candidate, first lady Sandra Colom. Once in office, the PP government quickly passed the Anti-Evasion Law (Decree 4-2012) and the Law for Tax Actualization (Decree 10-2012), including changes to the income tax, the tax on vehicle registration (known as IPRIMA) and vehicle circulation, new powers for the customs administration, reforms to the VAT, and new stamp duties.[22]

The reforms greatly simplified the income tax for both firms and individuals, eliminating many exemptions and thereby promising to raise revenues.[23] Still, the progressive potential of an increase in direct taxes was weakened because firms and individuals could opt into the previous system with lower rates of tax on net incomes or into a new dual-rate system with only two brackets, one set at 5 percent of income and the other at 7 percent.[24]

The reforms of the vehicle taxes eliminated customs duties and replaced them with an internal tax on the market value of vehicles. This addressed the problem of undervalued imported vehicles, such as when importers draw up receipts for a much lower price than the actual value of a car.[25] As in the case of the income tax, the progressive potential of this change was watered down somewhat through the lobbying efforts of used-car importers.

Pérez Molina was able to pass such sweeping reforms quickly because he had unified various right-wing factions, which softened some of their opposition to reform, perhaps to counter the populist appeal of UNE. Pérez Molina also represented the opposition of traditional business elites to the candidacy of Manuel Baldizón and the Renewed Democratic Liberty party (Libertad Democrática Renovada, LIDER), whose support base was rooted in local rural elites and their dependents, as well as private-sector factions dependent on state contracts.

The PP continued the pattern of minority support in Congress, mustering only 56 deputies, 35.4 percent of the total. Still, because most of the reforms had been designed during previous governments, the UNE and GANA deputies voted in favor, as they could claim some credit for designing the reforms. By following the traditional pattern of joining with the government on major votes, smaller parties—such as Commitment, Renovation, and Order (Compromiso, Renovación y Orden, known as CREO); Encuentro por Guatemala; and Vision with Values (Vision con Valores, known as VIVA)—brought the total to 122 votes.[26] As a party bloc, only LIDER opposed the reforms, aiming to identify itself as the loser of the presidential runoff, the main opposition, and therefore as the front runner in the next election.[27]

The government's legislative strategy included no effort to form a fiscal pact, even though the groundwork was laid during the election campaign with a group designated the Group of Forty, which was made up of ex-ministers and other experts in tax policy. Pérez Molina used the time between his election and taking office to negotiate directly with those portions of the private sector that had joined his campaign. The proposals presented were essentially those that had emerged from the GANA and UNE governments, securing their support, and the quick presentation and vote on the laws also avoided the rapid party-switching that beset all governments once they are two to three years into their mandate.

Still, despite initially high expectations for the reforms, the overall impact was weak, raising at most an additional 1.31 percent of GDP—to just over 12 percent. This was barely sufficient to meet the goals of the peace agreement and little more. The reforms also removed many exemptions from the income tax, but still left the tax structure highly dependent on indirect taxes. Most observers consider these results better than the absence of reform, but the impact has been extremely limited.[28]

Among the limits to the reform, last-minute negotiations opened room for changes, and the private sector continued legal challenges once the law was in place. The Chamber of Commerce and the Chamber of Agriculture pressed cases with the Constitutional Court to overturn specific articles. With respect to customs, the Superintendencia de Administración Tributaria (Tax Administration) was unprepared for some of the changes, so the government delayed implementation. Fiscal revenues were weakened by the lower-than-expected growth of exports, as well as lower prices and quantities of imports, and the delay and problems with implementation obliged the government to hold further negotiations with CACIF.[29] Ultimately, the Customs Law was never implemented, although some of its problems were corrected in the Customs Law of 2013. The final law extended exemptions, lowered fines, and eliminated transit insurance on goods. Administrative problems ultimately led the government to militarize customs administration, though even this produced no increase in customs collection of the VAT, import duties, petroleum, and other revenues.

The executive branch took its own steps to water down the reforms. First, the government lowered the tax on circulation of vehicles, almost to the same level as before the reforms. Second, as a result of negotiations over the reforms with business associations, the government offered generous exemptions for real estate transactions. In sum, despite initially high expectations for the impact of reforms, the PP government appears likely to leave the next government in the same position as all previous governments—with weak finances and a need for significant fiscal reforms.

CONTINUED REGRESSIVITY IN GUATEMALAN TAXES

Over the span of five episodes of reform, addressed in the previous section, there have been some important changes with respect to tax progressivity in Guatemala (table 4.3). Direct taxes have increased from 20 to 30 percent of the total revenue, with two moments of particular change. From 1995 to 2003, increases in direct taxes came exclusively from auxiliary taxes. Later, the inclusion of a tax on gross income allowed increases to come from the income tax. In fact, the tax on gross income has collected more than the tax on net income since 2007, as it both eases the cost of compliance for small businesses and offers a more favorable tax treatment to firms with high profits. The VAT has fluctuated, but remains the most important source of revenue, increasing from 36 to 48 percent from 1995 to 2012. By contrast, customs duties have fallen to a quarter of the 1995 proportion and excises have fallen by half.[30]

If one traces the evolution of Guatemala's taxes, there have been notable changes (table 4.4). From 1995 to 2006, revenues increased from 8.8 to 11.9 percent of GDP, but fell to 11.0 percent in 2013.

Table 4.3. Tax Proportions, Selected Years

Type of Tax	1995	2000	2003	2005	2012	2013
Direct						
Income	20.1	13.3	13.3	19.9	24.7	27.6
Auxiliary	0.0	8.6	12.6	8.1	6.6	7.0
Property	0.5	0.1	0.0	0.0	0.0	0.0
Indirect						
VAT	36.0	47.3	45.8	45.9	48.8	47.2
Trade	23.6	12.0	11.8	9.6	5.4	4.2
Excise	15.2	14.1	12.6	12.1	9.1	8.7
Royalties	0.1	2.6	2.5	2.5	2.5	1.9
Others	4.5	1.9	1.4	1.9	2.8	3.4
Total	100.0	100.0	100.0	100.0	100.0	100.0
Excises						
Oil	8.9	9.3	7.4	1.8	4.9	5.0
Vehicle circulation	1.9	1.2	1.3	1.2	1.3	0.9
Border crossing	0.1	0.9	0.8	0.7	0.5	0.5
Beverages	2.1	1.3	1.4	1.4	1.3	1.3
Tobacco	2.1	1.4	1.4	1.1	0.7	0.8
Cement	—	—	0.4	0.3	0.2	0.2
Total Excise	15.2	14.1	12.6	6.5	9.1	8.7

Source: Authors' elaboration.

To get a more accurate impression of the distributive impact of tax reforms, household surveys can be used to simulate the impact of specific reforms.[31] The simulation concentrates on the effect of changes to income, the VAT, and excise taxes (tobacco, beverages, cement), which produce 50 to 65 percent of total revenue.[32] The simulation indicates that the tax system remains slightly regressive. In fact, though the tax system in 1995 was slightly progressive, the changes that have occurred since then have turned the system regressive by increasing taxes with regressive effects. The important thing to note is that

Table 4.4. The Evolution of Taxes, Selected Years (percentage of GDP)

Type of Tax	1995	2000	2003	2006	2012	2013
Income	1.8	1.5	1.5	2.4	2.7	3.0
Corporate			1.3	2.0	2.3	2.7
Individual			0.2	0.3	0.4	0.3
Auxiliary	0.0	1.0	1.5	1.0	0.7	0.8
Property	0.0	0.0	0.0	0.0	0.0	0.0
VAT	3.2	5.3	5.3	5.4	5.3	5.2
Customs	2.1	1.3	1.4	1.1	0.6	0.5
Excise	1.3	1.6	1.5	1.4	1.0	1.1
Royalties	0.0	0.3	0.3	0.3	0.3	0.2
Others	0.4	0.2	0.2	0.2	0.2	0.3
Total	8.8	11.2	11.7	11.9	10.8	11.0

Source: Authors' elaboration.

most of the increases in the income tax have come from the corporate income tax, which unlike the individual income tax has ambiguous effects on distribution because firms can shift the burden of the tax onto their customers or employees. Further, the changes to the personal income tax that target gross income introduced a flat tax without progressive brackets.

The increases to the VAT had clearly negative effects on progressivity, as higher rates increased the burden on poorer households. Further, the application of VAT credits lowered progressive personal income tax obligations. Excises had virtually no impact on progressivity, in part because these gather few revenues, but also because some tend to be regressive (e.g., those on beverages and tobacco) while others tend to be progressive (those on cement, vehicles, and fuel).

The 2012 reforms have some distributive impacts through changes in the system for the income tax on salaried employees, the individual income tax, and the vehicle circulation tax. According to the simulations, the changes to the income tax on salaried employees have had a slight regressive impact, with a small positive impact for the highest 10 percent of incomes. Despite the elimination of the VAT and other credits, the generally low level of incomes means that the impact on distribution has been minimal. In the case of income tax on nonsalary incomes, virtually all levels of income have increased their contributions, though only the top 10 percent of income earners have increased contributions more than 1 percent. An important impact was felt by firms registered as individuals, which lost their VAT credits. At the highest levels of income, the increase in rates from 5 to 7 percent increased their obligations. The vehicle circulation tax would have had a progressive impact, though a minimal one (at most 0.2 percent of income), but this reform was reversed by the government's executive branch. Because of this reversal, the 2012 reforms would appear to have caused a slight but statistically insignificant drop in the Gini coefficient (0.006)—a measure of the income distribution ranging from 0 to 1 (figure 4.1).

Figure 4.1. The Impact of Tax Reforms on the Gini Coefficient, Selected Years

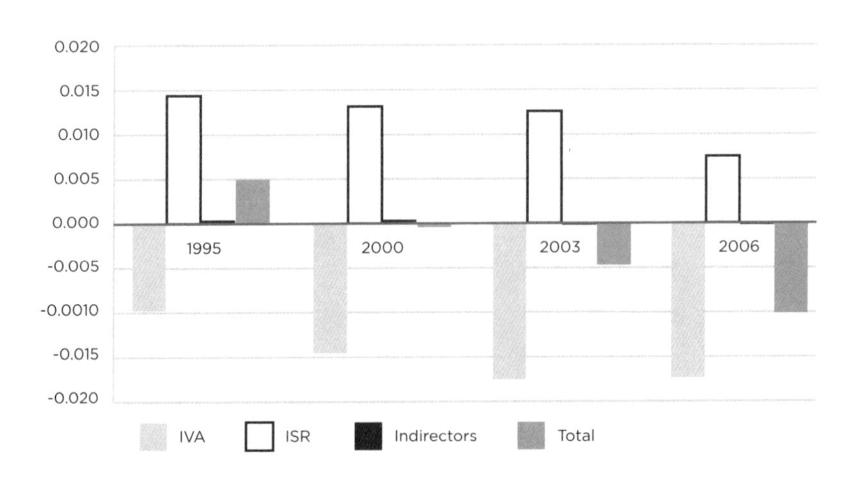

Source: Authors' elaboration, based on National Household Survey–Encovi, 2006.

CONCLUSION

The Guatemalan case offers lessons about the relationship between economic elites, political process, and state capacity—all reflected in the structure and changes to the tax system. Economic elites, despite their divisions, remain much more capable of articulating their interests with respect to taxes when compared with popular-sector actors. Still, economic elites have little cohesion, because they are riven by multiple cleavages, including those between emerging elites and traditional, oligarchic, local rural elites, and illicit actors. They can coordinate only sufficiently to veto efforts to build the state, and insufficiently to advance a project of their own.

This situation is reflected in the political system, exemplified in high levels of volatility and fragmentation in the party system. Governments are forced to build coalitions to pass legislation, and the rules of Congress offer multiple opportunities to block or dilute any reform proposal. Those reforms that do pass face subsequent obstacles in the Constitutional Court, whose politicized decisionmaking and privileged access allow opponents to overturn reforms. To confront this situation, various governments have attempted to form social pacts, hoping that direct dialogue with actors in society can secure agreement on fiscal policy that political elites would need to accept. Unfortunately, efforts to form pacts have simply opened additional opportunities for veto players to act, further demonstrating the interaction between weak elites and weak social cohesion.

Such political challenges do not mean that Guatemala has seen no reforms in recent years. In fact, each government has made a number of changes to the tax system. The more significant problem is that each reform has been temporary, shortsighted, and diluted by political processes, and thus has only had a limited impact on the tax system's capacity and progressivity. The result is a level of taxation between 10 and 12 percent of GDP.

The most recent reform of 2012 promises to raise revenues to the 13.2 percent level set in the peace agreement of 1996. But its history demonstrates both the strategies to navigate political obstacles along with structural limits on the impact of reform. It was the most significant set of reforms to date, taking advantage of the proposals designed by prior governments in drawn-out consultation campaigns. The parties of those previous governments backed the reform, which was introduced in the honeymoon period of high political capital at the beginning of the presidential mandate, and Pérez Molina could also take advantage of the temporary unity with the economic elite, who had feared the election of a candidate mobilizing popular sectors (Sandra Colom) or one representing rural, local elites and factions of the private sector dependent on the state (Baldizón).

Even as the reform indicated an opportunistic winning strategy, it also demonstrated the limits of any reform effort. Factions of the economic elite have rapidly sought to dilute the impact of reforms by overturning articles in the Constitutional Court or seeking special exemptions, and portions of the political elite have withdrawn their support, as indicated in struggles over the control of customs administration. Though the reform has been the most comprehensive ever, it has made only a limited impact on the progressivity of the fiscal system and it has not solved Guatemala's chronic fiscal shortfall. With the political capital of the current government largely spent, any additional reforms will likely fall to the government that enters in 2016, leaving the fiscal system once again subject to the vagaries of Guatemalan politics.

NOTES

1. Organization for Economic Cooperation and Development (OECD) / CEPAL / CIAT, *Estadísticas tributarias en América Latina* (Paris: OECD Publishing, 2012).
2. These levels of inequality have remained virtually unchanged since the end of the civil war, when the ratio was also 33 to 1, with the poorest 10 percent receiving 1.4 percent of national income and the richest 10 percent receiving 41.8 percent in 2011. United Nations and World Bank, *Socioeconomic Database for Latin America and the Caribbean (Sedlac)*, http://sedlac.econo.unlp.edu.ar/eng/statistics.php.
3. Aaron Schneider, *State-Building and Tax Regimes in Central America* (New York: Cambridge University Press, 2012).
4. Omar Sánchez, "Tax Reform Paralysis in Post-Conflict Guatemala," *New Political Economy* 14: 1 (2009): 101–31.
5. $N=1/\sum_{k=1}^{n} p_k^2$ in which n is the number of parties with seats and p_k is the proportion of the kth party. See M. Laakso and R. Taagepera, "Effective Number of Parties: A Measure with Application to West Europe," *Comparative Political Studies* 12, no. 1 (April 1979): 3–27. The effect of squaring the proportions gives additional weight to

larger parties to avoid overcounting small parties that perhaps hold little importance to coalitions and political negotiation.

6. Morgens N. Pedersen, "The Dynamics of European Party Systems: Changing Patterns of Electoral Volatility," *European Journal of Political Research* 7, no. 1 (1979): 1–26.
7. The only election when volatility decreased, in 1999, coincided with a significant increase in the number of congressional seats, from 77 to 113. The increase meant that the party exiting the presidency, PAN, could keep a large number of seats, depressing the volatility index even as the party of the incoming president, FRG, gained proportionally.
8. Mark P. Jones, "Weakly Institutionalized Party Systems and Presidential Democracy: Evidence from Guatemala," *International Area Studies Review* 14, no. 4 (2011): 3–30.
9. The Rice index varies between 0 (in which the same number of deputies in each parties for and against a bill) and 1 (in which all the deputies vote in the same way). Javier Fortín, "Of the Party, by the Party, and for the Party: A Study of Congress and the Deputies of the Guatemalan Congress" (thesis, Universidad de Francisco Marroquín, Guatemala, 2007), 19.
10. The Constitution established "severe limits on the tax powers of Congress and created in the tribunals an additional battlefield on the issue of tax legislation." CEPAL, *Fortalezas, Debilidades, y Desafíos del Pacto Fiscal* (Santiago: CEPAL, 1998).
11. One example is the presidential candidacy of Efraín Ríos Montt. On previous occasions, the Court had ruled against his eligibility, but new magistrates, named or beholden to the FRG, ruled in his favor, and as a result he ran for the presidency and barely lost in 2003. Gustavo Porras, *Instituciones políticas, proceso de formulación de políticas públicas y resultados de las políticas en Guatemala* (Guatemala: ASIES, 2005). A similar politicization of the judiciary, with negative effects on fiscal reform, has been noted in the Mexican case in a Wilson Center study by Carlos Elizondo; see http://www.wilsoncenter.org/event/ReformaFiscalMexico.
12. CEPAL, *Fortalezas, Debilidades, y Desafíos del Pacto Fiscal.*
13. SIN-Guatemala, *Guatemala: El financiamiento del desarrollo humano* (Guatemala City: PNUD, 2001).
14. Excises tend to be fixed in value according to units of consumption, and lose their significance over time as a result of inflation if they are not adjusted.
15. ICEFI, *Equidad del Sistema Tributario en Guatemala 2006* (Guatemala City: BID-BCIE, 2007).
16. ICEFI, "Incentivos fiscales y su relación con la inversión extranjera en Guatemala y Nicaragua," *Boletín de Estudios Fiscales* no.8 (Guatemala: ICEFI, 2008).
17. ICEFI, *Historia de la tributación en Guatemala: Desde los mayas hasta la actualidad* (Guatemala City: SAT-ICEFI, 2007).
18. This section draws on Maynor Cabrera, "Evasión y equidad en Guatemala," *Serie Macroeconomía del Desarrollo* (Santiago: CEPAL, 2009).
19. As a party close to the military, the FRG was close to the PAC, and the GANA decision to honor the commitment was seen as an attempt to curry favor with this constituency, though neither this government nor the next fully implemented the required payments.

20. The program was entitled PACUR, Program for the Support of Urban and Rural Communities, perceived by most observers to be heavy with patronage.
21. Alberto Barreix y J. Roca, "Reforzando un pilar fiscal: El impuesto a la renta dual a la uruguaya," *Revista de la CEPAL*, no. 92 (2007).
22. The income tax created a dual system for capital income and profits, and improved control on tax rebates as well as incorporating international best practices on transfer prices and reductions in the nonresident income tax. An important change was to apply a 5 percent tax on dividends and dropping the rate on total income from 31 to 25 percent—previously labeled the Optional Regime and now the Regime for Profitable Activities. ICEFI, *Análisis breve de la reforma tributaria guatemalteca de 2012* (Guatemala: ICEFI, 2012).
23. Almost all exemptions were eliminated, including those for social security contributions, the legally obligated end-of-year bonus for a fourteenth-month payment (Bonus 14), insurance premiums, and charitable contributions. Also, the system of claiming VAT payments as a credit toward personal income tax was eliminated, applying instead a 12,000-quetzal deduction for VAT receipts from taxable income.
24. The previous general regime (now the Simplified Regime) applied a 5 percent tax to incomes below 30,000 quetzales per month (approximately $4,000) and higher incomes, paying 1,500 quetzales, along with 7 percent on all income above 30,000 quetzales. Businesses or individuals that opted for the former alternative regime on net profits saw their rates drop from 31 to 25 percent. For the income tax, the number of brackets lowered and the minimum threshold increased from 36,000 to 48,000 quetzales.
25. The problem had been particularly acute since the 2004 Guatemalan adherence to Article VII of the General Agreement on Tariffs and Trade.
26. Floor votes have been available only since 2012, with the installation of electronic voting.
27. There was also support from the UCN (14), Independent Bloc (9), Frente Amplio (1), FRG (1), independents (1), PAN (2), Unionista (1), Victoria (1), and URNG (1).
28. ICEFI, *Análisis breve de la reforma tributaria guatemalteca de 2012.*
29. The weak results reveal the inability of the main revenue stream, VAT, to make up for shortcomings in other areas.
30. The fall in customs is due to trade liberalization, while the share of excises has eroded primarily through inflation.
31. Instituto Nacional de Estadística Guatemala, *Encuesta Nacional de Condiciones de Vida* (Guatemala City: Government of Guatemala, 2006).
32. The simulation calculates the pretax market per capita income for each household in the survey and then applies the rates, bases, and exemptions for each year. Following standard economic practice, direct taxes are assumed to be paid by those who receive income streams, and indirect taxes are borne according to patterns of consumption. To estimate progressivity, the Kakwani coefficient compares the Gini coefficient for the market distribution of income to a coefficient of concentration on respective taxes. To define redistribution, the simulation compares the Gini before and after taxes, or the Reynolds-Smolensky coefficient. For a demonstration, see Nora Lustig

and Sean Higgins, "Commitment to Equity Assessment (CEQ): A Diagnostic Framework to Assess Governments' Fiscal Policies Handbook," January 2013; Alberto Barreix and G. Bes y J. Roca, "Equidad Fiscal en Centroamérica, Panamá y República Dominicana," BID-Eurosocial Fiscalidad, Washington, 2009; and Maynor Cabrera, Nora Lustig, and Hilcías E. Morán, *Fiscal Policy, Inequality, and Ethnic Divide in Guatemala*, CEQ Working Paper 20 (New Orleans: Commitment to Equity Project at Tulane University, 2014), http://www.commitmentoequity.org/publications_files/Guatemala/Cabrera_Lustig_Moran_Oct_17_2014.pdf.

Commentary: Improving Guatemala's Tax System

Foundation for the Development of Guatemala (FUNDESA) and Coordinating Committee of Agricultural, Commercial, Industrial, and Financial Associations (CACIF)*

In any country, taxation is extremely important for the proper functioning of the state. Guatemala has faced countless challenges in this area. Among Latin American countries, it has some of the lowest rates of total revenues flowing into the treasury. It is also a country with a very young population with educational needs and high rates of chronic child malnutrition (49 percent), among other problems. Guatemala also faces a series of obstacles that limit its development, such as the poor quality of education. According to a study published by the Foundation for the Development of Guatemala (Fundación para el Desarrollo de Guatemala, FUNDESA) and the Coordinating Committee of Agricultural, Commercial, Industrial, and Financial Associations (Comité Coordinador de Asociaciones Agrícolas, Comerciales, Industriales, y Financieras, CACIF), the five major factors hampering growth in Guatemala are chronic malnutrition, the opaqueness of government, insecurity, impunity, and serious deficiencies in infrastructure.

* This commentary is drawn from the study *Hacia el Mejoramiento del Sistema Fiscal* (Guatemala City: Fundación para el Desarrollo de Guatemala and Comité Coordinador de Asociaciones Agrícolas, Comerciales, Industriales, y Financieras, 2014). The editors are grateful to Juan Carlos Zapata, executive director of Fundación para el Desarrollo de Guatemala (FUNDESA), for permission to reprint sections of the document, and to FUNDESA research associate Fernando Spross for editorial assistance.

Overcoming such limitations requires effective public investment, which up until now has fallen far below expectations. For example, current investment in education is 2.8 percent of gross domestic product (GDP). According to 2011 UNESCO data, Guatemala ranked 119th among 122 countries in per capita investment in education. Certainly there are significant opportunities in terms of the quality of spending, but the country must urgently recognize the need to implement comprehensive solutions to address these shortcomings.

It is important to recognize that Guatemala has a strong tax-paying culture within the formal private sector. This sector has been actively committed to playing a constructive role in this process for the betterment of the country, and has been involved in critical initiatives to help shape the public policy agenda. Unlike at other times in the country's history, today entities such as CACIF and FUNDESA are collaborating on technical proposals to find solutions to the problems affecting the country, as is the case with low tax collection.

Guatemala's taxation system is deeply flawed, a fact evidenced by the state's inability to adequately carry out its functions. We should mention that Guatemala has a very unusual population pyramid—first, because its annual growth rate is about 2.5 percent; and second, because four of every ten people are under fifteen years of age, while six of every ten are under twenty years old. This implies a current need to invest in youth, and a future growth in demand for employment, housing, food, and services.

In nominal terms, tax collections have increased more than 110 percent in the past decade, from around 22 billion quetzales (Q) in 2004 to Q46 billion in 2013. In this period, tax collections have remained around 11 percent of GDP. However, Guatemala has a tax structure that includes eight indirect and five direct taxes. The former are imposed on consumption and the latter are imposed on income, profits, and assets.

This structure shows that the value-added tax (impuesto al valor agregado, IVA) represents 52 percent of net tax revenues, while the income tax (impuesto sobre la renta, ISR) represents 27 percent and the "solidarity tax" (impuesto de solidaridad, ISO) 7 percent. The share of customs duties, meanwhile, has been decreasing, to about 4 percent of the total. Other revenues (selective taxes) account for 10.5 percent of tax collections.

In analyzing the composition of tax revenues in relation to GDP in Latin America, Guatemala ranks fifteenth out of eighteen countries, with an average tax burden of 11.2 percent between 2000 and 2013. If social contributions (social security) are factored in, the country ranks sixteenth out of eighteen, as one of the countries with the lowest tax burden, at 12.93 percent, outranking only Paraguay (12.57 percent) and Mexico (11.17 percent).

The IVA rate in Guatemala (12 percent) is the third lowest among the 18 Latin American countries, with only Paraguay (10 percent) and Panama (7 percent) lower. In 2013, IVA tax collections amounted to the equivalent of 5.7 percent of GDP. Income tax collections, for their part, came to the equivalent of 3.1 percent of GDP in 2013, with the majority (89 percent) collected from companies and 11 percent from individuals. Guatemala's population distribution, unlike that of other countries, means that it must allocate a greater amount of financial resources to address basic education and health concerns.

To summarize, looking at the current tax structure and the characteristics of the taxation system, the areas where Guatemala falls short the most are shown in table 1.

Contraband and customs fraud are two factors that directly affect Guatemala's fiscal situation, primarily due to their impact on tax collection and the losses to the national economy. These have been recurrent practices in the country; one can see evidence of efforts to combat them since colonial times. Today there are more than 150 informal border crossings to which merchandise can be diverted to avoid controls, compared with 20 existing customs offices.

For customs purposes, removing or introducing merchandise into the country without paying any duties is considered contraband, as is smuggling banned merchandise. However, our interest mainly focuses on how significantly contraband and customs fraud reduce the collection of taxes, which could be used to finance the public spending required for the state to meet certain basic obligations. There is confusion when it comes to estimating losses to the treasury from contraband.

Contraband and customs fraud represent a loss to the country's economy of 2.8 to 4.4 percent of GDP. Moreover, 74.5 percent of the economically

Table 1. Summary of the Deficiencies in Guatemala's Current Tax Structure and Taxation System

Area	Deficiency
1. Weak customs controls	This is a problem that includes contraband and customs fraud, which affects collections not only of duties but also of value-added taxes on imports, and taxes all the way down the product marketing chain. Uncollected taxes in this category were estimated at 3.6 percent of GDP in 2012 (based on a study of economic activities representing 62 percent of the country's total economy).
2. Corporate income taxes	Guatemala has a rate similar to other Latin American countries in terms of income tax collections as a percentage of GDP. However, the option to choose a simplified income tax system should be limited to companies with a certain level of sales. This would make it more difficult to arbitrage tax rates among related companies and could improve tax collection.
3. Individual income taxes	In this category, Guatemala collects about half of what other Latin American countries collect and one-tenth of what developed countries collect. It is not a matter of raising rates for people with the highest incomes but of expanding the tax base. As in other countries, people should be required to use the same declaration of income for tax purposes as for banking transactions.
4. Social security contributions	Guatemala collects about half of what other countries in the region do. This has to do primarily with two factors. The first is the low percentage of the population affiliated with the social security system, close to 1.2 million people (20 percent of the economically active population). Second, there is a disincentive for higher earners (more than Q6,000 per month) to pay into the Guatemalan Social Security Institute (IGSS), since 5.5 percent of their salary is deducted even though they only have the right to the same retirement income as what someone earning up to the maximum Q6,000 would receive.
5. Property taxes	The low collection rate in this category (0.12 percent of GDP) is due to the fact that the very high tax rate (0.9 percent) is imposed on a property value that is not real. Property valuations are very low, and the municipalities (which are in charge of administering the tax) do not have effective tools to enforce this tax.
6. Nontax income and income from natural resources	The lack of a modern law on the development of renewable and nonrenewable natural resources, the general unwillingness to carry out a dialogue on environmental issues, and divisiveness among communities have all meant that the potential for tax collections on this front is minimal. However, the opportunity to improve revenues from natural resources does exist.

active population is in the informal sector. The problem is complex due to the number of people who depend on contraband for a living.

It is clear that the state of Guatemala is very weak on this issue, with an erosion of governance, institutional weakness, and porous borders among the main problems. One telling factor is the fact that 90 percent of tax-related crimes reported to the Public Prosecutor's Office are not resolved, and the amounts recovered through the criminal justice system are equivalent to only 2.7 percent of the complaints filed. The fact that this problem is worsening is of concern. In 2013, the IVA on imports grew by 0.23 percent, while imports themselves grew both in value (3 percent) and in volume (5.4 percent).

A Big Data analysis could provide part of the solution to the problem. This refers to the processing and analysis of massive amounts of data to produce information about some good or service of significant value. The development of an electronic platform of this type will make it possible to register, in real time, information about what types of containers enter the country, as well as the volume of merchandise and other specifications, to help counter the problem of contraband and customs fraud.

In November 2011, CACIF made public a proposed State Compact to ensure a new institutional framework, one that would make it possible to put the public finances in order and break the cycle of endless talks on the lack of resources for public institutions. This State Compact is based on four essential components: (1) a high-quality civil service, (2) balanced and healthy public finances, (3) accountability, and (4) transparency and oversight over public spending.

As a first step under the State Compact, the organized business sector proposed a Grand National Agreement on Development. This included aspects such as (1) an agreement on efficiency, compliance, and tax adjustments; (2) development of natural resources and state economic assets; (3) a pact on formal employment; and (4) a pact on economic growth. Separately, implementation of an Agenda on Quality of Spending and Transparency was also proposed; on this point, it was recommended that certain legal frameworks be modified, including, among others, the Organic Budget Law, the Comptrollership of Accounts Law, and the Probity Law.

On February 10, 2012, the Tax Modernization Law (Decree 10/2012) was approved as a national emergency. That led to a tax reform, which was established with regard to different types of taxes. Precedents for this reform date back to the peace agreements (1996) and the Fiscal Pact (2000). Through the Fiscal Pact, the Group to Promote Fiscal Dialogue prepared a proposed comprehensive fiscal reform, which included changes to improve the quality and priorities of public spending, fiscal transparency, and tax reforms.

Back in 2011, FUNDESA and CACIF joined forces to prepare a proposal to counteract the erosion of public finances in Guatemala. This process was carried out by the Fiscal Commission, made up of a strong team of members of these organizations. Not all the proposals made were accepted, and it was not possible to provide feedback on the final bill presented to Congress.

Changes included in the reform passed in 2012 include modifications to the various taxes detailed in the Tax Modernization Law. These include the Income Tax; the Specific Tax on First Registration of Motor Vehicles; the Value-Added Tax Law; the Law on Taxes on Circulation of Land, Sea, and Air Vehicles; the National Customs Law; and the Law on Taxes on Revenue Stamps and Special Stamped Paper.

There were many expectations with regard to the Tax Modernization Law. It was expected to have the biggest impact on income taxes collected, followed by the tax on newly registered imported vehicles and the tax on circulation of vehicles. With respect to the IVA, the main change involved eliminating the tax on the transfer of real estate applicable to second and subsequent sales, which would now be imposed through the tax on revenue stamps and special stamped paper. Exemptions to this tax were also restricted for educational facilities. Finally, with regard to the tax on revenue stamps and special stamped paper for protocols, changes were made to levy taxes on second and subsequent transfers of ownership of real estate in certain cases and to exclude the distribution of dividends from this tax.

Despite the reform, the haste with which it was approved and enacted meant that the law included a series of errors and inconsistencies, which led to ambiguous and contradictory regulations. As a result, the reform was subject to numerous appeals on grounds of unconstitutionality, and parts of the original text were no longer valid.

In terms of the results obtained from the reform, the collection of tax revenues increased by 8.1 percent, mainly due to the increase in direct taxes. As to indirect taxes, the reform was not designed to improve collection of the IVA, although an improvement in domestic IVA collection was expected due to the widening of the tax base and the implementation of controls through the Customs Law.

The effect of spending also needs to be taken into account. The main problem here is the lack of systematic information with respect to the beneficiaries of government-run social programs—above all in education, health, and ground transportation. Without a doubt, allocative and technical efficiency must be substantially improved, but that requires the implementation of results-based management throughout the state. One project that has provided support to the government in this regard is called "Transformation of Government for Results-Based Public Management," part of an initiative known as Mejoremos Guate (Let's Improve Guatemala).

A system of performance indicators is also needed, to help improve the way goods and services are provided and delivered, as are more efficient oversight systems for the General Comptroller's Office and mechanisms to try to eliminate fiscal practices that constitute additional burdens for companies, among other things. Another proposal for consideration is to conduct a national crusade against informal economic practices. Economic informality creates an effect of exclusion and a series of other negative aspects. The goal of this crusade would be to double the number of those affiliated with the IGSS—in other words, the number of formal workers—within the next thirty-six months.

To carry out these proposals, it is necessary to take into account certain principles laid out in the Fiscal Pact, which should characterize the tax system and cause the fewest distortions possible in the economy:

- *Promotion of growth and equity:* Having an efficient tax system should be one of the main objectives of any fiscal policy. Any tax generates distortions in the economy, and the goal should be to keep these at the minimum needed to achieve the tax collection target.

- *Fairness in the tax system:* The concept of a "fair" tax system refers to horizontal equity (treating those who are in similar situations equally) and vertical equity (treating those in different circumstances differently).

- *Regulatory transparency:* It is important for tax rules to be clearly understood by the taxpayers. This means that tax rules must be transparent. Transparency allows individuals and companies to make informed decisions, thus reducing the inefficiency that taxes introduce into the economy.

- *Neutrality:* The aim of the tax system is to collect resources to fund government spending. Redistribution of wealth and subsidies to different sectors of the economy are not goals of the tax system.

- *Broad bases:* Having a broad base for each tax is a key goal; this means ensuring that the taxpayers are spread out across the widest possible base and therefore the tax burden does not fall on just a few. This makes it possible to have more moderate rates and also makes the tax system fairer, by treating all taxpayers equally.

- *Stability:* Stability in the tax system reduces the distortions caused by the system. If rules changes frequently, investment decisions are affected by uncertainty.

- *Efficiency:* Beyond the level of tax collection, the tax structure (makeup of rates and collection of different types of taxes) is key to growth. The aim is, first, to give priority to administrative steps (without legal changes) and, second, to make legal changes to current taxes to close loopholes and correct existing errors.

Clearly, without sufficient resources the people of Guatemala will not have access to the public goods that are required to cover their most basic needs—nutrition, health, and education. Further, without sufficient resources Guatemala's businesses will not have the public goods and services they require to be competitive in the global economy—security, infrastructure, an educated and trained workforce, and speedy and effective justice.

However, beyond the subject of taxes, actions should also be considered to provide for a higher quality of public spending, reasonable management of public debt and public assets, and a stronger environment for controlling and monitoring fiscal activity. It is necessary to work intensely on improving transparency and the quality of spending, controlling corruption and tax evasion, and reducing informality in the economy. All these aspects must be addressed at the same time.

That is why we insist on a comprehensive approach to fiscal issues. The Fiscal Pact, signed in 2000, is a comprehensive policy proposal with perspectives for the short, medium, and long terms. It constitutes a broad, representative social accord on the rights and obligations of citizens and the state, and entails an extremely important commitment to enable the state to carry out its basic functions. This is a comprehensive agreement that addresses the range of fiscal policy issues: public spending, public debt, state revenues, state assets, tax administration, and control and evaluation of spending. We at FUNDESA and CACIF believe it is both necessary and urgent to once again take up the discussion on the implementation and fulfillment of the Fiscal Pact.

CHAPTER 5

The Political Economy of Progressive Tax Reforms in Mexico

Vidal Romero

This chapter examines successful and unsuccessful attempts to institute progressive tax reforms in Mexico from 2000 to 2013.[1] The goal is to understand which specific conditions allow or impede progressive tax reforms.

Mexico's political and economic institutions have undergone significant transformations since the 1990s. Mexico's political landscape is more pluralist, and its institutions have become more democratic.[2] The country has opened up its economy; the state has gradually reduced its participation in nonstrategic sectors of the economy; and in-depth, far-reaching, telecommunications, energy, and education reforms were approved during the first two years of President Enrique Peña Nieto's administration.

Even after an important effort in 2013 to overhaul the tax system, it remains plagued by a multitude of special tax arrangements and by high levels of evasion. These traits introduce severe horizontal and vertical inequities into the system. Horizontal equity implies that individuals or corporations with identical income characteristics should pay the same taxes. Vertical equity implies that individuals or corporations that have higher earnings should progressively pay more taxes. These are not entirely independent dimensions. Ideally, a tax system should have both types of equity.

Mexico's tax system is a blend of progressive and regressive taxes, focused on short-term necessities. The reasons for this are explored in this chapter. Many specialists on this topic have determined that progressive tax systems would help to improve economic conditions and reduce inequality in Latin America.[3]

The next section provides a brief, general description of Mexico's tax system. The chapter then describes the main changes in the system from 2000 to 2013, focusing on the progressive taxation aspects, and identifies the factors that may lead to successful and unsuccessful reforms. The conclusions include policy recommendations to increase the likelihood of implementing progressive tax reforms.

MEXICO'S TAX SYSTEM

As is the case in many Latin American countries, Mexico's tax system is the result of decisions—made under pressure from organized groups upon a relatively weak state—aimed at solving urgent, short-term revenue problems.[4]

Two main issues plague the Mexican tax system: a multitude of confusing tax arrangements, riddled with loopholes and tax exemptions; and high rates of tax evasion.[5] Special exemptions in the income tax (IT) are estimated to represent 1.52 percent of gross domestic product (GDP); and special arrangements for the value-added tax (VAT), are estimated at 1.53 percent of GDP.[6] According to the political economist John Scott, subsides to gasoline, electricity, and cooking gas add up to another 3.3 percent of GDP.[7] It is estimated that 2004 tax evasion levels for the VAT were 40 percent of the VAT maximum potential revenue—which is high in absolute terms, yet below the region's average of almost 50 percent.[8] For the special arrangement created for small businesses (REPECOS), Jiménez and coauthors estimated an evasion level of almost 96 percent (this tax arrangement was eliminated in 2013). Evasion has a strong negative impact on equity.[9]

Exemptions and evasion reduce tax revenue. In 2013, Mexico's tax revenue was 10.2 percent of GDP, compared with Colombia's 17 percent, Brazil's 39 percent, and Argentina's 27 percent. Figure 5.1 shows Mexico's tax revenues and GDP changes.

Low tax collection in Mexico is compensated for by oil revenue, which has been growing in recent years thanks to high oil prices. Because this is not sustainable in the long term, it is not an ideal situation. Mexico's

Figure 5.1. GDP Changes and Tax Revenues: Oil, Income Tax, and the Value-Added Tax

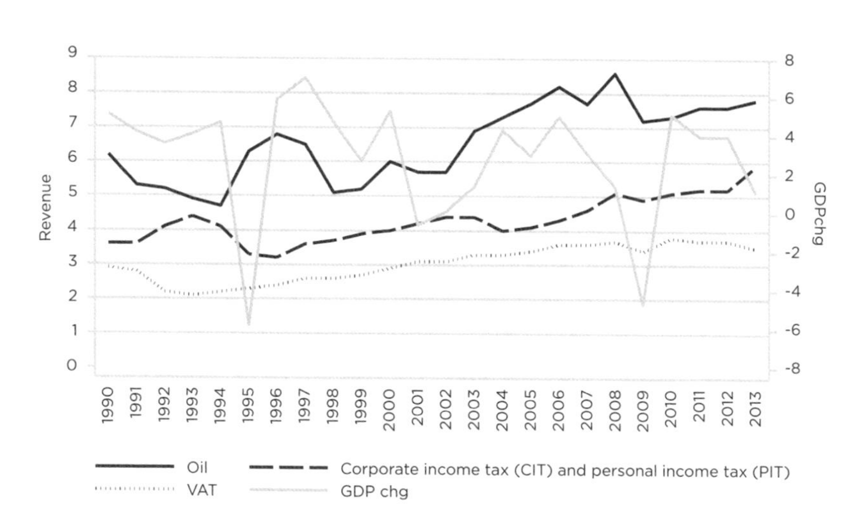

Source: Instituto Nacional de Geografía y Estadística, Banco de Información Económica, http://goo.gl/iswem0.

oil production has been decreasing, and international oil prices cannot be counted on to remain high (as seen by decreases in 2014).

Fiscal federalism is also deficient in the country. Subnational governments collect less than 5 percent of all tax revenue, yet they account for almost 60 percent of all spending. There is a fiscal disconnect in the system, creating incentives for inefficient spending. Monitoring and evaluating governments' fiscal performances are complicated by this fact.[10]

Most fiscal reform in Mexico has taken place during times of economic crisis. The result has not been the construction of a "better" tax system, with greater vertical and horizontal equity, but a set of uncoordinated measures taken to solve urgent necessities.[11] As in many countries in the region, the focus has been on maximizing revenue from those sources that are easiest to tap, and then to redistribute revenues to organized interests through spending.

Due to its high tolerance for evasion and the promotion of exemptions, the current tax structure in Mexico compensates for those who do not contribute by relying disproportionally on a relatively small number of captive taxpayers.[12] Additionally, Mexico's democratization has not been able to provide the median voter with enough influence to counteract organized interests seeking tax breaks.[13]

PROGRESSIVE TAX REFORMS IN MEXICO, 2000–2013

What follows is a discussion of the most significant changes that Mexico's tax system underwent from 2000 to 2013. There are different patterns across presidential administrations, very much as a function of the different environments that they faced and the goals they pursued. All bills, both those initiated and those approved, have had a mix of progressive and regressive tax elements, which in turn have had mixed effects upon the tax system as a whole (even as they have been advertised to the public as progressive changes).

Main Tax Changes

I constructed a data set that included what I considered to be the main changes in the tax system from 2000 to 2013. The changes I included satisfied one of two criteria: They modified who paid taxes, and/or they modified the VAT or IT rates.[14] Every change is coded by the year it was approved by Congress, not the following year in which it would take effect, since timing and context determine the political logic of every change.

Changes to tax laws are coded in three dimensions. First, they are coded by the expected equity effect: progressive-regressive, with the understanding that in many cases the multiple distortions of Mexico's tax system may neutralize or modify the expected equity effect. Second, they are coded by the direction of the expected equity effect; that is, whether it is vertical, horizontal, or both. And third, they are coded by the inferred government's motive behind the change: to create incentives for economic activity, to increase revenue, or to reduce tax evasion.

Table 5.1. The Progressivity of Tax Changes, 2000–2013

Type of Tax Change	Percentage of Changes
Progressive	53.9
Progressive-regressive	10.8
Regressive	27.7
Neutral	7.7
Total (n = 65)	100

Source: Author's coding.

Data from the subsample analyzed show that about two-thirds of tax changes in the period were potentially progressive changes. Of those, 10.8 percent combined progressive and regressive measures (table 5.1).[15]

Table 5.2 adds direction in terms of equity (horizontal and/or vertical) to every observation in our sample. The first four rows consider our basic categories of analysis: the potential effect on equity (progressive or regressive), and its direction (vertical or horizontal). These four rows do not add to 100 percent because there are some observations that I deem that have both progressive and regressive effects and others that have both vertical and horizontal directions. The remaining rows in table 5.2 show the disaggregated percentages, which add up to 100 percent.

As can be observed, the majority of changes in the period were progressive. This is understandable, given the multiple distortions in the tax system inherited from the hegemonic regime of the Partido Revolucionario Institutcional (PRI), which lasted seven decades. The regime was very much sustained by organized groups that received payment partly in the form of tax benefits, which were formalized in the tax code to allow the government to credibly commit with these groups. Combine this with multiple economic crises that demanded tax changes to deal with urgent revenue needs.[16] Once these changes were formalized, as with any benefit granted to a specific group, their elimination has proven to be difficult. As a result, the system has become institutionalized in its regressivity.

Table 5.2. Tax Changes' Equity (Expected) Effect, 2000–2013

Type of Tax Change	Percentage of Changes
Progressive-horizontal	26.1
Progressive-vertical	44.6
Regressive-horizontal	27.7
Regressive-vertical	27.6
Disaggregated	
Progressive-horizontal	15.4
Progressive-horizontal/vertical	7.7
Progressive-horizontal/regressive-vertical	3.0
Progressive-vertical/regressive-horizontal	7.7
Progressive-vertical	29.2
Regressive-horizontal	4.6
Regressive-horizontal/vertical	15.4
Regressive-vertical	9.2
Neutral	7.7
Total (n = 65)	100

Source: Author's coding.

Nevertheless, it is also obvious from the data that there was no master plan for tax reform in terms of the system's progressivity. Tax changes took a wide variety of forms, many of them regressive. Over time, the potential effects of changes to tax laws seem to be clustered by presidential administration, which faced different short-term necessities.

Figure 5.2 shows a significant concentration of regressive measures during the administration of President Vicente Fox (2000–2006). There are fewer of these during the governments of presidents Felipe Calderón (2006–12) and Enrique Peña Nieto (2012–present). This is a most likely a response to both clientelism, and to different conceptions of the role of the state in the economy.

Regarding motive—economic stimuli, revenue increases, or tax evasion reduction—a relatively similar share of changes have been made on

Figure 5.2. Tax Changes' Motives Over Time, 2000–2013

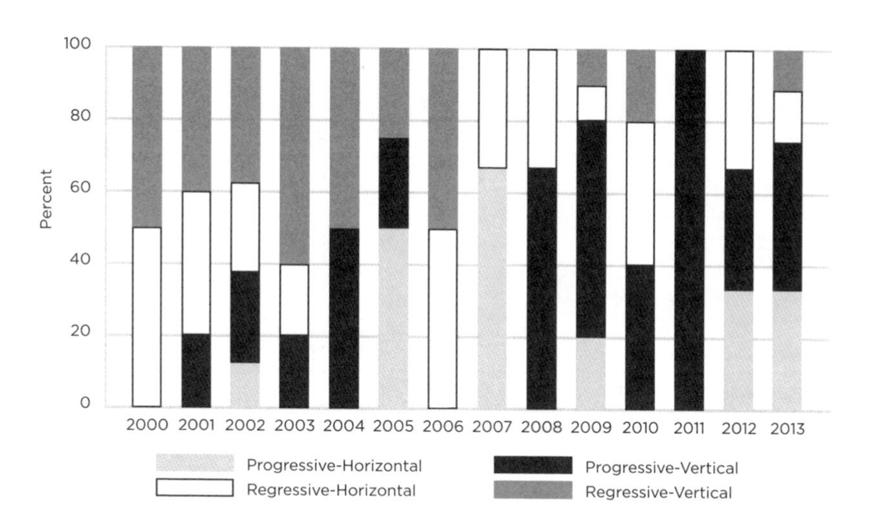

Source: Author's coding.

the first two fronts, and fewer have been focused on reducing evasion (table 5.3).

The patterns here are clearer: Economic stimuli (e.g., reductions in IT rates for agriculture) tend to make the system more regressive. Measures to increase revenue or to reduce evasion tend to have the positive externality of improving equity in the tax system, the former mainly in vertical terms, and the latter in horizontal.

As it can be seen in figure 5.3, motives seem to correlate with presidential administrations. During the Fox administration, the emphasis was on measures to promote economic activity. The main clientele of the Partido Acción Nacional (PAN), and of Fox especially, were businessmen and the upper middle classes, who demanded less state intrusion in the

Table 5.3. Tax Changes' Equity (Expected) Effect, 2000–2013

Type of Tax Change	Motive (percent)		
	Economic Stimuli (39.7%)	Increase Revenue (47.6%)	Reduce Evasion (12.7%)
Progressive-horizontal	0.0	13.3	75.0
Progressive-horizontal/ vertical	0.0	16.7	0.0
Progressive-horizontal/ regressive-vertical	0.0	6.7	0.0
Progressive-vertical/ regressive-horizontal	4.0	13.3	0.0
Progressive-vertical	28.0	36.7	12.5
Regressive-horizontal	12.0	0.0	0.0
Regressive-horizontal/vertical	28.0	6.7	12.5
Regressive-vertical	20.0	3.3	0.0
Neutral	8.0	3.3	0.0
Total (n = 63)	100	100	100

Source: Author's coding.

economy. Fox's agenda was clearly economic but, most important, President Fox enjoyed a significant increase in oil revenue thanks to high oil prices, despite decreasing production (see figure 5.1).

The pattern changed with the Calderón administration. At the beginning of his administration, there were few changes, and no pattern to the ones that did exist. However, the financial crisis of 2008–9 and decreasing oil proceeds induced the government to change the tax laws in 2008 to increase revenue in the short term. Figure 5.3 also shows that there were very few measures directed at reducing tax evasion between 2000 and 2013.

In the following subsections, I discuss in greater detail what I consider to be the main reforms and nonreforms during this period. I focus my analysis on the progressive components of the bills.

Figure 5.3. Tax Changes' Motives Over Time, 2000–2013

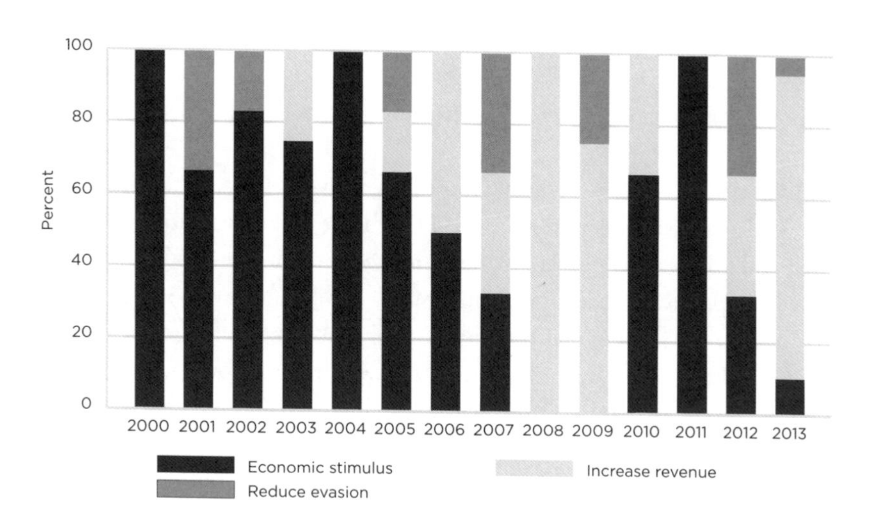

Source: Author's coding.

The Failed Reform of 2001

A few months after his arrival in office, President Fox sent Congress an ambitious bill called the "New Public Treasury" (Nueva Hacienda Pública). In tax terms, the original bill was hardly progressive. The bill was widely rejected by all opposition parties, and it did not pass, as the president's party did not have an absolute majority in either chamber of Congress.

Not only did the opposition disapprove, but many members of the president's own party (the PAN) also openly rejected the tax proposal, arguing that Fox had not bothered to reach agreements within the party. Some *panistas* even stated that they had no knowledge of the bill until it arrived in Congress.

The bill in question proposed eliminating many VAT exceptions and increasing the VAT rate for some products that had not paid the tax before.

These last products included groceries, medicines, tuition fees, newspapers, magazines, and books. This change was designed to increase revenue, but it increased the VAT regressivity, because these products are consumed in higher proportions to their income by the poorer. The bill was highly unpopular in the media, among politicians, and among the general population, and thus it failed.

In its place, Congress approved more progressive changes, which increased the VAT rate on luxury items such as yachts, expensive motorcycles, and high-end groceries like caviar, eel, and smoked salmon. This tax change may have been progressive, but it was quite minor and had little real impact.

The new bill was not planned; it was a populist reaction to Fox's regressive proposal. Fox's public communication strategy had acknowledged that the VAT increases for food and medicines was highly regressive, but he promised government compensation for the poorer sectors of society by increasing social programs. The campaign promised a return via spending *completo y copeteado* (complete and overflowing). Given the Mexican government's reputation for inefficient spending, this promise was hardly credible.[17]

As for the IT, President Fox proposed a mixed reform. The individual IT maximum rate would decrease from 40 percent to 32 percent, which benefited the middle and upper classes—Fox's clientele. Technically, this would serve to give incentives to economic activity. To compensate for lost revenue, Fox proposed an increase in the corporate IT rate from 30 percent to 32 percent. Congress rejected this last proposal, probably under pressure from organized business groups. Eventually, the Fox administration and Congress agreed to reduce the individual IT tax rate from 40 percent to 35 percent, and a subsequent gradual reduction to 27 percent by 2007. However, the IT rate increased back again in 2009. Ceteris paribus, this change should have had a vertically regressive effect in the system relative to the previous scheme (not in absolute terms). Individuals in the lower income categories do not pay IT; they get a credit on their salaries (if they are in the formal economy). Thus, the rate reduction results in that those who earn more pay less than before.

The 2007 Reform

In light of a decelerating economy and decreasing oil production, President Felipe Calderón's administration lobbied for a fiscal reform that explicitly aimed at increasing revenue. The bill was named "Fiscal Reform for Those Who Have Less" (Reforma Hacendaria por los que Menos Tienen). But despite the equity reference in its title, the tax changes that it proposed were a blend of progressive and regressive measures. The progressive component was in spending, not in taxation.

The explicit goals of the bill were to increase revenue, improve public spending, fight tax evasion, and strengthen fiscal federalism by further decentralizing spending. The original bill proposed increasing the VAT rate to 15 percent on groceries and medicines (more or less the same proposal that Fox had presented in 2001). When the media got wind of this, however, it triggered such uproar from the PRI and the Partido de la Revolución Democrática (PRD) that this proposal never even reached Congress. Taxing groceries and medicines is taboo in Mexico.

The other two relevant proposals, which did reach Congress, were the Single Rate Business Tax (IETU), and the Tax on Cash Deposits (IDE). The IETU taxed cash collected from the sale of assets, independent services, and property rentals. It was aimed at reducing evasion and reducing exemptions from corporations and individuals, because this tax allowed for few deductions. As expected, there was significant opposition from potentially affected individuals and corporations. However, the PRI and the PRD did not show strong opposition to this tax and agreed to it, most likely because their political bases of support were not directly affected. As part of the bargain to pass this part of the bill, the VAT increase was dropped. Additionally, Calderón's proposal was amended in Congress to exempt payroll salaries and benefits, donations, and social security contributions from this tax. This added to the tax's progressivity, and PRI and PRD voters were affected far less.

The IDE imposed a 2 percent tax rate on cash deposits above 15,000 pesos (about $1,100), applied to all bank accounts. The IDE could later be credited to the IT. This tax had the straightforward goal of reducing tax evasion. At least in its design, the IDE was a bold attempt to improve horizontal equity. This tax did have an impact upon PRI and PRD voters, such as street and public market vendors, and taxi drivers, whose organizations are related to these parties. However, it was difficult to justify not supporting this measure, because it was clearly directed at reducing tax evasion. Tax evasion may be widely practiced in Mexico, but it is unpopular. The IDE also had a component of public security, because organized crime is mainly a cash business. Even businesspeople, a powerful interest group, could not state a coherent opposition to this measure. The IDE proposal passed.

The 2009 Reform

In the midst of the 2008–9 global financial crisis and a grave domestic security crisis, President Calderón attempted a second fiscal reform. There was an urgent need to raise more resources to compensate for the noxious effects of the economic crisis in the poorer—or at least this was the formal justification for the bill. In its initial proposal, the government proposed a flat 2 percent tax on the consumption of all goods and services, with no exemptions, which was in addition to the current VAT. The government explicitly acknowledged that this would be a regressive measure, but that it was necessary to increase the available resources to help the poor.

The proposal was rejected. In 1995, Congress had approved a VAT increase in the middle of a severe economic crisis. This time, however, the tax increase was a hard sell; the economy was in bad shape, but it was far from collapsing. The opposition did not buy the president's arguments. Opposition parties did agree to relatively more progressive proposals that considered a 1-point increase to the VAT general rate, without eliminating exemptions or 0 percent rates. A 2-point increase to the IT maximum rate was also agreed to.

Both measures were relatively benign for PRI and PRD voters, and the PAN shouldered most of the blame. In a sense, the PAN and the executive had no other choice given income distribution in Mexico, where a majority of the population lives in precarious conditions.

The 2013 Reform

The 2013 fiscal reform promoted by President Peña Nieto was explicitly presented to the public as a progressive reform. It emphasized that those who have more should contribute more to the well-being of the country, and it was billed as the "just" thing to do.

Nevertheless, it was not originally a fully progressive reform; its main goal was to increase revenue. The bill included some vertically progressive measures, such as increasing the individual IT, and other horizontally regressive measures, such as eliminating the IETU and the IDE. There is sufficient evidence from the media to believe that the executive was lobbying for a VAT increase on groceries and medicines.[18] There were strong reactions against this potential change from the main opposition parties, the PRD and the PAN. The PRI needed support from at least one of these parties to pass the bill. A VAT increase for food and medicines was not included in the bill that was sent to Congress.

The PRI and President Peña Nieto failed to get an increase in the VAT rate on groceries and medicines, just as presidents Fox and Calderón had failed to do in 2001 and in 2007. Increases in the VAT have only been possible during economic crises in Mexico.[19] However, Congress did approve an increase in the VAT rate in northern border cities from 11 percent to the general VAT rate of 16 percent.

Another controversial proposal, at least for the middle classes, was eliminating the VAT exemption on tuition fees and mortgage payments. The middle and upper classes strongly rejected this measure. Even though they are not organized lobbying groups, the pressure in the media was so strong that the government had to pull back the proposal. This is clearly a sign of democratization in Mexico, and the opening of new roads to influence government.

The party that ended up supporting the PRI's bill was the PRD, a party of the left. Technically, the PRD was a natural ally, because the reform mostly affected the middle and upper classes and businesspeople. However, regarding tax bills, and many other laws, the norm in Mexico had been an alliance between the PRI and the PAN. The PRI and the PRD were usually natural enemies, because the PRD was born as a splinter group from the PRI, and was its main detractor. In all likelihood, the PRI's concession to the PRD was to not propose a change to the 0 percent VAT rate on groceries and medicines in order to get this leftist party's support for the tax bill.

The alliance was also greatly facilitated by a pact (Pacto por México) that was signed by the main political parties soon after President Peña Nieto took office. The Pacto had the explicit goal of constructing a multiparty consensus in order to achieve the institutional reforms that the country needed. The exercise was very successful in this respect.

THE DETERMINANTS OF PROGRESSIVE TAX REFORMS IN MEXICO

Assessing the successful and failed reforms of the previous section, there is variance across presidential administrations regarding the progressivity of the tax system. Efforts to be progressive have focused on redistribution through spending, not taxation. Taxation has been used to increase revenue and/or grant specific groups favors. These groups return the favor by promising to invest in the country, or through political support.[20]

The high number of exemptions in the system and the tolerance for tax evasion are not random, but have their origins in structural issues and political motivations. The following subsections analyze the main constraints to reform that decisionmakers face in Mexico. The focus is on issues of vertical and horizontal equity and how these constraints apply to the reforms discussed above.

Structural Factors

Mexican decisionmakers are seriously limited by multiple structural constraints. Leverage to promote a more progressive system is limited by these constraints. Economic limitations are the key structural constraints.

The first constraint is capital. Capital in Mexico is scarce (relative to the country's needs), mobile,[21] and concentrated.[22] This circumstance puts the Mexican government at relative disadvantage vis-à-vis businessmen. Additionally, the globalization of markets has increased Mexico's competition for foreign investment with other emerging economies, such as China, India, or Brazil. As a result, businessmen usually enjoy preferential treatment. This is hardly a new circumstance in Mexico—and other countries, such as Guatemala and Uruguay.[23] Elizondo shows that this has been the case even during the PRI regime's "golden years" in the 1960s and early 1970s.[24]

As a result, the implementation of truly progressive reforms in Mexico that would hurt the rich, if they aimed at vertical equity, or the powerful, if horizontal equity is pursued, is a challenging endeavor given capital constraints. Not only is it difficult for the government to set high tax rates on corporations, but it is also hard to eliminate exemptions, deductions, and legal loopholes.

Yet, there is a limit on the constraints that businessmen can set on the government. The 2007 reform that created the IETU and the IDE illustrate the circumstances under which the government was able to resist pressures from businessmen. As I explained in the previous section, Calderón's proposal was accepted by the PRI and PRD; it was an amended version, that did not seriously damage their support bases. And the PAN was willing to take full blame for the reform, given the expected benefits of increased revenue. The lesson in this case is that multi-party alliances can be formed to resist organized business, especially if one of them is prepared to shoulder responsibility.

The second constraint includes poverty and insufficient economic growth. Mexico's rate of economic growth is below the country's needs. This circumstance prevents the government from implementing equity measures.

Regarding tax evasion, the government cannot implement aggressive programs to reduce tax evasion and informality, which would improve the system's horizontal equity, because the potential impact upon many microenterprises and small businesses would be to force them to close. A significant share of the population—more than 50 million Mexicans (52.3 percent of the population by 2012) live in poverty conditions—those who are below the national poverty line—and many of these families are supported by microenterprises and/or informal economies.[25]

A gradual approach seems a more sensible alternative. The 2013 reform implemented a reasonable program that provides incentives for informal businesses to voluntarily formalize their fiscal situation. Those who apply will gradually start paying taxes with lower rates and better conditions than the formal sector for a period of ten years, when they will pay full taxes. Given the circumstances, this is a feasible, although lengthy, strategy to improve the system's horizontal equity.

Economic necessity also makes the government unable to credibly commit to long-term tax changes, because all actors know that if things go wrong economically, the government will renege.[26] The multiple changes to the VAT—many in contexts of economic crisis—illustrate this circumstance.[27] This creates perverse incentives for groups with some influence to systematically pressure the government to change tax laws, making horizontal equity a hard goal to achieve.

Widespread poverty means that the tax base is quite small; 60 percent of total income is concentrated in the two upper deciles of the population.[28] Revenue is concentrated in a small share of the population; the two upper deciles of the population pay 75 percent of IT.[29] It is thus problematic for the government to make a case for further taxation without being able to provide specific goods and services that benefit the middle and upper classes.[30]

The third constraint is oil revenue. Oil continues to be both a blessing and curse for Mexico's fiscal system. It is similar to what copper is to Chile, although to a lesser degree.[31] Oil provides a significant amount of public revenue, but it also allows the government to spare special interest groups, adding all sorts of distortions to the fiscal system's progressivity.[32] In 2014, an ambitious package of energy reforms was approved. These reforms partially tie the government's hands with respect to oil revenue and may help fix the equity component of Mexico's tax system. The changes to fiscal laws are explicit on how oil revenues are to be spent. Mexico's oil company, Pemex, must contribute to revenue with up to 4 percent of GDP. The excess of income is to be distributed, with clear rules, among various funds that will contribute to the country's development and to its macroeconomic stability.

Institutional Factors

The Mexican electoral landscape began democratizing in the early 1990s, and this process culminated in 2000, when the PRI lost the presidential election after seventy-one years in power. However, institutions have not been updated or reformed as fast as power has fragmented in the country. Many institutions inherited from the period of PRI hegemony have proven resilient and have not adapted to the new democratic context.

One such institution is reelection. During the period analyzed in this chapter, consecutive-term reelection of representatives was not permitted under the Constitution. This broke the electoral connection.[33] Without consecutive reelection, the political parties have a de facto monopoly over candidacies, decreasing representativeness, because politicians depend on their parties to get their next job, either in government or as candidates for a different office.[34] A political reform approved in 2013 allows immediate reelection for certain offices and further specifies the mechanisms for independent candidacies. As democratic representation improves, one could surmise that public pressures for a more progressive tax system would increase.

Another such institution is perverse fiscal federalism. Mexico's fiscal system suffers from a deep disconnect in which the federal government collects most taxes, but a majority of resources are spent by subnational governments. This introduces multiple inefficiencies into the system.[35] By not collecting taxes that could legally be collected at the subnational level, governments miss the opportunity to introduce an equity criterion into the system. Moreover, as Magar and colleagues show, state and municipal governments could implement and collect significant amounts of taxes, but choose not to do so.[36] One may suspect that political biases guide these decisions. There are also numerous exemptions and subsidies that subnational governments apply discretionally, which leaves the door open for decisions based on political motivations. For instance, in the Federal District, the military is exempt from paying property taxes. Esteban Tovar researched the determinants of subsidies to property taxes in the Federal District.[37] Controlling for all relevant economic characteristics that would determine a subsidy based on equity, he found a significant bias in this subsidy favoring PRD precincts (the PRD has governed the Federal District since 1997).

Still another such institution is the judicial system. Mexico's judicial system, and the institutions which cover fiscal issues, induce a bias in favor of those who are wealthy enough to hire lawyers and accountants. This seems to be a widespread problem in the region, as Arnson and Bergman indicate.[38] Elizondo argues that *amparos*—originally a legal recourse designed to protect citizens' basic guarantees and human rights from the power of the state—have been systematically abused in Mexico by corporations and individuals in order to avoid paying taxes.[39] This circumstance makes the system more regressive, because only relatively wealthier individuals and bigger corporations can afford to go to trial against the state. Trials are usually time consuming, and personal influences can be the key to get a positive verdict.

Finally, another such institution includes labor laws. Archaic labor legislation, which makes for a rigid labor market, generates incentives for business owners to operate informally and not to pay social security contributions. Antón and colleagues estimate that 79 percent of businesses operate informally.[40] This setting affects the horizontal equity of the system.

Instrumental Power

Much of the story of taxation has to do with organized groups' relative power. This is not exclusive to Mexico; it is a general feature of how states and societies interact.[41] Given the need to increase revenue, politicians have two—not mutually exclusive—options: to increase taxes on those who are already paying taxes, or to force those who do not pay taxes to contribute. The first alternative may be progressive, increasing vertical equity; whereas the second option would tend to contribute to horizontal equity. One would expect that, ceteris paribus, it is relatively less costly for a politician to choose the first alternative. And one would also expect that whether a group pays more taxes or not is a function of that group's relative power.

In Mexico, several factors come into play. To begin with, the structural conditions of Mexico's economy provide significant leverage to businesspeople vis-à-vis the government. From the PRI's hegemonic regime, successive Mexican governments have also inherited a series of commitments to organized groups, such as unions, street vendors, and taxi drivers. These groups were granted multiple benefits that have proven hard to take away. The PAN administrations of Fox and Calderón unsuccessfully tried to remove benefits directed to groups that constituted the PRI's support base. This failure negatively affected horizontal equity. The return of the PRI to the presidency suggests that this problem will not be fixed.

Formal Political Power

Power distribution matters. There are differences across political parties in their preferences for progressivity, as a function of their ideology and bases of support. Normally, one would expect that the PAN, a party on the right, would favor a horizontal equity that would benefit their unorganized supporters, and favor a vertical progressivity with a relatively flatter distribution, that is, with smaller marginal differences across income categories. The PRD is strongly for vertical equity, and would not mind horizontal equity if it benefited its organized groups. The PRD would strongly oppose benefits for corporations. The PRI favors vertical redistribution given to its supporters, but the mixed composition of these groups would probably induce the party to support many horizontal inequities.

The 2013 reform, which has a strong progressive component, was unusual in terms of party coalitions in Congress. The PRI, in the center, and the PRD, on the left, joined forces to push the reform forward. The center-left coalition clearly made a difference in terms of what was approved, as compared with the traditional center-right PRI-PAN alliance.

It is important to note that political capital substantively affects formal power distribution. Executives tend to have more popular support, and lesser enemies, when their administrations begin. Of the four main reforms and attempts of reform in the period that this chapter analyzes, three were in the first year of a presidential administration—2001, 2007, and 2013.

Cultural and Behavioral Considerations

As Marcelo Bergman states, an individual's decision to pay taxes is heavily mediated by the expected return in government spending.[42] In Mexico, not paying taxes is a widely practiced behavior. Elizondo explains this by the common belief that the government's public spending is deficient and opaque, and thus does not uphold its end of the contract with citizens.[43] Survey data from the Americas Barometer shows a strong resistance to pay more taxes to support further social spending. Table 5.4 shows a widespread resistance across income quintiles to paying more taxes for increased spending on education, health, and the social program Oportunidades. It is telling that even the lower quintiles have a strong resistance to paying more taxes to support social spending, when this is this segment that both stands to benefit the most and pays fewer taxes.

However, there is significant variance across quintiles and across topics. The richer quintiles show relatively more support for raising taxes to fund education and health, which some may use if quality improves, and strongly oppose more taxes to fund Oportunidades, which is a program that they will never join. This is highly suggestive as to how to frame progressive reforms.[44] Poorer sectors have a relatively stronger preference for more health services. As compared to the richer quintiles, those who are less well off are less willing to pay more taxes for financing education (table 5.4).

Table 5.5 shows that about two-thirds of Mexicans prefer more efficiency to further increases. It supports the argument that spending needs to be made more efficient and transparent before asking Mexican citizens to pay more taxes.

The 2013 reform explicitly appealed to equity as a sufficient reason to approve the reform. One of the main slogans of the government's campaign was that the tax reform should be approved "because it is just" (*porque es lo justo*). In 2001, President Fox appealed to an equity component in spending to justify a (failed) increase in the VAT on groceries and medicines.

If politicians cannot "sell" additional taxes on the grounds that more social spending will be possible, it seems complicated to sell higher taxes on the grounds of greater equity in the tax system. Moreover, there does not seem to be full agreement in any quintile that the government should act boldly to reduce inequality (table 5.6). It seems that the government needs to build a better case in public opinion if it wants to gather citizens' strong support.

Exogenous Factors

This subsection considers two exogenous factors in this situation. *The first factor is the 2009 global financial crisis.* During most of the period examined in this chapter, Mexico's economy was relatively stable, except for the 2009 global financial crisis. Even though this crisis was not as negative as the crises of the 1980s and 1990s, it reduced oil demand and decreased public revenue, which induced the government to increase tax revenue by increasing the IT and VAT rates, among other measures. As expected, these measures were not well taken by the public and businesspeople.

The second factor is public security. Beginning in 2007, Mexico faced a public security crisis that is continuing. In a span of five years, homicides went from a rate of 9 murders per every 100,000 inhabitants in 2006 to 24 murders per 100,000 in 2011.[45] This unfortunate circumstance has

Table 5.4. Willingness to Pay More Taxes (percentage who answered "yes")

Would you be willing to pay more taxes than you do currently so that the government can spend more on ...?

Topic	Income Quintile (percent)					
	1	2	3	4	5	Total
Primary and secondary education	21.0	23.7	20.5	23.8	30.3	23.7
Health	27.0	23.4	21.1	25.0	29.5	25.1
Social program Oportunidades	23.7	18.2	17.7	12.2	13.3	17.0

Source: Latin American Public Opinion Project, *Americas Barometer 2012*; *n* = 749 for education, *n* = 758 for health. and *n* = 742 for Oportunidades.

Table 5.5. Efficiency versus More Spending

In your opinion, to improve the quality of education/health in Mexico, what should the government do?

Topic and Subtopics		Income Quintile (%)					
		1	2	3	4	5	Total
Primary and secondary education	Better use the money that it is currently spending on education	65.8	71.4	70.0	65.7	67.7	68.1
	Spend more money on education, even if it has to raise taxes	21.5	17.7	16.2	21.9	20.2	19.5
Public health services	Better use the money that it is currently spending on health	64.9	67.8	70.0	65.5	61.3	66.0
	Spend more money on health, even if it has to raise taxes	21.2	20.3	20.0	25.7	23.4	22.1

Source: Latin American Public Opinion Project, *Americas Barometer 2012*; *n* = 749 for education, and *n* = 758 for health.

Table 5.6. Efficiency versus More Spending

The Mexican government should implement strong policies to reduce income inequality between the rich and the poor. To what extent do you agree or disagree with this statement?

Opinion	Income Quintile (%)					
	1	2	3	4	5	Total
Strongly disagree	0.6	0.9	2.0	1.7	1.2	1.3
2	1.6	1.2	0.7	1.1	0.8	1.1
3	3.2	1.9	1.4	2.6	4.4	2.6
4	8.3	7.4	7.1	9.9	16.2	9.6
5	15.4	16.4	21.4	19.0	17.0	17.8
6	22.1	17.7	20.7	18.7	19.8	19.7
Strongly agree	48.7	54.6	46.8	47.0	40.7	47.9
Total	100	100	100	100	100	100

Source: Latin American Public Opinion Project, *Americas Barometer 2012*; *n* = 1,538.

had negative effects on the prospects for a comprehensive progressive tax reform from the fiscal viewpoint. Public security policies are expensive. Mexico's security budget has significantly risen to cope with crime. This places additional pressures on the government to increase revenue. Its inability to provide security places the government in a weak position to bargain with organized groups, especially businesspeople. It makes it difficult to fix horizontal inequities and to create a more strict progressive system in vertical terms.

POLICY LESSONS

This last section summarizes what can be learned from the Mexican case in order to suggest policy recommendations that may increase the likelihood of moving toward a more progressive tax system.

The first policy lesson is to improve public spending. To reduce opposition to tax reform, the government must be able to credibly commit to efficient and honest spending. This is particularly important in progressive tax reform.[46] Public opinion polls show that there is significant distrust for the Mexican government's spending capacities and efficiency, along with as serious suspicions of corruption. Changing these opinions is not going to be easy, and it would seem that only actual improvement could change attitudes. There should be an explicit and credible commitment to the middle and upper classes regarding what they are going to receive from the government (i.e., better public education and citizen security), thereby renewing the social contract.

The second policy lesson is to reduce organized groups' influence in the process. It is relatively obvious and widely agreed that the freer the government and the opposition are from clientelistic political deals, the easier it will be to promote a more progressive tax system. However, it is impossible to devise a political party without political biases and pressure from all sorts of groups. The period analyzed demonstrates the growing influence of public opinion upon policy choices. However, organized groups are still the main actors influencing tax decisions. As long as there are politically motivated exemptions, evasion, and elusion in the system, parties will push to include their preferred exemptions in order to benefit the groups that constitute their base of support. Therefore, a strategy of gradual elimination of exemptions is not sustainable.

One solution is to make the system more transparent—report who pays taxes and how much, and report which legislator supports each tax change. This will actually free representatives from a lot of pressure to deliver to organized groups, improving the system's vertical and horizontal equity.

In addition, a fragmented economic elite is fundamental to make the system more progressive. Democratization is starting to induce this fragmentation. We just recently observed fierce public battles between two of the most powerful businessmen in Mexico, Carlos Slim and Emilio Azacárraga, regarding the regulation of telecommunications. Political parties somehow aligned with one or the other. This is a circumstance that governments can use to eliminate preferential treatments in the tax code.

The third policy lesson is to promote broad coalitions and make the process more transparent. The support of the leftist PRD for Peña Nieto's tax reforms helps to account for the elimination of many tax exemptions for corporations and wealthy individuals. If all three parties needed to approve the reform, they may have served as checks on one other to block special tax treatments to specific societal groups. This requires that bargaining be monitored; otherwise, parties may exchange favors instead, creating even more exemptions in the system.

Again, transparency is the key. The recent approval of immediate reelection for members of Congress should reinforce this mechanism to improve horizontal equality, because many more voters would have now influence over legislators, which should induce politicians to decrease tax exemptions. The Pacto por México proved to be a good bargaining setting for the main political parties, as it facilitated bargaining. This exercise could be replicated to improve the overall system.

The fourth policy lesson is to fix fiscal federalism and reduce evasion. Mexico's fiscal system should be simpler, and there should be a better connection between who collects and who spends. The disconnect between revenue and spending at the national and subnational levels creates negative incentives. State and municipal governments barely tax their citizens, distorting the progressivity of the system. This disconnect also creates political incentives to determine who does pay local taxes, creating favoritism and increasing clientelism. The property tax is a great example. It is estimated that municipalities collect less than 0.5 percent of GDP, about a quarter of the average for the countries that belong to the Organization for Economic Cooperation and Development.

Gradual, sustained, and public measures to reduce tax evasion should also help the government make its case to taxpayers that horizontal inequity is being reduced, thereby generating support for further reforms that will also reduce exemptions.

The fifth policy lesson is that framing of the issues matters, but has its limits. Framing issues is important. The equity argument is limited by the government's inability to spend efficiently and to significantly reduce tax evasion. In the period I have studied, some changes that imposed further taxes on the middle and upper classes were rejected not by organized groups but by wider society. The media reflected this opposition.

The security crisis opens a window of opportunity to promote reforms that improve equity by imposing tighter controls on corporations and individuals in order to better combat money laundering and other illicit activities, which would add to the system's progressivity.

In conclusion, there is ample room to improve the progressivity of Mexico's tax system. The fact that the system is in relatively bad shape is not a random circumstance, but the result of specific power distributions, predispositions, and structural constraints. Actions are needed to change these things. The multiple recent changes in Mexico's political and economic institutions should help to improve the fiscal structure, especially if they succeed in making the system as a whole more transparent and, as a consequence, more trustworthy.

NOTES

1. The author expresses thanks for excellent research assistance from José Alberto García Huitrón, helpful comments from Alexandra Uribe Coughlan, and support from the Asociación Mexicana de Cultura AC and the Sistema Nacional de Investigadores of Conacyt.
2. For a good overview and explanation of Mexico's changes in recent decades, see Beatriz Magaloni, *Voting for Autocracy* (Cambridge: Cambridge University Press, 2006).
3. Cynthia J. Arnson and Marcelo Bergman, "Introduction," in *Taxation and Equality in Latin America*, ed. Cynthia J. Arnson and Marcelo Bergman (Washington, D.C.: Latin American Program of the Woodrow Wilson International Center for Scholars, 2012); Giovanni Andrea Cornia, Juan Carlos Gómez-Sabaini, and Bruno Martorano, "A New Fiscal Pact, Tax Policy Changes and Income Inequality: Latin America in the Last Decade," working paper, World Institute for Development Economics Research, 2011, 70; Nora Lustig, Carola Pessino, and John Scott, "The Impact of Taxes and Social Spending on Inequality and Poverty in Argentina, Bolivia, Brazil, Mexico, Peru and Uruguay: An Overview," Tulane Economics Working Paper Series, 2013; Ana Corbacho, Vicente Fretes Cibils, and Eduardo Lora, eds., *More Than Revenue: Taxation as Development Tool* (Washington, D.C.: Inter-American Development Bank, 2013); James Mahon, "Tax Incidence and Tax Reforms in Latin America," Latin American Program of the Woodrow Wilson International Center for Scholars, 2012.
4. See Eric Magar, Vidal Romero, and Jeffrey F. Timmons, "The Political Economy of Fiscal Reforms in Latin America: Mexico," (*SSRN Electronic Journal*, 2009), doi:10.2139/ssrn.1963863; and Carlos Elizondo, "In Search of Tax Revenue: Tax Reform in Mexico under the Administrations of Echeverría and Salinas," *Journal of Latin American Studies* 26 (1994).
5. For a good assessment of Mexico's fiscal situation and perspectives, see Instituto Mexicano para la Competitividad AC, "Perspectivas para una Reforma Fiscal," 2013, http://goo.gl/Gj4c96.

6. Luis César Castañeda and Juan E. Pardinas, *Sub-National Revenue Mobilization in Mexico*, Working Paper IDB-WP-354 (Washington, D.C.: Inter-American Development Bank, 2012).
7. John Scott, "Gasto público para la equidad: Del Estado excluyente hacia un estado de bienestar Universal," Programa Presupuesto y Gasto Público en México, México evalúa, Centro de Análisis de Políticas Públicas, 2010.
8. Corbacho, Cibils, and Lora, *More Than Revenue.*
9. Juan Pablo Jiménez, Juan Carlos Gómez Sabaini, Andrea Podestá, eds., *Evasión y Equidad en América Latina* (Santiago: CEPAL and Deutsche Gesellschaft für Technische Zusammenarbeit, 2010).
10. Alberto Díaz-Cayeros, Kenneth McElwain, and Vidal Romero, "Fiscal Decentralization and Particularistic Spending," paper presented at the 2008 American Political Science Association annual meeting, Boston; Barry R. Weingast, Kenneth A. Shepsle, and Christopher Johnsen, "The Political Economy of Benefits and Costs: A Neoclassical Approach to Distributive Politics," *Journal of Political Economy* 89 (1981).
11. Magar, Romero, and Timmons, "Political Economy of Fiscal Reforms."
12. Karla Breceda, Jamele Rigolini, and Jaime Saavedra, "Latin America and the Social Contract: Patterns of Social Spending and Taxation," *Population and Development Review* 35 (2009).
13. Carlos Elizondo, "Progresividad y eficacia del gasto público en México: Precondición para una política recaudatoria efectiva," Latin American Program of the Woodrow Wilson International Center for Scholars, 2014; Magar, Romero, and Timmons, "Political Economy of Fiscal Reforms"; Scott, "Gasto público para la equidad."
14. I acknowledge that my description of the changes in the period is a function of the selection and coding criterion that I utilize. Further research could improve both the selection criteria and coding. An alternative would have been to exhaustively code all changes to tax laws in the period. This exercise, however, would have contained too much noise (i.e., many small reforms that do not cause any significant change in terms of who pays taxes and how much, which are counted equal than reforms that do change who pays taxes and how much).
15. E.g., taxes on specific luxury items would make the system more vertically progressive, because the richer would be paying more taxes, but horizontally regressive because many other equivalent items have a different tax rate.
16. Magar, Romero, and Timmons, "Political Economy of Fiscal Reforms."
17. Elizondo, "Progresividad y eficacia del gasto público."
18. See, e.g., http://goo.gl/qN1Knd.
19. Magar, Romero, and Timmons, "Political Economy of Fiscal Reforms."
20. Elizondo, "In Search of Tax Revenue"; Elizondo, "Progresividad y eficacia del gasto público."
21. For a good explanation on how mobile capital conditions the government's decisionmaking, see Carles Boix, *Democracy and Redistribution* (Cambridge: Cambridge University Press, 2003); and Arnson and Bergman, "Introduction."
22. For a better understating on the problems of concentrated capital, see Robert Bates, "A Political Scientist Looks at Tax Reform," in *Tax Reform in Developing Countries*,

ed. Malcom Gillis (Durham, N.C.: Duke University Press, 1989); and Daniela Campello, "The Politics of Redistribution in Less Developed Democracies," in *The Great Gap*, ed. Merike Blofield (University Park: Pennsylvania State University Press, 2011); Mahon, "Tax Incidence."

23. Maynor Cabrera and Aaron Scheneider, "Instituciones, Impuestos, y Desigualdad en Guatemala," Latin American Program of the Woodrow Wilson International Center for Scholars, 2013; Andrés Rius, "The Uruguayan Tax Reform of 2006: Why Didn't It Fail?" Latin American Program of the Woodrow Wilson International Center for Scholars, 2013.
24. Elizondo, "In Search of Tax Revenue."
25. Data available at the World Bank site: http://wdi.worldbank.org/table/2.8
26. For a good explanation of commitment problems that rulers face, see Douglas North and Barry Weingast "Constitutions and Commitment: The Evolution of Institutions Governing Public Choice in Seventeenth-Century England," *Journal of Economic History* 49 (1989).
27. Magar, Romero, and Timmons, "Political Economy of Fiscal Reforms."
28. Secretaría de Hacienda y Crédito Público, "Distribución del Pago de Impuestos y Recepción del Gasto Público por Deciles de Hogares y Personas. Resultados para el año de 2012," http://goo.gl/XCqUhX.
29. Ibid.
30. Breceda, Rigolini, and Saavedra, "Latin America and the Social Contract"; Mahon, "Tax Incidence"; Corbacho, Cibils, and Lora, *More Than Revenue.*
31. Tash Fairfield, "The Political Economy of Progressive Tax Reform in Chile," Latin American Program of the Woodrow Wilson International Center for Scholars, 2014.
32. Instituto Mexicano para la Competitividad AC, "Perspectivas."
33. The term "electoral connection" refers to the incentives that elections provide to representatives to follow, or not, their constituents' preferences.
34. Changes in the law enacted in 2013 allow for reelection and independent candidacies, beginning with the representatives elected in the 2015 elections.
35. Corporación Andina de Fomento / Development Bank of Latin America, *Public Finance for Development: Strengthening the Connection between Income and Expenditure: Economy and Development Report* (Caracas: Corporación Andina de Fomento / Development Bank of Latin America, 2012); Saulo Santos de Souza, "The Political Economy of Tax Reform in Latin America: A Critical Review," Latin American Program of the Woodrow Wilson International Center for Scholars, 2013.
36. Magar, Romero, and Timmons, "Political Economy of Fiscal Reforms."
37. Esteban Tovar, "Política Redistributiva Fiscal: El Caso del Impuesto Predial en México" (undergraduate thesis, Instituto Tecnológico Autónomo de México, 2011).
38. Arnson and Bergman, "Introduction."
39. Carlos Elizondo Mayer Serra, "La industria del amparo fiscal," *Política y Gobierno* XVI (2009).
40. Arturo Antón, Fausto Hernández and Santiago Levy, *The End of Informality in Mexico? Fiscal Reform for Universal Social Insurance* (Washington, D.C.: Inter-American Development Bank, 2012).
41. Margaret Levi, *Of Rule and Revenue* (Berkeley: University of California Press, 1988).

42. Marcelo Bergman, *Tax Evasion and the Rule of Law in Latin America: The Political Culture of Cheating and Compliance in Argentina and Chile* (University Park: Pennsylvania State University Press, 2009).
43. Elizondo, "Progresividad y eficacia del gasto público."
44. Jeffrey F. Timmons, "Taxation and Representation in Recent History," *Journal of Politics* 72 (2010).
45. For a good assessment of Mexico's security situation, see Javier Osorio, "Democratization and Drug Violence in Mexico," Working Paper, Mario Einaudi Center for International Studies at Cornell University, 2013.
46. Arnson and Bergman, "Introduction"; Elizondo, "Progresividad y eficacia del gasto público."

CONCLUSION

The Political Economy of Progressive Tax Reform in Latin America's Recent Experience

James E. Mahon Jr. and Marcelo Bergman, with Cynthia J. Arnson

This conclusion has two principal sections. The first reviews and analyzes the main findings of the case studies, comparing them with one another to derive some provisional generalizations about conditions that might favor reform. The second section draws a series of lessons for reformers involving tactics and strategies, which, unlike structural or political institutional factors, are more likely to be open to their influence and control. We also offer some final thoughts as we look ahead.

GENERAL CONCLUSIONS ABOUT THE POLITICAL ECONOMY OF PROGRESSIVE REFORM

In recent years, there have been two general types of reforms in Latin America and the Caribbean: revenue-enhancing and progressive. The first mainly sought higher revenues, the second to shift the tax burden. Tax initiatives sometimes included both goals (Chile and, to a lesser extent, Mexico), sometimes the first one alone (Guatemala), or sometimes only the second one (Uruguay and Colombia in 2012).

With regard to successful progressive reforms, formal political power and conjunctural factors appear to have been most influential in the case studies presented in the preceding chapters. In explaining negative results (i.e., failed or very limited reforms), the instrumental and structural power of the organized private sector also seems to have been quite important. A general summary of the most important conditions accompanying the outcomes is shown in table C.1.

Let us begin with the most obvious pattern. The two major progressive reforms in the region—one undertaken in Uruguay by Vázquez and the Frente Amplio in 2006, and the other in Chile by Bachelet and the Nueva Mayoría in 2014—both took place under presidents from the left with strong electoral mandates. In each case, the president's party or coalition had a legislative majority. This meant that opponents focused their tactics outside the legislature, engaging in publicity campaigns and threats of disinvestment aimed at swaying public opinion. At the same time, both the Uruguayan and Chilean tax authorities enjoyed reputations for competence and honesty as well as autonomy from elected officials. Elite sectors could not reasonably argue that they feared arbitrary, politicized enforcement of the new tax regimes. Highly technocratic tax agencies also provided a neutral source of information on the likely effects of the proposed reforms. In Uruguay, patient, methodical reformers tapped this fiscal expertise to prepare detailed, credible, and (in retrospect) highly accurate estimates of the incidence of taxation under the proposed reform.

Recent experience also validates an older generalization about tax reform. In all four cases in which a reform proposed net increases in revenue—Chile, Mexico, Guatemala, and Colombia in 2014—the reforms took place in the first year of a presidential administration. (The Dominican Republic also adopted a revenue-enhancing reform in 2012, President Danilo Medina's first year.) This is consistent with the pattern described elsewhere regarding revenue-raising reforms of the first generation (c. 1967–94).[1] The fundamental concept is that a tax reform that increases revenue is harder to accomplish, because some or most contributors would be certain to have a higher tax burden. Hence, politicians find it easier to pass such reforms during the political "honeymoon" following their election, when their popular mandate is strong and before their political capital has dissipated.

Another pattern appears to support the reasoning above. Colombia (in 2012, but not in 2014) and Uruguay were the only cases in which the reforms aimed at revenue neutrality. As argued by Flores-Macías and Rius, this aided the passage of reform in both cases by diminishing taxpayers' expectations of a tax increase on themselves. As Rius argues in chapter 2, this was especially important for those who considered themselves "middle class," which turns out to include a distinct majority of the population. Here the mechanism might also involve another cognitive bias, in which a (credible) promise to maintain stable net revenues leads people to anchor their personal expectations at or near a change of magnitude zero. In other words, unlike the cases of revenue-positive reforms, those that are revenue neutral do not activate loss-aversion behaviors on the part of those who presume that their own taxes will rise.

The clout of business and private-sector organizations is also apparent in the cases considered in this volume. In a previous article, chapter 1 author Tasha Fairfield observes how the organized power of business constitutes an important explanation for differences between the Chilean and Argentine tax systems, and the political scientist Gabriel Ondetti cites a similar difference to help explain the disparity in tax burdens between Mexico and Brazil.[2] The case studies in this book illustrate the power of business sectors in Mexico, Chile, and Guatemala to block or limit reforms at various times

However, the cases presented in the preceding chapters also suggest a different dynamic: Even where business organizations were powerful enough to obstruct reform in the recent past, a movement or candidate from the political left later helped convince economic elites to accept tax reform. In Chile, it was the student protest movement of 2011–12, to which Fairfield ascribes the remarkable change in tax reform politics. In Guatemala, the threat was less dire—a potential presidential candidacy of first lady Sandra Torres de Colom—as was its ultimate effect. Although Torres de Colom's candidacy raised only a slight hint of populism, in chapter 4 Cabrera and Schneider count it as one of the factors that reduced opposition to the tax measures proposed by the new right-wing government of Otto Pérez Molina in 2012.

Where business interests were not frightened into compromise, this book's cases suggest that success was more likely when elites were fragmented (as in 2006 in Uruguay) or when reformers took a gradual and flexible

Table C.1. Tax Reforms and Conditions in Five Latin American Countries

Condition	Chile, 2014	Uruguay, 2006	Colombia, 2012
Did the reform propose to increase revenue?	++	0	0
Was the reform progressive?	++	++	+/0
Had the president received a strong mandate?	+	+	+
Did the president's party have a majority in the legislature?	+	++	++
What political orientation of the president and legislature?[a]	L/L	L/L	CR/C
In what year of the administration was reform passed?	1	2	3
Competent and autonomous tax administration?	++	++	+
Were elite and business interests well organized?[b]	++ CPC links with UDI, RN	0/+ Except rural	+ ANDI, Consejo Gremial
Are there fiscal resource rents?	+	0	+
Did the reformers communicate effectively?	++	++	+
Was there a movement or active candidacy to the left of the reformers?	++ Big student demonstrations on this issue	0	0
Was the country in a broadly felt economic crisis?	0	0	0

Note: ++ = the condition was strongly present; + = the condition was present; 0 = the condition was not present.

[a]L = left, R = right, CR = center-right, C = center.

[b]For the spelled-out names of the political parties and other entities abbreviated here, see the respective country chapters in the present volume.

Condition	Guatemala, 2012	Mexico, 2013	Other Notable Countries
Did the reform propose to increase revenue?	+	+	Dominican Republic (DR), 2012: + Costa Rica (CR), 2014: +
Was the reform progressive?	0	+/0	DR, 2012: 0
Had the president received a strong mandate?	0	0	DR, 2012: + CR, 2014: +
Did the president's party have a majority in the legislature?	0, but joined by party that proposed it under prior government	0, but pacts with other parties; tax reform ally on left	DR, 2012: ++ CR, 2014: 0
What political orientation of the president and legislature?[a]	R/R	C/C	Brazil, 2002- : L/C
In what year of the administration was reform passed?	1	1	DR, 2012: 1 CR, 2014: 1
Competent and autonomous tax administration?	0	+	DR, 2012: + CR, 2014: ++ Brazil, 2015: ++
Were elite and business interests well organized?[b]	+++ CACIF vs. strong	++ CCE, CMHN	DR, 2012: + CR, 2014: 0/+ Argentina, 2000-: 0 Brazil, 2000-: 0
Are there fiscal resource rents?	0	+	Venezuela, Bolivia: ++ Brazil: 0
Did the reformers communicate effectively?	0: Did not counter misinformation	0: Seen as deal by parties	DR, 2012: 0: not in platform CR, 2014: 0: ignored deficit
Was there a movement or active candidacy to the left of the reformers?	+ Sandra Colom, Unidad Nacional de la Esperanza	0	DR, 2012: 0 CR, 2014: + : Villela Brazil, 2015: 0
Was the country in a broadly felt economic crisis?	0	0	DR, 2012: 0 CR, 2014: debt Brazil, 2015: slump

approach (as in Chile before 2014). These tactics could often be combined, as in the initiative passed in 2012 in Colombia, where a measure to reduce informality by shifting the burden from payroll to corporate taxes won the support of labor-intensive businesses. In cases such as this, governments need to display flexibility in order to bargain with a fragmented elite.

Several chapter authors also highlight a relatively new and important aspect of the politics of taxation in the region: the role of political institutions beyond the executive. Although tax reforms were traditionally conceived and debated by the tax authorities and the treasury, recently legislatures and judicial powers have become increasingly prominent players. For many leaders, it was not enough to assemble coalitions in the legislature to pass reforms. As the cases of Mexico, Guatemala, Colombia, and Uruguay demonstrate—and as President Laura Chinchilla in Costa Rica painfully discovered[3]—leaders must also consider the role of independent courts that can overturn tax reforms. Because powerful private sectors are the most likely players to mobilize judges and courts, judicial power has become another effective resource in the resistance against tax reforms.[4]

Finally, in contrast to reforms of the first generation, the most recent period does not show a connection between broadly felt economic crises and tax reforms. None of the countries explored in this book had a major crisis during the period examined. In the only instance of severe crisis in the region—Venezuela—the government has not proposed any tax reforms. Resource rents did complicate tax reform efforts, often by sapping reform energies after commodity prices increased in Chile, Mexico, and Colombia. However, as chapters 3 and 5 make clear, the decline in fiscal rents from petroleum in 2013–14 has also made raising revenue an indispensable part of tax reform's design in Colombia and Mexico.

ADVICE FOR REFORMERS

Undoubtedly, the first rule for reformers must be to "strike when the iron is hot"; this implies that the most crucial part of any reform strategy is to recognize those moments when conditions are ripe. The previous section supplied some suggestions in this regard. But just as obviously, reformers usually must accept structural factors (as well as institutional ones) as given. So what can they do when conditions are less favorable?

Let us assemble lessons from two sources. First are several examples from the literature on past progressive reforms, lessons about which the authors of this book seem to agree:

1. Reformers fare better when they advocate subtle, piecemeal policies whose impact is ambiguous or "predictably contained," because tax reforms engender an atmosphere of uncertainty that puts key societal groups on the defensive. In these circumstances, it is more helpful to avoid stirring up opponents than to mobilize supporters.[5] From recent Colombian experience, Flores-Macías supports the argument that understated reforms are more likely to avoid activating opposition. Fairfield uses similar terms to describe the benefits of phase-in and gradualism in Chile.

2. Tactically, it is also important to isolate those hurt by redistribution from their potential allies, to gain nonpoor allies for reform. Rius seconds this, based on Uruguay's process, while Romero also points to broad reform coalitions as likely to improve the odds of success.

3. It is useful to project an image of quiet technical competence. In the Chilean case, tax increases were sometimes justified with reference to the importance of fiscal discipline, as Fairfield notes.

4. Good data on tax incidence are helpful in identifying potential allies and opponents.[6]

5. More concretely, tax increases whose revenue is earmarked or linked to particular programs have been the most successful ones (also noted by Fairfield in chapter 1).[7]

6. The vigorous, public, and effective prosecution of tax evasion is more popular than other kinds of reforms.[8] Several of the chapter

authors further suggest that it also advances progressive goals. In the argot of tax specialists, the pursuit of "horizontal equity" also aids reforms focused on "vertical equity."

Here are additional suggestions from this book's contributors:

7. Referring to Mexico, Romero argues for the indispensability of credible reforms on the spending side. Citizens do not want to pay higher taxes to fund government waste.[9]

8. Romero also suggests that in order to mobilize public opinion against the special interests that benefit from tax loopholes, these parts of the tax code should be more widely publicized.

9. Rius argues, from the experience in Uruguay, that it helps to maintain a public focus on benefits to the "middle class," because this is what both the rich and poor often consider themselves, and to publish detailed and credible estimates of the reform's likely incidence.

10. Flores-Macías's description of the national alternative minimum tax (Impuesto Mínimo Alternativo Nacional, known as IMAN) in Colombia, at least in the tax's original form, suggests that limits on the benefits obtainable from tax exemptions could be a more politically feasible way to reduce the effect of loopholes on corporate income taxes.[10]

11. Noting the "war emergency" aspect of Colombia's temporary wealth tax, Romero also speculates that Mexico's security crisis could be used to encourage compliance among wealthier taxpayers. This approach could be used by any country facing dire problems of insecurity.

LOOKING AHEAD

A major conclusion that can be drawn from the foregoing is that progressive tax reforms are best accomplished when times are good economically. Insofar as Latin American governments have become more dependent on exports of primary products—whether through state owned company income, taxes on particular exports, or the general health of their economies—a period of declining commodity prices appears to present a less favorable climate for such reforms. As noted above, the challenge of declining resource rents has hit Venezuela hard since 2013, and it has also affected fiscal management in Colombia and Mexico. Falling commodity prices and tax revenues can be expected to dominate fiscal politics in Argentina, Brazil, and Ecuador in the near future. In addition, several other countries—Costa Rica and Honduras most insistently—face major long-postponed fiscal adjustments.

Does this mean that the "wave" of progressive tax reform should be considered a historical anomaly? Probably not. First of all, the intellectual consensus about efficiency-with-progressivity is now broad and deep. Second, there are good reasons to think that, with the incipient rise of the middle-class sectors in the region, the base of support for efficient progressivity has expanded.[11] Where the tax reform on the agenda involves simplification as well as progressivity—as it does now in Brazil—the need for fiscal adjustment might just provide the spur needed to move the reform project beyond the point of being something that everyone agrees is necessary but nobody regards as probable.[12] Finally, and most important, there are other ways to pursue progressivity.

For one thing, something very important is missing from this book's case studies and from recent fiscal history elsewhere in the region: significant reforms of property taxation, above all on real estate. Of the major reforms and proposed reforms considered here, all mainly involved actions to be taken by the central government, and none involved major changes to the taxation of property. As was noted in the book's introduction, property taxes are low, and little progress has been made in changing this. It appears that resistance to progressive reform is even stronger at the local level. This remains the biggest item on the agenda of tax reformers.

For another thing, as the private-sector comments on Guatemala testify, in several countries across the region business, civil society, and politicians are calling for new or renovated "fiscal pacts" that would encompass spending as well as taxation reforms within a set of institutionalized rules. As the contributors to this volume have observed about taxation in Mexico, the key to increasing tax revenue lies in improving effectiveness and reducing corruption on the spending side. If convened, negotiations over new fiscal pacts could offer opportunities for an exchange of additional tax revenues for improved transparency, better design and efficiency, and greater progressivity in program expenditures. In this kind of bargaining, the prospect of a progressive reform of taxation—which has been demonstrated to be possible, above all by recent events in Uruguay and Chile—could help direct the energy of its elite opponents into another, long-neglected channel: the pro-poor reform of government expenditures.

Finally, the dominant discourse of politicians seems to indicate that the political climate in the region now favors progressive changes in fiscal policy. We heard this with the Mexican initiative of 2013, when a mantra of "those who make more will pay more" obscured the disappointing projections of new revenue from it. Even more was it evident in the Colombian reform of December 2014, whose primary purpose—closing a fiscal gap created by falling oil revenue, rising expenditures, and the commitments of a fiscal responsibility law—could easily have been missed amid the invocations of fairness and social conscience that dominated the public remarks of President Juan Manuel Santos and Finance Minister Mauricio Cárdenas. In other words, whether or not Latin American tax reforms actually shift the fiscal burden in a progressive way, we may have entered a period when officials and politicians increasingly feel obliged to claim that they do.

NOTES

1. J. Mahon, "Causes of Tax Reform in Latin America," *Latin America Research Review* 39 (2004): 1–29.
2. T. Fairfield, "Business Power and Tax Reform: Taxing Income and Profits in Chile and Argentina," *Latin American Politics and Society* 52, no. 2 (2010): 37–71; G. Ondetti, "Tax Burdens and Historical Legacies in Brazil and Mexico," paper prepared for American Political Science Association's 2012 Annual Meeting. Paper available at http://ssrn.com/abstract=2110920.

3. In April 2012, Sala IV of the Constitutional Court struck down her government's large and multifaceted tax law after a constitutional challenge by an opposition legislator. Reuters, April 10, 2012.
4. Carlos Elizondo and Luis Manuel Pérez de Acha, "Separación de poderes y garantías individuales: La Suprema Corte y los derechos de los contribuyentes," *Cuestiones Constitucionales* 2006 (14).
5. W. Ascher, *Scheming for the Poor: The Politics of Redistribution in Latin America* (Cambridge, Mass.: Harvard University Press, 1984), 217–18, 229, 309–11, 315; W. Ascher, "Risk, Politics, and Tax Reform: Lessons from Some Latin American Experiences," in *Tax Reform in Developing Countries*, ed. M. Gillis (Durham, N.C.: Duke University Press, 1989), 417, 419. At *Scheming*, 309–10, Ascher's implicit but entirely plausible premise is that the likely opponents command more resources than likely supporters.
6. R. Bates, "A Political Scientist Looks at Tax Reform," in *Tax Reform in Developing Countries*, ed. M. Gillis (Durham, N.C.: Duke University Press, 1989), 478.
7. Ibid., 220–22, 228, 307, 311, 319; cf. Bates, "Political Scientist Looks at Tax Reform," 479.
8. W. Ascher, *Bringing in the Future: Strategies for Farsightedness and Sustainability in Developing Countries* (Chicago: University of Chicago Press, 2009), 22, 85; the key here is that the benefit from a rate reduction may be more easily calculable than the cost of the simplification (100–101).
9. See also C. Elizondo, *Progresividad y eficacia del gasto público en México: Precondición para una política recaudatoria efectiva* (Washington, D.C.: Latin American Program of the Woodrow Wilson International Center for Scholars, 2014), http://www.wilsoncenter.org/publication/PoliticaFiscalMexico.
10. See also N. Salazar, *The Political Economy of Tax Reforms: The Case of Colombia*, Latin American Program of the Woodrow Wilson International Center for Scholars, http://www.wilsoncenter.org/publication/TaxationColombia.
11. R. M. Bird and E. Zolt, "Fiscal Contracting in Latin America," Rotman School of Management, University of Toronto, September 2014, 22, http://ssrn.com/abstract=2496576.
12. Roberto B. Piscitelli, "Reforma Tributária," *Jornal dos Economistas* 301 (August 2014): 5. "A necessidade de uma reforma tributária é uma aparente unanimidade e, ao mesmo tempo, algo extremamente improvável."

Contributors

Cynthia J. Arnson is director of the Latin American Program of the Woodrow Wilson International Center for Scholars. She is editor of *In the Wake of War: Democratization and Internal Armed Conflict in Latin America* (Stanford University Press, 2012); coeditor (with Carlos de la Torre) of *Latin American Populism in the 21st Century* (Johns Hopkins University Press, 2013); and author of *Crossroads: Congress, the President, and Central America, 1976–1993* (2nd ed., Pennsylvania State University Press, 1993)—among other publications. She is a member of the editorial advisory board of *Foreign Affairs Latinoamérica*. She is also a member of the advisory boards of the Social Science Research Council's Conflict Prevention and Peace Forum and of Human Rights Watch / Americas, where she served as associate director from 1990 to 1994. She received an M.A. and Ph.D. in international relations from the Paul H. Nitze School of Advanced International Studies at Johns Hopkins University.

Marcelo Bergman is professor and researcher at the Universidad Nacional de Tres de Febrero in Buenos Aires, and an affiliated professor at the Centro de Investigación y Docencia Económicas (CIDE) in Mexico City. Beginning in 2005, he served as the founder and academic director of the Study of Security and Rule of Law Program (PESED) at CIDE. He has held other teaching and research positions at the University of Oregon, the United Nations Development Program, and the Hebrew University of Jerusalem. He is the author of numerous works, including *Tax Evasion and the Rule of Law in Latin America: The Political Culture of Cheating and Compliance in Argentina and Chile* (2010); *The Challenges of Rising Criminality to Democracy and Rule of Law in Latin America* (2009); and *La Confianza y el Derecho en América Latina* (2007). He received his B.A. and

M.A. in political science from the Hebrew University of Jerusalem and his Ph.D. in sociology from the University of California, San Diego.

Maynor Cabrera has been a senior economist at the Fundación Economía para el Desarrollo (FEDES) since 2014. He has also worked as economic adviser for the *National Human Development Report* of the United Nations Development Program (UNDP) in Guatemala, technical adviser to the Guatemalan government, and technical secretary of the Fiscal Pact Commission. His areas of specialization are tax policy and macroeconomics. He has worked as a consultant for the UN Economic Commission on Latin America and the Caribbean (ECLAC), the UNDP, the World Bank, the Central American Institute for Fiscal Studies (ICEFI), and the Inter-American Development Bank. He studied economics at Guatemala's Universidad de San Carlos and received an M.A. from the Catholic University of Chile.

Tasha Fairfield is an assistant professor in international development at the London School of Economics and Political Science. She received a Ph.D. in political science from the University of California, Berkeley, and degrees in physics from Harvard University and Stanford University. She is the author of *Private Wealth and Public Revenue in Latin America: Business Power and Tax Politics* (Cambridge University Press, 2015). Her research interests include democracy and inequality, business politics, policy formulation, and the political economy of development. Previously, she was a Hewlett Fellow at Stanford University's Center on Democracy, Development, and the Rule of Law and a visiting fellow at the University of Notre Dame's Kellogg Institute for International Studies. Her research has been supported by the Social Science Research Council, Fulbright-Hays, and the International Centre for Tax and Development.

Gustavo A. Flores-Macías is an assistant professor in the Department of Government at Cornell University, specializing in the politics of economic reforms, taxation, and state capacity. Before joining Cornell's faculty, he was a fellow at Cornell's Polson Institute for Global Development between 2008 and 2010. He also served as director of public affairs in Mexico's

Consumer Protection Agency. His research has appeared or is forthcoming in the *American Political Science Review*, *Comparative Politics*, *Journal of Democracy*, *Journal of Politics*, *Peace Review*, *Political Science Quarterly*, and *Studies in Comparative International Development*. He has also contributed chapters to several edited volumes. His book, *After Neoliberalism? The Left and Economic Reforms in Latin America* (Oxford University Press, 2012), won the Latin American Studies Association's Tomassini Award in 2014. He received a Ph.D. in government from Georgetown University and a master's in public policy from Duke University, where he was a Fulbright scholar.

James E. Mahon Jr. is the Woodrow Wilson Professor of Political Science at Williams College, and lectures on a host of topics including political economy, comparative politics, United States–Latin America foreign relations, and Latin American politics. He has written extensively on Latin America and is the author of various articles on political economy, comparative social inquiry, and U.S. foreign policy, as well as *Mobile Capital and Latin American Development* (Pennsylvania State University Press, 1996). His current research examines fiscal politics and the reform of the state in Latin America.

Andrés Rius is an associate professor and chair of the Economics Department in the School of Economic Sciences and Management of Uruguay's Universidad de la República. He also coordinates the Economics Department's Development and Institutions Research Group. He has held several teaching and research positions, including posts at the International Development Research Centre from 1997 to 2010. He has contributed chapters on investment promotion, economic development, and public policy to several recent books as well as a recent article to *World Development*. He received an M.A. and Ph.D. in economics from the University of Notre Dame as well as an undergraduate degree in economics from the Universidad de la República.

Vidal Romero is chair of the Political Science Department of the Instituto Tecnológico Autónomo de México (ITAM). He received a master's degree in public policy from ITAM and a Ph.D. in political science from Stanford

University. His research has focused on presidential decisionmaking, fiscal reforms, and crime and violence. He has collaborated on different research projects with the World Bank and the Inter-American Development Bank. He was a visiting professor at the Center on Democracy, Development, and the Rule of Law at Stanford University and Tinker Professor at the Center for Latin American Studies at Stanford University. His work has been published in multiple edited volumes and journals, including *Latin American Research Review*, *Política y Gobierno*, *Revista de Ciencia Política*, *International Journal of Public Opinion Research*, *Revista Latinoamericana de Opinión Pública*, and *Political Research Quarterly*.

Francisco Rosende is a professor of Economics at the Pontificia Universidad Católica de Chile and served as dean of the School of Economics and Business Administration from 1995 to 2013. Between 1985 and 1990 he was chief of research of the Central Bank of Chile. In 2012 President Sebastián Piñera appointed him as chairman of a committee to evaluate Chile's antitrust legislation. He is the author of a textbook on macroeconomic theory and editor of *La Escuela de Chicago: Una mirada histórica a 50 años del convenio Chicago: Ensayos en Honor a Arnold C. Harberger* (Santiago: Ediciones Universidad Católica de Chile, 2007), among other works, and writes monthly economics columns for the Chilean daily *El Mercurio* and for Uruguay's *El País*. He holds a degree in commercial engineering from the Universidad de Chile and a Master's in Economics from the University of Chicago.

Aaron Schneider holds the Leo Block Chair in the Josef Korbel School of International Studies at the University of Denver. He teaches subjects including political economy, comparative state building, and international development, and he has written extensively on Latin America, development, public finance, and social mobilization. His book *State-Building and Tax Regimes in Central America* was a *Foreign Policy* Western Hemisphere Book of the Year in 2012, and its Spanish translation was a Best Books of 2014 selection by *Contrapoder*. His current research compares Brazil and India on issues of democratic deepening, state capacity, and the role of emerging powers in the international political economy.